NEW
FREE FROM THE SEA

FOR STEPHEN
WHO LOVED THE SEA AND ALL THE
CREATURES THAT LIVE THEREIN

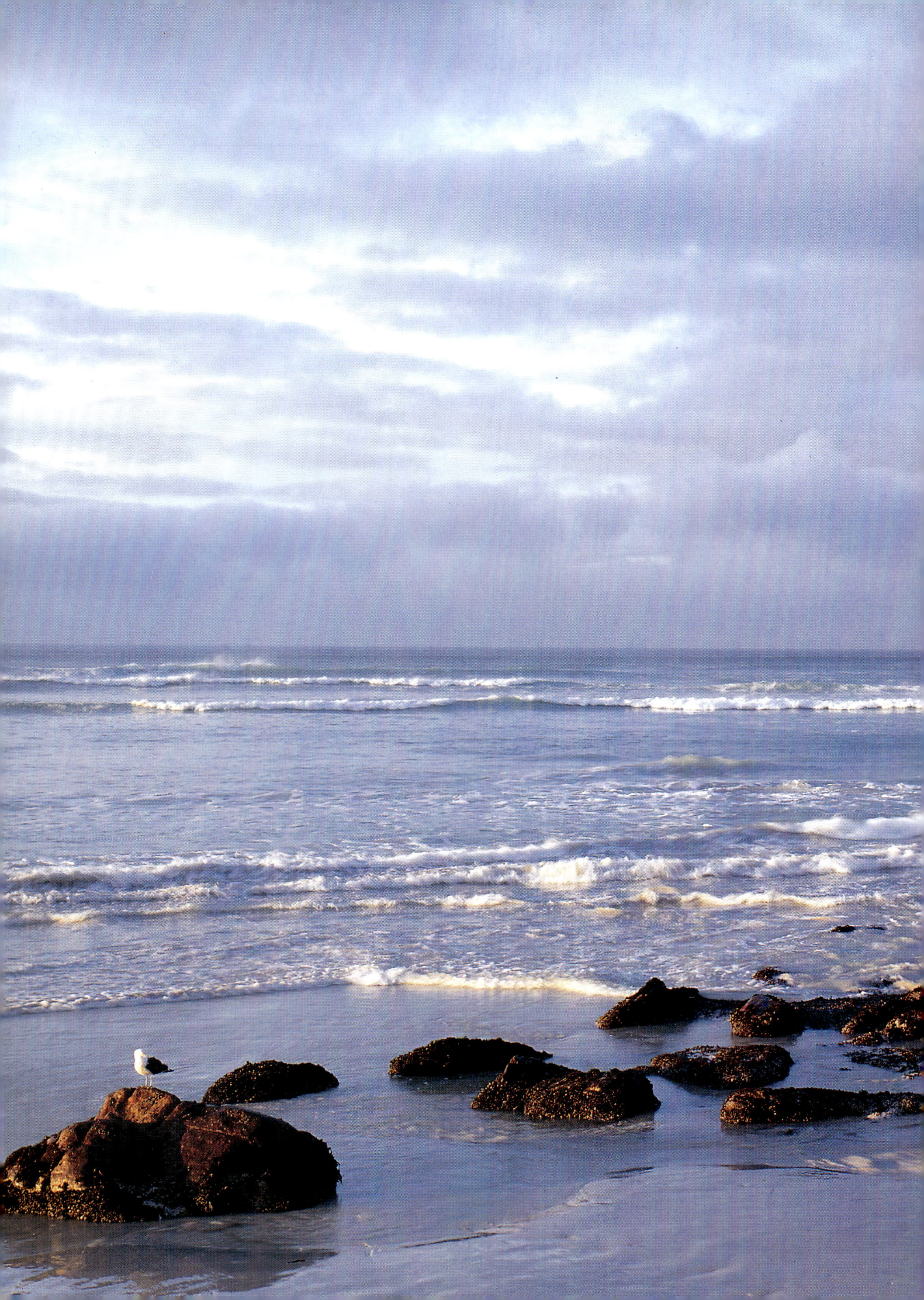

NEW
FREE FROM THE SEA

Lannice Snyman & Anne Klarie
Photography by Volker Miros

BIBLIOGRAPHY

Smith's Sea Fishes
by Professor J L B Smith. Edited by Margaret M Smith
& Phillip C Heemstra (Macmillan South Africa)

A Guide to the Common Sea Fishes in Southern Africa
by Rudy van der Elst (Struik)

Sea and Shore Dangers
by Margaret M Smith (Icthos)

New Larousse Gastronomique
by Prosper Montagne (Hamlyn)

Leipoldt's Cape Cookery
by C Louis Leipoldt (W J Flesch & Partners)

Hilda's Diary of a Cape Housekeeper
by Hildagonda J Duckitt
(Macmillan South Africa)

PO Box 26344, Hout Bay 7872, South Africa

The Publishers would be happy to hear from readers at the following e-mail address: lannice@iafrica.com

First Edition published by Struik Publishers (Pty) Ltd 1994
Second Impression published by S&S Publishers 1999

Text, photographs and illustrations © Lannice Snyman and Anne Klarie 1994

All rights reserved. No part of this publication may be reproduced, stored in a retrieval system or transmitted, in any form or by any means, electronic, mechanical, recording or otherwise, without the prior written permission of the copyright owners and publisher.

EDITOR: Glynne Williamson
DESIGNER: Petal Palmer
ASSISTANT DESIGNER: Lellyn Creamer
COVER DESIGN: Petal Palmer
PHOTOGRAPHER: Volker Miros
PHOTOGRAPHER (TITLE PAGE): Alain Proust
FOOD STYLIST: Anne Klarie
ASSISTED BY: Lannice Snyman
LINE DRAWINGS: Anne Klarie

Typesetting: Struik DTP
Cover reproduction: Disc Express Cape, Cape Town
Reproduction: Hirt & Carter (Pty) Ltd, Cape Town
Printing and Binding: Tien Wah Press (Pte.) Ltd, Singapore

ISBN 0-620-23839-9

Contents

Introduction 6

Selecting, Preparing and
   Storing Fish 8

Cooking Methods for Fish 9

Seafood and Poisoning 11

Snacks, Starters and Salads 12

Soups 26

Fish Dishes 34

Shellfish Dishes 66

The Seafood Braai 82

The Seafood Lover's Pantry 88

Seafood A-Z 99

Index 127

Introduction

OUR LOVE OF SEAFOOD DATES BACK TO OUR CHILDHOOD, AND IN
THE EARLY SEVENTIES WE FORMULATED THE IDEA TO WRITE
A BOOK ABOUT ALL THE DELICIOUS GOODIES WE WERE FISHING,
DIVING AND COAXING FROM OUR WATERS.

The first edition of *Free From The Sea* was published in 1979. This book ran to a further eleven impressions – a total of 50 000 books. The second edition was published in 1991 and when this, too, sold out we decided the time was right for a total revamp.

It made sense to incorporate *Free From The Sea's* sequel, *More From The Sea*, published in 1986, a collection of new seafood recipes inspired by the unprecedented interest in seafood as a desirable alternative to red meat.

New Free From The Sea, therefore, becomes the definitive reference book for the identification and preparation of everything edible in our seas, and the ultimate collection of the very best seafood recipes to suit all occasions.

Many new recipes have been incorporated in this revised edition, as our work is influenced by the changes that continually affect all areas of cookery; new trends that require us to constantly revise our approach to cooking methods, food presentation and the combination of ingredients.

Our kitchens have been many and varied – from the comfort of our own homes to the primitive kitchens at campsites we've shared along much of our coastline. Here, on occasions too numerous to recall, we have enjoyed the ultimate seafood experience – a just-caught fish, freshly cooked in the simplest possible way. In sea-shore cooking, necessity truly has been the mother of invention. We've used beach-rubbed rocks to tenderize perlemoen, crushed cornflakes to coat the steaks, diving knives to prise open oysters, and leafy twigs as basting brushes for crayfish sizzling over open coals.

The book is divided into three sections: the first section deals with selecting, preparing, storing and methods of cooking seafood.

Then there's the recipe section. Here we have devised many original recipes, as well as adapting some classic dishes to accommodate local seafood.

The third is an alphabetical index of each type of seafood relevant to this book. We have included common names, a line drawing to help you to identify your catch, interesting information about it, what we consider to be the most successful cooking methods, and a list of recipes.

Compiling this index involved painstaking research. South Africans have a habit of endowing their fish with different names in each part of the country, resulting in many a headache for naturalists and anglers – as well as ourselves! There have been occasional attempts to standardize these names, many of which came to naught. Happily so, for many descriptive nicknames will remain part of our heritage.

The enjoyment of seafood is rather like the enjoyment of wine – everyone has his or her own particular favourites. So, too, in the preparation of seafood. We have cross-referred many different types that can be substituted in each recipe, taking into account texture, flavour and – in the case of fish – size as well.

We encourage you to experiment even further; only by so doing will cooking seafood become for you what it is for us – constantly challenging, always fulfilling and incredibly rewarding.

Through our books, we have happily made many friends country-wide, and we hope most sincerely that with *New Free From The Sea* we will reach an even wider audience of new readers, for whom these recipes will provide as much pleasure as we have had in their creation.

Lannice Snyman and Anne Klarie
Hout Bay, September 1994

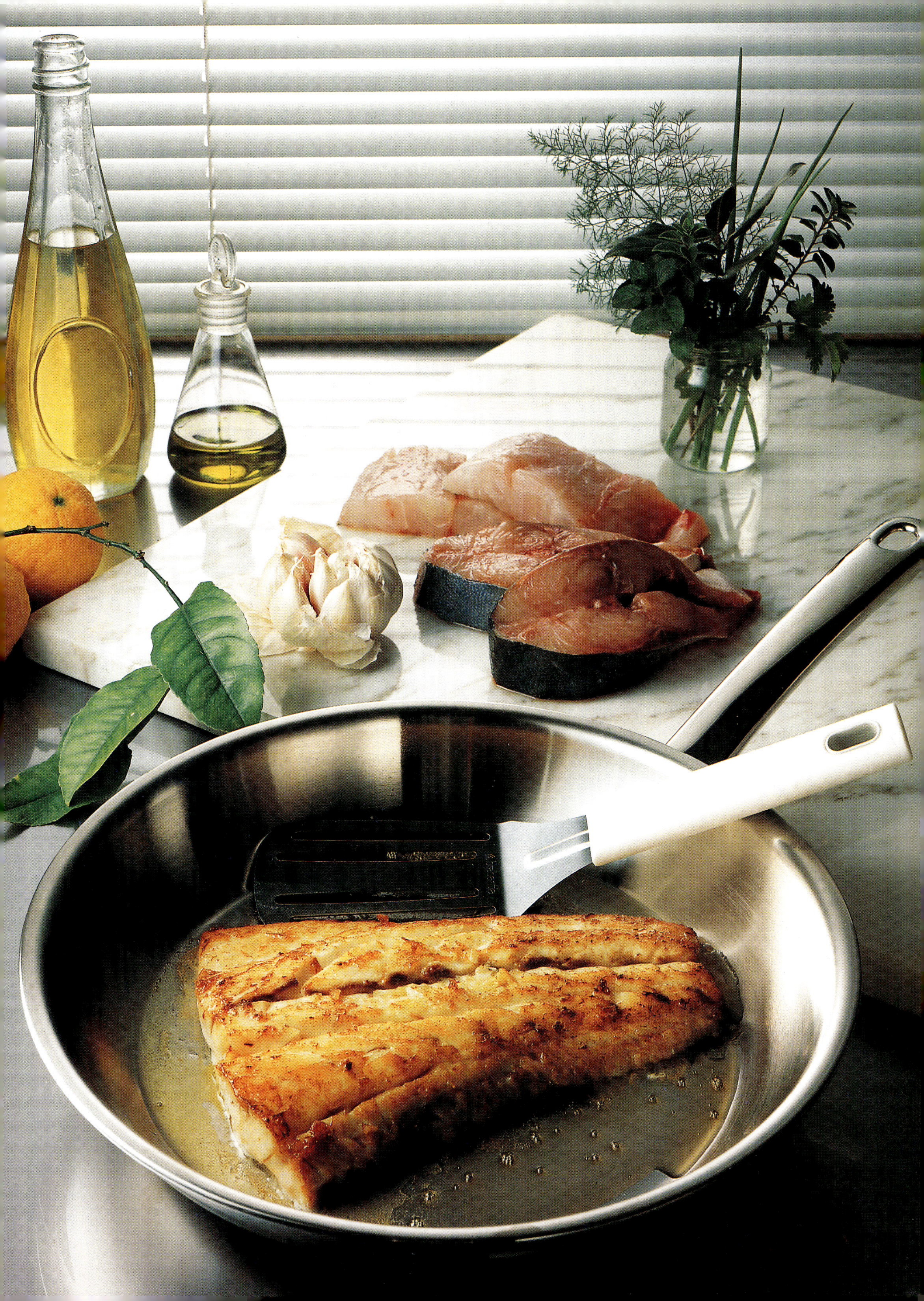

Selecting, Preparing and Storing Fish

Our fishing industry is thankfully getting better and better at bringing high quality fresh and frozen seafood to all parts of the country, enabling everyone to enjoy it even if geographical restrictions deny one the pleasure of catching one's own. Still, it's vital for the consumer to know as much as possible about the correct handling of fish.

Selection

Freshness is the keyword when choosing fish, but it's the one factor so often overlooked by restaurateurs, housewives and suppliers. Before you even think of cooking fish, get to know what fresh fish should look/smell/taste like – firm flesh, red gills, bright, bulging eyes and almost no fishy smell. If possible feast just once in your life on a fish you've caught yourself and cooked within a few hours. It's an unforgettable experience!

When it comes to spoiling, nothing compares with fish! From the moment it stops wriggling, the quality deteriorates. Add to this rough handling, freezing and defrosting, languishing in the car en route to the kitchen: the complexity of the problem is not to be underestimated.

Seafood is seasonal and your enthusiasm for choosing a specific type of fish should be tempered by this knowledge. Take note of the alternative choices in each recipe or change your menu rather than buy fish that is less than perfect for the recipe you have in mind.

It still amazes us that so much elderly fish is displayed at fish shops and supermarkets, awaiting the hapless purchaser. Yet there's no need to buy lousy seafood – walk away and go to a fishmonger you can trust.

'Fresh' and 'Frozen' Fish

These terms are explicit and mutually exclusive, a fact often ignored by fishmongers and restaurateurs. (Most diners-out have had at least one encounter with less-than-perfect fish!) 'Fresh' means never having been frozen, though fresh fish may have been kept chilled for a time – sometimes far too long.

'Frozen' fish may have been rendered thus on the trawler or once the catch reaches the factory. Yet defrosted fish is all too often termed 'fresh' by the fishmonger.

Storing

Cook fish within a day or two of purchasing, especially fish that has been frozen. If possible, avoid freezing fresh fish in a home freezer. Unless you have a 'quick blast'

The keyword when choosing fish is freshness

button, the process takes too long causing ice crystals to form, spoiling the texture. Of course the rule may be bent if you've caught or purchased a still-wriggling creature and wish to enjoy some of it immediately and save some for later. Cut the surplus fish into serving portions, clean thoroughly, wrap well and freeze as quickly as possible.

Optimum Storage Time

Though some types of fish last better than others (kob, for instance, spoils very much faster than tuna), it's safe to say that a freshly-caught fish may be refrigerated for up to three days. Make sure it's quite clean, cover with clingfilm and keep it away from crushed ice and ice blocks which will spoil the texture of the flesh. As a general rule, the maximum storage time for frozen fish is three months.

Bleeding Fish

Some types of fish should be bled soon after catching to get rid of all traces of blood and improve the flavour. To do this, cut the gills and let the blood flow freely into a pool of water. Some fishermen do this as a matter of course with any fish they catch; some don't bother. In our experience some species must be bled. These have been marked in their sections in the Seafood A-Z.

Scaling

Hold the fish by the tail and, with the blunt edge of a knife, scrape away scales with swift movements from tail to head. If you have difficulty in scaling – perhaps the fish isn't perfectly fresh – plunge it into boiling water for a few moments, then proceed.

Cleaning

Slit fish along the belly, remove the entrails and rinse clean. Clip off the gills with scissors or cut off with a knife. Leave on the head and tail if you're cooking it whole. If it's to be stuffed, there's no need to slit the belly: the entrails may be removed from the head cavity.

Flatfish – like soles – have their entrails in a cavity behind the head. Slit it open here, remove entrails, remove the fins and clean well.

Filleting

Lay the fish on a board. Use a sharp knife to carefully slice down the length of the backbone and cut the fillets from either side.

Skinning

Some fish – like rock cod, gurnard, shark and other fish with tough skins – may have their skin pulled off: make an incision with a knife at the head. Grip the skin with a dry cloth and pull off the skin quickly in one deft movement.

Soles are skinned from tail to head. Lay the fish, dark side up, on a board and make a slit just above the tail. Hold the tail and pull the skin off towards the head. Remove the white skin in the same way.

Most fish are best skinned like this: after cleaning, scaling and filleting, place the fillet skin-down on a board. Pin the skin with a fork and cut it away from the flesh, keeping the knife as close as possible to the board.

NOTE: Specific preparation of shellfish is treated in their sections in the Seafood A–Z.

Cooking Methods for Fish

Despite the wealth of fine fish in our country, fish cookery is probably the least understood and most frequently abused form of cookery in our homes and restaurants. Yet it's the easiest thing in the world to become an expert – just follow a few simple rules!

To avoid loss of flavour and succulence, fish should be cooked for a minimum amount of time and over as low heat as possible. This also applies to frying and braaiing when a moderate heat is preferable – though it's nice to brown the fish quickly at the start to improve flavour, texture and appearance.

Always bear in mind that you're dealing with exquisite, delicate flavours, so when following our recipes, don't take liberties with the herbs and spices. You'll overpower the flavour of the fish with too heavy a hand.

Frying

Stand over your frying pan to ensure perfect timing and avoid excessive heat.

Season fish with salt and pepper before frying in hot ghee, butter and oil (this prevents the butter burning), or hard margarine. Wait until it starts to brown, add a little crushed garlic if you wish, then brown the upper side of the fish. Turn the fish and reduce the temperature for the remainder of the cooking time. Cover the pan after browning the fish, to make it even more succulent.

It's impossible to give exact timing estimates; your heat and the thickness of the fish must be taken into account. As a guide, fish fillets 3-4 cm thick should take two minutes on each side. Another way is to watch until the fillet becomes opaque half-way up, then flip it over to complete the cooking process.

Various coatings can be used when frying fish:
- Seasoned flour, or milk and flour (fish browns better when first dipped in milk).
- Flour, egg and breadcrumbs. A tasty variation is to add ground almonds to the crumbs.
- Batter – see recipes starting on page 90.

Grilling

First allow the grill to become piping hot. Brush both the grill-pan and the fish with butter or oil to prevent the fish from sticking. Score the fish's skin to prevent it from twisting and, after browning, season with salt, pepper and lemon juice. Don't forget that pan-juices make a delicious sauce: simply boil on the stovetop to reduce and thicken slightly, or add it to the sauce you're preparing.

As a timing guide, grill fish 3 cm thick for 3-4 minutes on each side.

For added flavour, sprinkle the fish with freshly chopped herbs. Afterwards pour over a couple of tablespoonfuls of warmed brandy, ignite and flame. The burning herbs give the fish an irresistible flavour.

Fish may be marinated prior to grilling and basted while it cooks. See the recipes from page 93 onwards.

BAKING

Baking is best for drier types of fish which may be baked whole, stuffed, in cutlets or fillets.

Add a minimum of liquid, as fish forms its own juice while baking. For a special touch, add cream to the baking juices and use as a sauce.

Various ingredients such as onion, tomato, mushrooms, garlic, bacon, wine and herbs can be added to make baked fish even more interesting.

Baking in foil is quick and easy. It seals in the natural flavour and keeps fish succulent. Season the fish, dot with butter and seal in well-oiled foil. No liquid need be added, though one may sprinkle over a little lemon juice or dry white wine before closing the foil.

With baked fish it is always a good idea to serve a separate sauce. Our recipes start on page 93.

STEAMING

This is the gentlest way of cooking fish – in the steam over simmering water. Use a proper fish steamer if you have one, or simply place the fish on a rack in a covered saucepan. The Chinese steam fish to perfection in special bamboo baskets or in a wok.

We're inclined to associate steamed fish with cooking for invalids – easy to digest but dull and insipid. Yet many purists consider steaming to be the ultimate cooking method for fish. With intelligent use of herbs, seasoning and sauces, steaming can bring out the most delicate fish flavours without any loss of moisture.

Instead of adding herbs, try steaming fish between layers of well-washed seaweed. The flavour of the sea comes through strongly.

POACHING

It is preferable to poach fish in Court-Bouillon (page 88) rather than either water or water with onion and seasoning added. Your fish will be much more tasty.

Always poach very slowly; the liquid should barely move. Your fish is cooked the moment it's opaque right through, and it can then be drained and served hot, or left to cool in the poaching liquid if it's to be served cold.

MICROWAVING

This method of cooking seafood is enormously successful and many of our recipes may be easily adapted for microwave cooking. Make sure that you follow these basic principles when microwaving fish:

- Always defrost fish first.
- Avoid over-cooking fish (which is so easy to do in the microwave oven).
- To ensure even cooking, the pieces of fish should be of a similar thickness. If necessary, fold thinner pieces over, or arrange with the thicker parts outwards. When cooking a whole fish, shield the tail section with foil.
- Don't add salt until afterwards. Season instead with fresh herbs and a squeeze of lemon juice.
- We have found that microwaving on 70% power is best, and as a rule of thumb, calculate 1 minute per 100 g fish. When there are other ingredients in the dish (vegetables; a stuffing), take this into account.

BRAISING

Unlike poaching, braising uses far less liquid in the cooking process and as a result less flavour is lost. The braising liquid is always served as part of the dish.

Place the fish in an ovenproof dish, season with salt and freshly milled black pepper and add herbs and vegetables of your choice. Add a few blobs of butter and either a little fish stock and white wine, or stock and water. Cover the dish tightly and cook in the oven or on the stovetop. Baste the fish occasionally with the braising juices.

ROASTING

This is a great way of cooking drier types of fish like tuna, which may be roasted plain or stuffed. First weigh the fish to calculate cooking time.

Set the oven at 200 °C, pour a little oil into your roasting pan and heat it in the oven. Dust the fish with flour and season lightly with salt and milled pepper. Brown all over in oil, taking care not to break the skin when turning. Reduce oven temperature to 180 °C and cook uncovered for 30 minutes per kilogram.

The secret of successful roasting is frequent basting. This keeps the fish from drying out and ensures crispness.

BRAAIING

Most types of fish can be cooked over the coals, though some are more successful than others. Fish braais can be as simple or elaborate as you like, from cooking a single, freshly-caught fish over a beach fire, to presenting a tempting array of different types of fish and seafood with marinades, basting sauces, side dishes and other delicious accompaniments.

Besides being cooked over the coals, seafood can be cooked on a solid plate or plough disc on which butter, garlic and herbs are sizzling.

Steamed, fresh mussels

More delicate-fleshed fish should be wrapped in foil before braaiing, and a whole fish cooked like this can first be stuffed. After it's cooked, remove the fish from the foil and carefully brown it in a hinged grid over the coals. This will help capture the lovely smoky flavour.

Nothing, though, can beat the flavour of a fish cooked open over the coals. Using a hinged grid solves the problem of the flesh breaking as the fish is turned. Place the tail towards the hinged part to further regulate the pressure of the grid on the flesh. Liberally brush both fish and grid with oil before cooking to prevent the fish from sticking. And for a gourmet touch, scatter fresh herbs on the coals to add a gentle herby flavour.

Remember that fish cooks surprisingly quickly over open coals. Keep the heat moderate and never, ever overcook it.

NOTE: Super seafood braai recipes start on page 82.

Smoking and Curing

These 'cooking' methods evolved before the time of refrigeration and fast transportation of foodstuffs – and remain popular to this day.

Smoked fish makes interesting hors d'oeuvres, sandwich fillings, snacks, dips and, of course, may be used in some of the recipes in this book.

Hot smoking Home-smokers are quick and economical to use for smoking many types of fish – there's a recipe on page 49.

Cold smoking No heat is used when fish is cold-smoked, simply the smoke which 'cooks' it through. Though some people have cold-smoking apparatus at home, this method is normally done commercially.

Curing and salting After cleaning the fish, fillet or vlek by cutting through past the backbone, leaving the fillets hinged together at the belly. Season the fish heavily with coarse salt and place in layers on trays. After 5-6 hours, wash thoroughly and hang the fish to dry where there is plenty of air circulation.

To make fish biltong, continue drying for up to 10 days, depending on the size of the fish.

NOTE: Smoking and curing are, in fact, methods of half-cooking, so don't expect the fish to keep for any longer than a week in the fridge. After that it may be wrapped and frozen.

Seafood and Poisoning

Common sense and the sea go hand in hand. The dangers of the sea and sea life must be understood and respected by all those who enjoy the pleasures of our shores.

Some people are allergic to seafood and should never eat it. The allergy can be limited to, say, shellfish, though some can't tolerate even the smallest portion of fish. The symptoms can vary from mild – a prickly feeling in the ears, mouth and throat – to so severe and traumatic as to make a tracheotomy necessary. The unfortunate thing is that the allergy can get worse every time you eat seafood so it's sensible to avoid that particular seafood to which you are allergic.

For the rest of us there is still the danger of poisoning, so follow these simple rules:

- Ensure your seafood is fresh and has been properly stored and frozen. It spoils quicker than any other type of food. Trust your sense of smell and taste – poisoned fish has a sharp, peppery flavour.
- Collect bivalves (like mussels, oysters, clams), periwinkles, redbait and sea urchins at low tide and as far as possible from the danger of shore pollution. Avoid all seafood that dwells close to areas like harbours and near sewerage or factory waste pipes.
- Never, ever eat bivalves from areas affected by a toxic tide. Check with the local Department of Sea Fisheries if you're in any doubt.
- Don't eat the liver of the steenbras, kob or shark; the high vitamin A content can cause poisoning.
- Never eat blaasop or sunfish.

Snacks, Starters and Salads

A SEAFOODY START TO A MEAL IS A GREAT IDEA.
SNACKY THINGS TO OFFER WITH DRINKS, LIGHT STARTERS
TO PRECEDE A SUBSTANTIAL MAIN COURSE, OR A
GOURMET CREATION TO IMPRESS THE PICKIEST GUEST.

Marinated Mussels

These plump and tender delicacies are popular in the snack-time stakes and ridiculously simple to prepare. Use a 900 g can of black mussels. Or gather them fresh from the rocks, clean and steam them open as described on page 111.

36 black mussels
French Dressing (page 94)
tiny sprigs of parsley or fennel for garnish

Remove the mussels from their shells, reserving the most perfect half-shells in which to serve each one. Scrub the shells well and gloss with a light spray of oil.

Place mussels in a bowl, pour over just sufficient dressing to cover them, and refrigerate for at least 24 hours to marinate. They'll be fine for up to 2 weeks.

Arrange the mussel shells on a large, flat platter. Drain the mussels, place one in each shell and garnish with herbs. Serve at room temperature.
Serves 6-8

Pickled Winkles

750 g freshly-gathered periwinkles
375 ml cider vinegar
375 ml water
24 peppercorns
12 whole allspice
10 cloves
6 small bay leaves
250 ml chopped spring onion
olive oil

Clean and cook the periwinkles as described on page 114. Remove from their shells, pile in a colander and rinse under running water. Pour over plenty of boiling water.

Mix together the vinegar, water, peppercorns, allspice, cloves, bay leaves and spring onion, add the periwinkles and pack into sterilized jars. If there isn't sufficient liquid, top up with equal quantities of water and vinegar.

Pour a film of olive oil onto the surface to seal, then close and refrigerate for at least a week before serving.

Calamari Crackling

400 g calamari tubes, well cleaned
60 ml water
40 g (40 ml) butter
fresh lemon juice
milled black pepper

Set the oven at 200 °C. Cut calamari into rings about 15 mm thick. Place in a baking dish, pour over the water and dot with butter. Season with a squeeze of lemon juice and a little pepper.

Bake uncovered for 1 hour, stirring occasionally with the buttery juices. After 30 minutes the calamari will be lightly browned (serve at this stage if you wish). After an hour it will be dark brown and crisp – watch carefully at this stage, as it burns in a flash. Cool and serve within a few hours of preparation.
Serves 8

Calamari Crackling, Marinated Mussels and Pickled Winkles

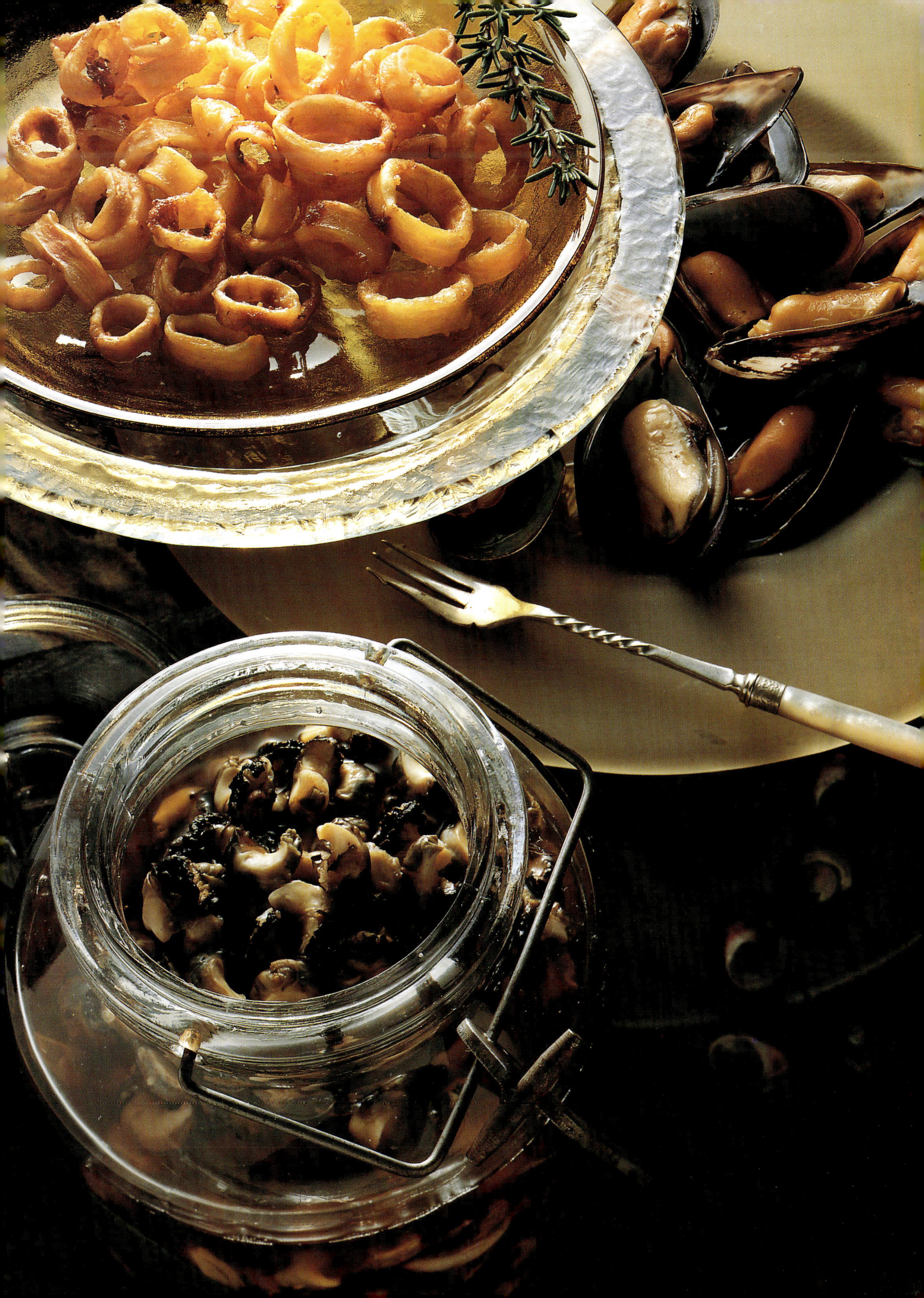

ROLLMOPS

Easy to buy, but fun to make yourself. Serve garnished with onion rings and parsley sprigs as a starter or as part of a cold table.

12 pilchards
500 ml cider vinegar
500 ml water
12 black peppercorns
6 whole allspice
6 cloves
3 small bay leaves
45 ml prepared English mustard
3 small onions, thinly sliced into rings
30 ml capers
3 dill pickled cucumbers, cut into wedges

Sterilize glass pickling jars with boiling water and set aside to drain. Fillet the pilchards, leaving the skin on (you'll have 24 fillets). Rinse with cold water, drain on a wad of kitchen paper and pat dry. Discard any remaining bones if you have the patience – and a pair of tweezers!

Combine the vinegar, water, peppercorns, allspice, cloves and bay leaves in a saucepan. Bring to the boil and simmer without the lid for 5 minutes. Cool the marinade to room temperature.

Lay the fish fillets skin down and spread each one sparingly with mustard. At the narrow end of each fillet place a few onion rings, 3-4 capers and a wedge of dill pickle. Roll up and secure with toothpicks. Pack in layers in the pickling jars, scattering a few onion rings between the layers and on top. Pour the marinade over, seal or cover with clingfilm and refrigerate for 5-7 days before serving.

Makes 12

Crayfish Cocktail, recipe page 15

MOCK CAVIARE

Cross the costly roe of the virgin sturgeon off your shopping list – here's a super substitute.

250 g fresh fish roe
fresh lemon juice
2 ml salt
milled black pepper
5 ml grated onion
15 ml brandy
lemon twists and parsley sprigs for garnish

Place the roe in a small saucepan, add water to cover and 5 ml lemon juice. Cover and poach very gently for about 10 minutes. Drain the roe, split it open, remove and discard the skin and crumble it into a small bowl. Season with salt and pepper and add grated onion, brandy and a squeeze of lemon juice. Mix lightly with a fork.
  Serve on biscuits or fingers of rye bread garnished with lemon twists and parsley sprigs.
Serves 4

MAKE AHEAD Mock caviare improves with keeping; store it in the fridge for 2-3 weeks.

CRAYFISH COCKTAIL

One of the most popular ways of serving crayfish as a starter. Monkfish, prawns and langoustines could be used instead.

2 small, freshly-cooked crayfish
Seafood Sauce (page 94)
lettuce leaves
parsley sprigs and lemon wedges
for garnish

Extricate all the flesh from the crayfish tails, bodies and claws. Dice it and mix gently into the sauce. Arrange lettuce on serving plates, top with crayfish cocktail and garnish with parsley and lemon wedges.
Serves 4

VARIATIONS
- *Avocado Ritz* Spoon crayfish cocktail into halved avocados which have been stoned, brushed with lemon juice and seasoned with salt and pepper.
- *Crayfish Melon Cocktail* Halve small, ripe sweet melons (spanspek), discard pips and spoon crayfish cocktail into the hollows. If melons are on the large side, skin first, then cut into quarters and fan the melon quarters onto the plate. Spoon the crayfish cocktail alongside.

CEVICHE

Tender, tangy slices of fish 'cooked' in lime or lemon juice. Serve as snacks, on biscuits or with mixed salad leaves and herbs as an interesting starter. Tuna is good in this recipe, so are other gamefish like yellowtail, marlin and snoek, but any fresh fish of your choice may be used.

400 g filleted, skinless fish

MARINADE
200 ml fresh lime or lemon juice
60 ml wine vinegar
60 ml olive oil
1 red or green chilli, seeded and finely sliced
10 ml sugar
2 ml crushed garlic
2 ml salt
2 ml milled black pepper
fresh coriander leaves for garnish

Trim the fish and, if using tuna, discard the dark meat, then slice into fine slivers. The task is a little tricky, but it helps to use a really sharp knife and hold the fish firmly while slicing. You will be left with several irregular bits and pieces that won't be pretty enough to serve to guests. Marinate them all the same and use in a seafood salad.
  Mix together the marinade ingredients. Layer the fish and marinade in a flat, glass dish, cover with clingfilm and refrigerate for at least 3 hours (up to 8 hours, if you wish), then drain the marinade and serve the fish. Each piece will be opaque and deliciously tangy.
Serves 8

KIPPER PÂTÉ

A delicious and quick-to-make pâté!

250 g smoked, boneless kippers
1-2 cloves garlic, crushed
100 g butter
milled black pepper
60 ml cream
squeeze of fresh lemon juice

Place the kippers, heads down, in a deep jug. Fill with boiling water and set aside for 5 minutes. Drain, cool and flake the flesh.
  Gently soften the garlic in butter. Remove from the heat, mix in remaining ingredients and whiz smoothly in a food processor or blender.
Serves 4-6

Smoked Fish Pâté

Any smoked fish will do; our favourites are snoek and angelfish.

200 g smoked fish
1 onion, chopped
150 g butter
juice of ½ lemon
milled black pepper
125 ml cream
few drops of red food colouring

Remove fish skin and bones and flake the flesh. Soften the onion in half the butter. Remove from the heat and mix in the remaining butter, flaked fish, lemon juice, plenty of pepper, cream and food colouring.

Whiz the mixture smoothly in a food processor or blender. Check the flavour, scoop the pâté into a bowl, cover and refrigerate until firm. Serve liberally spread on wholewheat bread.

Serves 3-4

Aegean Island Pâté

Variation on the taramasalata theme. It's great on biscuits in the company of other Greek snacky things like olives, cubed feta cheese and dolmades.

200 g fresh fish roe
or 198 g tin cod's roe
5 slices crustless, cubed white bread
80 ml olive oil
80 ml cream
15 ml gelatine
40 ml fresh lemon juice
10 ml grated onion
1 clove garlic, crushed
4 canned anchovies, finely chopped
15 ml tomato sauce
salt and milled black pepper

If using fresh roe, first poach it whole for 10 minutes in water to which a little lemon juice has been added. Remove the skin and crumble the roe.

Pop it into a food processor, add the bread and pour over the olive oil and cream. Sprinkle gelatine onto the lemon juice and warm gently until it dissolves (place it in a larger container of hot water or microwave for 20 seconds on full power). Add the gelatine to the roe with the onion, garlic, anchovies, tomato sauce and a little salt and pepper. Bear in mind, though, that anchovies are salty. Whiz until smooth, then tip it into a bowl and chill.

Serves 4-6

Pandora's Mussels

Frozen mussels are a good substitute in this recipe. Simply dispense with the steaming and opening step and replace the mussel stock with fish stock.

36 black mussels
1 onion, finely chopped
100 g butter
750 ml soft breadcrumbs
50 g nibbed almonds, toasted
salt and milled black pepper
15 ml chopped fresh herbs
or 5 ml dried herbs
60 ml mussel stock
squeeze of fresh lemon juice

TOPPING
100 g butter
250 ml soft breadcrumbs
60 ml chopped parsley

Scrub mussels clean, steam open, remove from the shells and cut each into 3-4 pieces. Strain and reserve the stock. Settle 36 mussel shells in a layer of coarse salt on a baking tray. Set the oven at 180 °C.

Soften the onion in butter. Remove from the heat and mix in the mussel bits, crumbs, almonds, salt, pepper, herbs, mussel stock and lemon juice. Pack the filling into the shells.

Melt the butter for the topping, mix in the crumbs and parsley and top the mussels with this mixture. Bake for 5-10 minutes until piping hot and the topping is crisp. Arrange the mussels on plates and garnish with lemon.

Serve with fresh, crusty bread.

Serves 6

Haddock and Leek Roulade

Whip up a savoury Swiss roll with a delicious fishy filling to serve as a starter, luncheon dish or at a buffet.

ROULADE
50 g (50 ml) butter
50 g (100 ml) flour
500 ml milk
2 ml dry English mustard
2 ml white pepper
2 ml salt
40 g (125 ml) mature Cheddar cheese, grated
4 large eggs, separated
fresh herbs for garnish

Haddock and Leek Roulade, recipe page 16

HADDOCK AND LEEK FILLING
400 g haddock
milled black pepper
125 ml milk
1 large leek, sliced
30 g (30 ml) butter
30 ml flour
10 ml lemon juice

ROULADE In medium saucepan melt the butter, then remove from the heat and blend in the flour and a little of the milk to make a smooth paste. Slowly add the remaining milk, stirring briskly to avoid the mixture becoming lumpy. Season with mustard, pepper and salt.

Stir over high heat until the sauce thickens. Remove from the heat and beat in the cheese and egg yolks. Allow the mixture to cool. Set the oven at 160 °C. Line a 30 cm x 40 cm Swiss roll tin or biscuit tray with well-buttered waxed paper or light foil and sprinkle it with flour.

Beat the egg whites until they form soft peaks and fold them gently into the roulade base. Spread the mixture in the prepared baking tray and bake for 45 minutes until golden and springy to the touch. Meanwhile lay out a dry tea towel and cover it with waxed paper. Turn the roulade out onto it and gently peel off the baking paper or foil.

Roll up the roulade while it's still warm, starting with the long side and aided by the towel. Cool it, still rolled up, so that it keeps its shape.

FILLING Prepare this while the roulade is cooking. Place the haddock in a wide saucepan. Season with pepper, pour over the milk, cover and poach gently for about 10 minutes until the fish is cooked and flakes easily. Remove the fish from the poaching liquid (reserve it for the sauce) and remove the skin while it is still warm. Flake the fish coarsely and place in a bowl.

Soften the leek in melted butter. Remove from the heat, stir in the flour, then slowly add about 125 ml of the poaching liquid. Stir over high heat until the sauce thickens, adding a little more liquid if necessary. Mix in the lemon juice and season with pepper.

Unroll the roulade, spread over the warm filling and roll up once more. Place on serving platter, garnish with a bunch of fresh herbs and serve warm.

Serves 8-10

MAKE AHEAD Prepare and fill the roulade several hours ahead of time and place on a baking tray. Cover lightly with buttered, waxed paper. Reheat gently in a warm oven before serving.

Perlemoen Croquettes

Delicious to serve as snacks or starters. Instead of perlemoen, you're welcome to use prepared octopus or finely chopped prawns or shrimps.

750 g raw perlemoen (weight without shell)
butter and oil for cooking
1 small onion, very finely chopped
30 g (30 ml) butter
20 ml cake flour
250 ml milk
salt and milled black pepper
40 ml finely chopped parsley
2 ml dried tarragon
1 egg, lightly beaten
oil for deep-frying
lemon wedges for squeezing

COATING
toasted crumbs
2 eggs
30 ml milk

Scrub the perlemoen nice and clean and slice vertically; there's no need to tenderize it. Fry it lightly in a little butter and oil to bring out the flavour. Remove from the pan and set aside. Deglaze the pan with water and boil until reduced to a light glaze. Mince the perlemoen or chop very finely.

Soften the onion in the butter in a medium saucepan. Remove from the heat and blend in the flour, milk and a little salt and pepper. Stir over high heat for a couple of minutes until the sauce is smooth and thickened. Stir in the glaze from the sautéed perlemoen.

Mix the perlemoen into the sauce with the parsley, tarragon and beaten egg. Form into 50 mm croquettes and coat with crumbs. The easiest way to do this is to half fill a small bowl with crumbs, drop in a croquette and rotate the bowl. Refrigerate the croquettes for about 2 hours to chill and firm up.

Beat the topping eggs with milk, dip the croquettes in this, then recoat with crumbs as before. Deep-fry in hot oil until crisp and golden. Drain on kitchen paper and serve with lemon wedges to add a touch of tartness.
Serves 6

MAKE AHEAD The crumbed croquettes may be refrigerated for up to 24 hours. Deep-fry just before serving.

Redbait Poffertjies

Intrepid redbait munchers cut fresh pods from the rocks and guzzle them raw. However, the less courageous prefer them cooked, and deep-fried is the best way to do it.

fresh redbait
milled black pepper
butter for frying
crushed garlic
sunflower oil for deep-frying

COATING
egg and milk
toasted crumbs

Remove the redbait from their pods and clean very well. Be sure to scrape out and discard the stomach from the soft lower portion. Rinse in cold water and cut into blocks about 25 mm square. Season lightly with pepper.

In a small saucepan melt a little butter and add garlic to taste. Gently fry the redbait until the colour lightens, tossing well in the garlicky butter. This will take about 2-3 minutes. Remove from the heat and drain the redbait.

Beat together the egg and milk, using as much as is necessary for the amount of redbait you're using (calculate 15 ml milk for each egg). Dip redbait in this, then toss in the crumbs and coat lightly. Deep-fry in medium-hot oil until very crisp and golden-brown. Unlike most other seafood, over-cooking is not too much of a problem; a crisp coating is more important.

Drain poffertjies well and serve hot with lemon wedges.

MAKE AHEAD It is vital that only the freshest of fresh redbait is used; the flavour tends to become stronger if it is kept for too long. If this is the case, use it as bait and catch a fish with it instead!

It may, however, be crumbed, covered and refrigerated for a few hours. Deep-fry just before serving so they are crunchy and piping hot.

Oysters Kilpatrick

24 oysters on the half-shell
4 rashers rindless streaky bacon
Worcestershire sauce

Line a baking tray with coarse salt and nestle the oysters to stand level. Chop the bacon into very tiny bits and divide it among the oysters. Sprinkle a few drops of Worcestershire sauce on top and sizzle under the oven griller until the bacon is crisp. Serve hot.
Serves 4

BAKED ANCHOVY AVOCADO

2 ripe avocados
20 g chopped walnuts or pecans, toasted
6 canned anchovies, finely chopped
250 ml Mayonnaise (page 94)
30 ml milk
250 ml soft breadcrumbs
stoned black olives or capers for garnish

Set the oven at 220 °C. Leaving the skin on, cut the avocados into thirds or halves. Slice these into 3-4 strips, cutting almost to the tip. Peel off the skin, fan the avocado on individual plates and scatter the nuts over.

Blend anchovies, mayonnaise and milk and spoon onto the avocado, leaving the tips exposed. Scatter over the crumbs, place the plates in the oven and reduce the temperature to 200 °C. Bake for 7 minutes. The topping should be golden, the crumbs toasted, and the avocado warm. Garnish each platter with olives or capers – serve at once.

Serves 4-6

SMOKED OYSTER BITES

Enfold canned oysters in crisp pastry for a quick and delicious snack that may be served warm or cool.

2 x 105 g cans smoked oysters, drained
Cream Cheese Pastry (page 92)

Set the oven at 200 °C. Lightly oil a baking tray. Roll out the pastry thinly and cut into circles about 8 cm in diameter. Place a smoked oyster onto each circle. Fold the pastry over and seal the edges with a little water, crimping lightly with a fork.

Place the oyster bites on the baking tray and bake for 15 minutes until golden-brown. Serve warm.

Makes about 20

MAKE AHEAD These snacks remain deliciously crisp for several hours after baking. They also reheat beautifully in a moderately warm oven should it be necessary to prepare them ahead of time.

Oysters Kilpatrick, recipe page 18

Steamed Crayfish with Tangy Butter, recipe page 21

CHEESE CRUST OYSTERS

Oysters nestled under a creamy, cheesy, crunchy blanket.

24 oysters on the half-shell
250 ml milk
1 bay leaf
1 small onion, quartered
5 black peppercorns
30 g (30 ml) butter
30 ml cake flour
60 ml cream
salt and milled black pepper
60 ml grated mild cheese (Gruyère or mild Cheddar)
60 ml soft breadcrumbs

Stand the oysters on baking trays, ready for cooking. A layer of coarse salt on the trays will keep the shells steady.

In a small saucepan combine the milk, bay leaf, onion and peppercorns. Bring to the boil, remove from the heat and allow to stand for at least 10 minutes for the flavours to infuse, then strain.

Melt the butter in a medium saucepan. Remove from the heat and blend in the flour and a little of the flavoured milk to form a smooth paste. Stir in the remaining milk, cream and a little salt and pepper. Stir over high heat until the sauce is smooth and thickened, then remove from the heat and stir in half the cheese. Mix together remaining cheese and crumbs for the topping.

Spoon about two teaspoonfuls of sauce onto each oyster, sprinkle with cheesy crumbs and brown under the griller. The oysters will be lightly cooked, the sauce piping hot, and the topping deliciously crunchy.

Transfer the sizzling oysters to four plates (six per serving), garnish with lemon wedges and serve at once.

Serves 4

Scallops in Creamy Leek Sauce

A delicious blending of flavours that compliments the delicate flavour of scallops. Mussels could be used instead.

500 g scallops
1 leek, sliced (white part only)
30 g (30 ml) butter

SAUCE
375 ml Fish Stock (page 88)
375 ml dry white wine
5 ml crushed garlic
250 ml cream
2 egg yolks
15 ml fresh lemon juice
salt and milled black pepper
fennel sprigs and paprika for garnish

Rinse the scallops with cold water (leave the roe intact), pat dry and set aside. Soften the leek in butter in a medium saucepan. Add scallops and cook for 2-3 minutes, turning occasionally. Remove from the heat and set aside.

Combine stock, wine and garlic in a clean saucepan and simmer uncovered until reduced by half. Meanwhile mix the cream and egg yolks together and mix in some of the simmering stock, a few spoonfuls at a time. Remove the stock from the heat and whisk in the egg mixture.

Heat the sauce gently, stirring all the while, just until it thickens slightly. Don't allow it to boil; the sauce will curdle if it does. Pour the sauce over the scallops, stir in the lemon juice and a little salt and pepper. Reheat gently.

Spoon the scallops onto four plates, garnish with fennel and dust with paprika. Serve with crusty bread to mop up the delicious sauce.
Serves 4

Nut-Crust Oysters

16-20 shucked oysters
60 ml cake flour
milled black pepper
2 ml ground allspice
150 ml toasted crumbs
80 ml finely chopped walnuts
2 eggs, lightly beaten

Mix together flour, pepper and allspice. Combine crumbs and walnuts in another small bowl. Dip oysters in flour, in egg, then in crumbs. Deep-fry in hot oil for about 1 minute until golden-brown. Drain and serve with lemon wedges.
Serves 4

Steamed Crayfish with Tangy Butter

Simplicity is the essence of this stunning starter: crayfish steamed in wine, vinegar and herbs, which is then reduced to form the base of a simple butter sauce.

4 crayfish tails
125 ml off-dry white wine
60 ml white wine vinegar
1 fresh or dried bouquet garni
(parsley, fennel, thyme)

TANGY BUTTER
stock from poaching crayfish
125 g cold butter, cut in small cubes
milled black pepper

TO SERVE
oak or butter lettuce
sliced melon or paw-paw
sprigs of fennel

Slice the crayfish tails by snipping down the length of the shell – both back and belly – with a pair of scissors. With a sharp knife, cut through the flesh and remove alimentary canal. (Doing it this way is preferable to simply slicing through the shell, which is inclined to damage the flesh.)

In a medium saucepan combine the wine, vinegar and herbs. Bring to the boil and add the crayfish, shells down. Cover and simmer very gently for 4-5 minutes until the crayfish is perfectly cooked. Remove from the stock and cover with foil to keep warm while preparing the sauce.

TANGY BUTTER Increase the heat and boil the stock uncovered until it is reduced to 30 ml. Remove from the heat, discard the herbs and whisk in the butter, bit by bit, until the sauce is silky smooth. Season with a little pepper.

Arrange the lettuce leaves on four serving plates. Remove crayfish from the shells, place each piece on the lettuce and spoon over just a touch of the butter sauce. Garnish each serving with sliced melon and a sprig of fennel and serve warm.
Serves 8

MAKE AHEAD To preserve the wonderful flavour, the crayfish must be freshly steamed and should not be refriger-ated between steaming and serving. The sauce, too, should be freshly made and spooned over the crayfish while it is still warm.

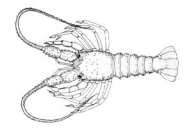

CRAYFISH MOUSSELINES WITH RED PEPPER PURÉE

There's an air of delightful decadence about this classy starter – individual mousselines served with a pretty purée.

CRAYFISH MOUSSELINES
250 g crayfish tail flesh (weight without shells; reserve shells for garnish)
250 g skinless hake fillets
2 eggs
250 ml cream
250 ml milk
15 ml chopped parsley (optional)
5 ml salt
2 ml white pepper

RED PEPPER PURÉE
2 large red peppers (about 300 g)
125 ml cream
1 onion, finely chopped
2 large, ripe tomatoes, skinned and chopped
50 g (50 ml) butter
2 ml crushed garlic
5 ml salt
5 ml paprika
1 ml sugar
milled black pepper
lobster tail segments and fresh herbs for garnish

First prepare the shell garnishes: cut off the fanned part of each tail shell and poach in simmering water for about 5 minutes until bright orangey-red. Scrub under cold running water and cut off the two outside segments on each side. Gloss lightly with a spray of oil.

MOUSSELINES Set the oven at 160 °C. Oil eight mousseline dishes (teacups are a fine substitute). Cut the crayfish and fish into large cubes and purée in a blender or food processor with the eggs, cream, milk, parsley, salt and pepper. Divide the mixture evenly between the prepared baking dishes. Place them in a larger baking dish, pour in enough boiling water to come half-way up the sides and cover with foil to prevent the mousselines hardening as they cook. Bake for 20 minutes until cooked and the tip of a sharp knife comes out clean.

RED PEPPER PURÉE Slice the peppers into wide strips, discarding seeds and filaments, and place skin-up on a baking tray. Grill until the skin blisters and starts to blacken (please don't burn the flesh!). Remove from the oven, cover with a damp tea towel and leave to cool. Peel off and discard the skin. Purée the peppers with the cream.

In a small saucepan soften the onion in butter without allowing it to brown. Stir in the tomato, garlic, salt, paprika, sugar and pepper, cover and simmer gently for 5 minutes. If you prefer your sauce smooth, purée the onion mixture with the red pepper, otherwise simply mix it together and heat through. Adjust the seasoning.

Pour pools of pepper purée on eight serving plates, place a piping hot lobster mousseline on each, and garnish with segments of lobster tail shell and sprigs of herbs.
Serves 8

MAKE AHEAD The mousselines remain hot for up to an hour after cooking if left in the hot water. Or prepare them a day ahead, seal with clingfilm and refrigerate before cooking. The purée may be prepared several days ahead of time and reheated before serving.

PERLEMOEN TIMBALES WITH PINK HOLLANDAISE

A wonderful way to serve perlemoen when the diving season is in full swing and inventive cooks are searching for a new way to serve the super stuff. These timbales are incredibly easy to prepare (provided you have a food processor). They are equally delicious hot or cold.

TIMBALES
1 large perlemoen (about 250 g cleaned weight)
1 egg
125 ml cream
125 ml milk
5 ml finely chopped herbs (parsley, thyme, origanum) or 1 ml dried mixed herbs
2 ml salt
milled black pepper

PINK HOLLANDAISE
30 ml white or red wine vinegar
30 ml dry white wine
milled black pepper
3 XL egg yolks
15 ml tomato purée
200 g butter, cubed
30 ml thick cream
fresh herbs for garnish

Set the oven at 160 °C. Oil four ramekins or suitably shaped cups.

Scrub the perlemoen clean, trim it and cut into smallish cubes. Place it in a food processor and whiz as smoothly as possible. Blend in the egg, cream, milk, herbs, salt and a little pepper. Divide the mixture between the prepared ramekins, cover loosely with foil (don't seal; this will cause excess moisture to accumulate) and place them in a large baking tray. Pour in sufficient boiling water to come

Crayfish Mousselines with Red Pepper Purée, and Perlemoen Timbales with Pink Hollandaise, recipes page 22

half-way up the sides and bake for 20 minutes. Test with the tip of a sharp knife, piercing only to the centre of a timbale. If it comes out clean, it is cooked; if not, bake for a further 5 minutes.

HOLLANDAISE In the top of a double boiler combine vinegar, wine and a little pepper. Place directly on the heat and boil uncovered until reduced to 30 ml. Meanwhile bring water to simmering point in base saucepan. (The water should neither boil nor touch the top saucepan.)

Into the wine reduction beat the yolks and tomato purée, place over simmering water and cook, whisking continuously, until the sauce thickens. Whisk in the butter cube by cube, then remove from the heat immediately. Continue whisking for a further minute or so to cool the sauce slightly, then stir in the cream.

Spoon a little sauce onto four serving plates. Slide a knife round the edge of each timbale, tip out onto the sauce and garnish with fresh herbs.

Serves 4

ALTERNATIVE SERVING SUGGESTIONS

Combine two different sauces on each plate and place timbales in the centre. The flavour and colour of Fennel Sauce (page 97) or Mushroom Cream Sauce (page 98) contrast beautifully with the hollandaise.

- Another way of serving the timbales is to slice each vertically into 4 slices. Fan them onto the sauce and top with a sprig or two of herbs.
- For extra special entertaining: Before baking, insert into each timbale 2-3 large, uncooked, shelled prawns – tails up. Besides enhancing the flavour, the prawns create a colourful pattern as the timbales are sliced.

MAKE AHEAD The timbales may be kept warm in the hot water for up to an hour after baking. Hollandaise sauce should be served as soon as it has been prepared, but it won't mind too much if returned to the double boiler base after cooling slightly, where it may remain for up to an hour without spoiling in any way.

Salad Niçoise

200 g can light tuna
200 g slim green beans
crisp mixed salad greens
3 firm tomatoes, cut in wedges
¼ English cucumber, sliced
1 green or red pepper, seeded and sliced
3 hard-boiled eggs, quartered or chopped
6 canned anchovy fillets
black olives
chopped parsley
French Dressing (page 94)

Drain and flake the tuna. Cook the beans in salted water until tender (but not too floppy), refresh in iced water and drain well.

Arrange the salad greens on a large platter. Scatter flaked tuna on top and decorate with beans, tomato wedges, cucumber, green or red pepper, hard-boiled eggs, anchovies and a few black olives. Garnish with a generous scattering of chopped parsley.

Sprinkle the dressing over the salad, or offer it separately if some of your guests prefer an undressed salad. It makes a great starter or luncheon dish. If it's available, poach or steam fresh tuna instead of using canned fish.

Serves 6

Cool Calamari Salad, recipe page 25

COOL CALAMARI SALAD

Tender calamari in a light and spicy dressing with a salad and a garnish of fruit makes a delicious summer starter. If there's no paw-paw or melon about, use slim wedges of apple or pear.

400 g calamari tubes
fresh salad greens
paw-paw or melon balls

SPICY FENNEL DRESSING
125 ml Crème Fraîche (page 90)
15 ml snipped chives or spring onion
2 ml ground cumin
2 ml finely chopped fennel
or 1 ml dried fennel
salt and milled black pepper
fennel fronds for garnish

Clean the calamari tubes thoroughly, inside and out, in cold water. Slice into rings and place in a large bowl. Pour over plenty of briskly boiling water, stirring the calamari in the water. Allow to stand for 1 minute, then test it; it should be opaque yet meltingly tender. Allow to stand in the water for 30-60 seconds more if it's still slightly chewy, then tip it into a colander to drain.

Pile the calamari in a bowl. Mix together the dressing ingredients, pour over and toss well.

Arrange salad greens prettily on four plates. Pile the calamari salad into the centre and garnish with paw-paw or melon balls and fennel fronds.
Serves 4

MAKE AHEAD Calamari may be dressed, covered and refrigerated for up to 2 days.

HADDOCK SALAD O'NEILL

Homely haddock and crunchy prawns combined in the most heavenly salad. If you're feeling particularly parsimonious, leave out the prawns (be sure to increase the amount of fish if you do), but don't leave the recipe lying around. You'll not want your guests to know what they're missing.

500 g haddock
400 g prawns, heads off (optional)
6 carrots, cut into matchsticks
6 ribs celery, cut into matchsticks
2 green peppers, seeded and cut into matchsticks
½ English cucumber, cut into matchsticks
250 ml chopped spring onion
8 large lettuce leaves
chopped parsley for garnish

DRESSING
250 ml Mayonnaise (page 94)
125 ml cream
30 ml fresh lemon juice
10 ml coarse mustard
salt and milled black pepper

Poach the haddock, then drain, skin and flake. Poach prawns in boiling water (about 3 minutes, depending on size); shell and devein.

Place the carrot, celery, green peppers and cucumber in a large bowl. Toss with the spring onion, flaked haddock and prawns.

Blend the mayonnaise, cream, lemon juice, mustard and seasoning together until smooth and of pouring consistency (add a little milk if it's too thick). Pour over the salad and toss very well to coat every morsel thoroughly.

Line a pretty salad bowl with lettuce leaves, pile the salad into the centre and garnish with chopped parsley. Alternatively, place a lettuce leaf on each serving plate, fill the leaves with salad and garnish with parsley.
Serves 8

MAKE AHEAD This salad keeps well for up to a day.

SALMON CHANTILLY SALAD

Canned salmon is a marvellous stand-by, and in here forms the centrepiece of a summer salad platter. If grapes are unobtainable, substitute melon balls or mandarin orange segments.

210 g can pink salmon
30 ml finely chopped red pepper
15 ml chopped parsley
90 ml Mayonnaise (page 94)
30 ml sour cream
5 ml fresh lemon juice

SALAD
4 butter lettuce leaves
4 large button mushrooms, sliced
watercress
12 seedless grapes
whole chives

Drain the salmon and flake on kitchen paper, which will absorb the excess moisture. Discard the skin and tiny bones. Mix the fish with the red pepper, parsley, mayonnaise, sour cream and lemon juice.

Place lettuce leaves on four plates, spoon a quarter of the salmon mixture into each and garnish with sliced mushroom, watercress, peeled grapes and chives.
Serves 4

SOUPS

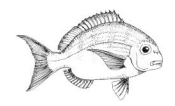

Seafood may be magicked into a wide variety of soups, from humble, hearty potages like Beggar's Bouillabaisse, to an elaborate concoction like Velvety Scallop Soup suitable for a show-off occasion.

BRETON FISH SOUP

Recipes from the French province of Bretagne are fairly simple when compared with the more complicated and highly-seasoned bouillabaisse from Provence. The fish which may be used in this recipe are the same, though – red steenbras, geelbek, kob, kingklip, yellowtail, musselcracker, silverfish and stumpnose.

1,5 kg firm fish fillets, skinned and cut
into pieces
80 ml olive oil
3 onions, chopped
2 cloves garlic, very finely chopped
4 potatoes, peeled and sliced
4 ripe tomatoes, skinned and chopped
or a 400 g can
125 ml dry white wine
1 litre Court-Bouillon or Fish Stock (page 88)
5 ml turmeric
5 ml salt
milled black pepper
1 bay leaf
2 sprigs thyme
or a pinch of dried thyme
chopped parsley for garnish

In a large pot fry the onion, garlic and potato in oil until golden. Add the tomato (use the liquid, too, if using a can), wine, stock and seasoning. Cover and simmer for about 15 minutes until the potato is nearly cooked.

Add the fish, cover and simmer for about 5 minutes more until cooked. Check the seasoning, then tip the soup into a hot tureen, garnish with chopped parsley and serve with lots of crusty bread.

Serves 8-10

HADDOCK AND ORANGE BROTH

300 g haddock
500 ml water
butter for cooking
500 g carrots, sliced
1 large onion, chopped
125 ml orange juice
2 ml grated orange rind
1 ml milled black pepper
60 ml medium dry sherry
125 ml cream
salt
coriander leaves or chopped parsley for garnish

Poach haddock in water, drain, flake and set aside. Reserve the poaching liquid.

Heat a little butter in a large saucepan, add carrot and onion, cover and sweat over low heat for about 6 minutes. Stir in the poaching liquid, orange juice, rind and pepper. Cover and simmer gently for 30 minutes until the vegetables are very soft.

Purée the soup, return it to the saucepan and add the sherry, cream and haddock. Heat through gently and check the seasoning and consistency, adding a touch of salt if necessary and a little milk if the broth is too thick.

Ladle the soup into warm bowls and garnish each serving with coriander leaves or chopped parsley.

Serves 6-8

Haddock and Orange Broth, and Breton Fish Soup

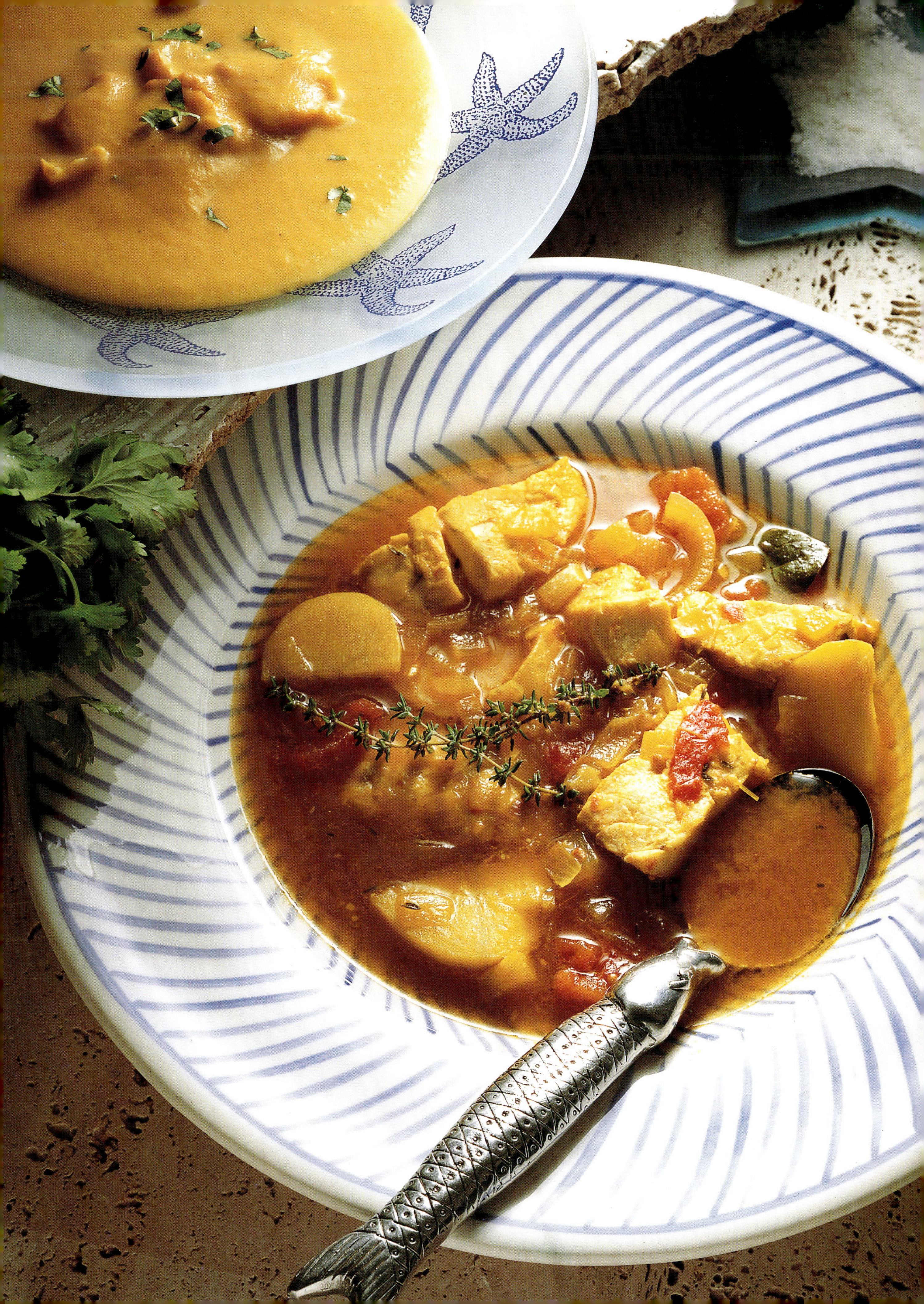

Cream of Perlemoen Soup, recipe page 29

Black Mussel Soup

Fresh or canned mussels work equally well in this recipe but do keep to the exact measurements of the flavourings – it's so easy to overpower the delicate mussel flavour.

36 black mussels
or a 900 g can
50 g (50 ml) butter
1 onion, chopped
2 ml crushed garlic
30 ml chopped parsley
30 g (30 ml) cake flour
125 ml mussel liquor
125 ml Fish Stock (page 88)
500 ml milk
125 ml dry white wine
5 ml chopped origanum
or 2 ml dried origanum
1 bay leaf
milled black pepper
125 ml cream

Steam the mussels open in a little water, drain (reserve 125 ml of the liquor) and pull out the beards, leaving the mussels attached to the shells. If using canned mussels, drain them and strain the liquor through a fine strainer (even in the can, it tends to be gritty). Rinse mussels under gently running cold water, rubbing the shells to remove sand and grit. Drain, open side down, in a colander.

In a large pot gently soften the onion, garlic and parsley in butter. Remove from the heat and blend in the flour, then add the mussel liquor slowly, making sure there are no lumps. Add the stock, milk and wine and cook, stirring, until the soup begins to thicken. Add the origanum, bay leaf and pepper. Cover and simmer very gently for 10 minutes. Check the seasoning. Just before serving, add the cream and mussels to the soup and heat through without allowing it to boil.

Serves 6-8

MAKE AHEAD This soup may be prepared up to 2 days ahead of time. Store the broth and mussels separately, covered and refrigerated. Before serving, reheat the broth and add the mussels and cream.

CREAM OF PERLEMOEN SOUP

A heavenly soup, the flavouring gently understated so as not to mask the perlemoen in any way.

400 g perlemoen (weight without shells)
60 g (60 ml) butter
1 large onion, finely chopped
2 ml crushed garlic
30 ml cake flour
250 ml cream
375 ml milk
125 ml dry white wine
juice of 1 small lemon
salt and milled black pepper
30 ml brandy
grated nutmeg for garnish

Scrub the perlemoen until squeaky clean, taking extra care with folds and crevices in the skirt. Slice this off and chop roughly. Cut out and discard the black alimentary canal. Cut the perlemoen vertically into slices about 5 mm thick. Select 8 slices and tenderize each with a mallet. These will be added to the soup just before serving.

Heat the butter in a heavy frying pan, and fry the tenderized slices very quickly – 1 minute's cooking time is all that's required. Set aside.

Fry remaining perlemoen for 1 minute, then remove from the pan and set aside. Mix the onion and garlic into the buttery pan-juices, adding a touch more butter if necessary. Cook until tender, then remove from the heat and blend in the flour. Purée the soup smoothly with the cream, milk, wine, lemon juice, seasoning and perlemoen. (Not the 8 selected slices.)

Pour the soup into a clean pot, cover and bring to the boil. Stir and simmer gently. Meanwhile cut the reserved perlemoen slices into smaller strips and place in a small bowl. Warm the brandy, pour over, flame, then stir the pieces into the soup. Check the seasoning and serve immediately, garnishing each serving with grated nutmeg.
Serves 8

MAKE AHEAD This soup may be refrigerated for up to 3 days. Store the reserved perlemoen separately. Flame with brandy and add to the soup just before serving.

SEAFOOD IN A CLAY POT

A sensational seafood supper for two. Prepare and serve in individual casseroles to allow more time to enjoy the candlelight – and the company! Beg, borrow or filch two matching clay pots in which to prepare this dish. Or use one larger casserole, nestle all the ingredients together, and enjoy the meal cuddled up close. The best fish to use in this recipe include red steenbras, geelbek, kob, kingklip, angelfish or stumpnose.

1 large crayfish tail, shelled and deveined
200 g filleted fish
4 medium prawns (heads off)
6 black mussels
1-2 small calamari tubes (optional)
milled black pepper

SAUCE
2 leeks, finely sliced
1 large ripe tomato, skinned and chopped
100 g butter
5 ml crushed garlic
125 ml Fish Stock (page 88)
125 ml dry white wine
30 ml chopped parsley

Set the oven at 200 °C. Cut the crayfish in half vertically and slice each half into 3-4 chunks. Skin the fish and cut into similarly proportioned pieces.

Devein the prawns and discard the shells, leaving the last tail segment intact to improve the appearance of the dish. Scrub the mussel shells and pull out the beards. Slice the calamari into rings.

Place the crayfish, fish, prawns and mussels into the pots or casserole. Season generously with pepper. (The calamari will be added towards the end of the cooking time.)

SAUCE In a small saucepan heat a little of the butter and fry the leek until tender. Stir in the tomato and garlic and cook for a minute more. Add the remaining butter, stock and wine and bring to the boil.

Pour the sauce over the seafood, cover with the lids or with foil. If the lids aren't tight fitting enough, place foil under them to ensure a good seal. Bake the seafood pots for 18 minutes.

Add the calamari, immersing it in the sauce. Replace the lids and bake for a further 2 minutes, which is all the time it should take for the seafood to be cooked to succulent perfection.

Garnish with a sprinkling of chopped parsley, light the candles and pour the wine. Serve the pot with plenty of crusty bread to dunk into the sauce; it's far too delectable to waste a drop.
Serves 2

QUISSICO BISQUE

Extravagant, but really special. Substitute canned oysters if you must – but don't use smoked oysters.

18 shucked oysters
2 onions, chopped
100 g button mushrooms, thinly sliced
30 g (30 ml) butter
850 ml Fish Stock (page 88)
400 g shelled, deveined prawns
1 potato, peeled and thinly sliced
salt and milled black pepper
200 ml cream
chopped parsley for garnish

Soften the chopped onion and mushrooms in butter. Add the stock, prawns, potato and a little salt and pepper. Cover and simmer gently just until potato is tender – about 10 minutes. Cool slightly, then whiz the soup in a blender or food processor until smooth.

Pour the soup back into the pot, add the cream and oysters – whole or cut into halves if you prefer. Simmer for 2-3 minutes (just long enough to cook the oysters). Check the flavour and tip the soup into a hot tureen or serving bowl and garnish with chopped parsley. Serve with wholewheat bread.

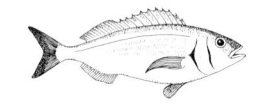

Serves 8-10

BOUILLABAISSE

This speciality of Marseilles in France has its origins in the mists of time. It is said that the ancient Phoenicians were the first to introduce this classical combination of fish, shellfish and herbs, with tangy rouille as an optional garnish.
Use whatever fish is available – the best types are red steenbras, geelbek, kob, kingklip, yellowtail, musselcracker, silverfish and stumpnose. Other seafood may also be added – like scallops and langoustines.

SEAFOOD
2 kg firm white fish fillets
500 g prawns (weight in shell)
24 black mussels
4 crayfish tails

BOUILLON
2 onions, finely sliced
3-4 leeks, finely sliced
125 ml olive oil
1,5 litres water
500 ml dry white wine
1 kg fish bones and trimmings
1,25 kg ripe tomatoes, skinned and quartered
1 fresh or dried bouquet garni
3-4 large sprigs fennel
or 2 ml dried fennel
5 threads of saffron
or 2 ml turmeric
2 cloves garlic, roughly chopped
3 strips orange peel
salt and milled black pepper

ROUILLE
2 red or green peppers, seeded and chopped
1 fresh red or green chilli, seeded and chopped
or a few drops of Tabasco
500 ml water
4 cloves garlic, chopped
80 ml olive oil
30-45 ml soft breadcrumbs

ROUILLE Simmer the green pepper and chilli in water for about 10 minutes until tender. Drain and pat dry, then whiz in a food processor or blender with the garlic and olive oil. Add enough crumbs for the rouille to hold its shape. Add Tabasco at this stage if you haven't used a chilli. Season with salt and pepper.

SEAFOOD Skin the fish and cut into large cubes; devein the prawns; steam open the mussels and remove the beards; remove the crayfish meat from the shells if you wish and cut into cubes.

BOUILLON In a large pot soften the onion and leek in olive oil. Add the remaining ingredients and simmer uncovered for 30 minutes. Strain into a clean pot, pressing on the solids to extract all the flavour. Check the seasoning.

Bring the bouillon to simmering point, add the fish and cook for 2 minutes. Add the prawns, crayfish and mussels and simmer for 5 minutes more until all the seafood is cooked. Check the seasoning.

WATCHPOINT Always start timing when the liquid reaches simmering point again.

Bouillabaisse is traditionally served in deep bowls with seafood and broth separate, a spoonful of rouille added to each serving. Alternatively divide the seafood between the bowls, top with the broth and offer the rouille separately for your guests to help themselves.

Serves 8-10

Bouillabaisse, recipe page 30

CRAYFISH BISQUE

A stunning, subtly-flavoured soup.

1 crayfish tail (250 g-300 g in the shell)
300 ml Fish Stock (page 88)
125 ml water
1 small onion, finely chopped
30 g (30 ml) butter
15 ml cake flour
15 ml tomato purée
125 ml milk
5 ml medium dry sherry
salt and milled black pepper
60 ml brandy
200 ml cream
paprika for garnish

Remove the crayfish from the shell and place the shell in a small saucepan with stock and water. Cover and simmer for 20-25 minutes. Strain the stock; discard the shell.

In a medium saucepan fry the onion in butter until golden. Mix in the flour and slowly blend in the stock. Add the tomato purée, milk, sherry and a little salt and pepper. Cover and simmer gently for a few minutes.

Meanwhile devein the crayfish, cut the meat into small pieces and place it in a small bowl. Warm the brandy, pour it over the crayfish and flame. As soon as the flames subside, add the crayfish to the pot and simmer for 3 minutes.

Add most of the cream (reserve a little to garnish the soup), heat the soup and check the seasoning. Ladle it into warm bowls and top each serving with a swirl of cream and a light sprinkling of paprika.

Serves 6

Red Sails in the Sunset, recipe page 33

RED SAILS IN THE SUNSET

A delicious soup that is strong on visual appeal too.

24-32 black mussels, well scrubbed
8-12 prawns shelled, deveined and halved lengthwise
250 ml water
125 ml dry white wine
10-12 spring onions, finely chopped
1 rib celery, finely sliced
4-5 ripe tomatoes, skinned and chopped
or a 400 g can
2 bay leaves
½ chicken stock cube
milled black pepper
chopped parsley for garnish

In a large saucepan combine the water, wine, spring onion, celery, tomato, bay leaves, crumbled stock cube and pepper. Cover and simmer gently for about 10 minutes.

Add the mussels and prawns, cover and simmer for a few minutes more – just long enough to open the mussels and cook the prawns. Debeard the mussels and check the seasoning of the broth. Tip the soup into a hot tureen, garnish with chopped parsley and serve with crusty bread.
Serves 4

MAKE AHEAD Cook the broth a day ahead. The seafood must be added and cooked just before serving.

VELVETY SCALLOP SOUP

A simply stunning soup for when posh nosh is called for. It's rich, so choose a light main course to follow. If scallops aren't easy to come by, substitute shelled prawns.

250 g shelled scallops
30 g (30 ml) butter
30 ml chopped fennel
30 ml finely snipped chives
125 ml champagne or dry white wine
125 ml cream

VELOUTÉ SAUCE
100 g butter
100 g (200 ml) cake flour
1,25 litres hot Fish Stock (page 88)
salt and white pepper

TOPPING
250 ml cream
5 ml Burmese Curry Mix (page 90)
or mild curry powder

Rinse the scallops lightly under running water and pat dry. Cut them into halves or thirds if you wish. Heat 30 g butter in a medium saucepan and lightly fry the scallops with fennel and chives for 1 minute. Remove the scallops from the pot with a slotted spoon and set aside. Add the champagne or wine to the pot and boil uncovered until reduced by half. Add the cream and reduce again by half.

VELOUTÉ SAUCE Melt the butter in a large saucepan. Remove from the heat and blend in the flour. Slowly add the hot fish stock, stirring constantly, until smoothly blended. Stir over high heat for a couple of minutes and season with a little salt and pepper. Strain this into the reduction, add the scallops and heat through.

Lightly whip the topping cream and mix in the curry powder. Ladle the soup into hot soup bowls, float the curry-cream on top and glaze under a hot grill.
Serves 4-6

MAKE AHEAD Prepare the soup prior to the point of adding the scallops. Cover and chill the soup and scallops separately for up to a day. Reheat the soup before adding the scallops to avoid overcooking them. Glaze the topping just before serving.

BEGGAR'S BOUILLABAISSE

2 onions, finely sliced
10 ml crushed garlic
45 ml olive oil
2 large potatoes, peeled and cubed
4 ripe tomatoes, skinned and chopped
or a 400 g can
small strip of orange peel
1 bay leaf
5 ml each turmeric and sugar
1,5 litres Fish Stock (page 88)
60 ml chopped parsley
salt and milled black pepper
1 kg filleted fish, skinned
and cut into 30 mm cubes

Soften the onion and garlic in a large saucepan. Add the potato, tomato, orange peel, bay leaf, turmeric, sugar, stock and half the parsley. Season with salt and pepper. Cover and simmer until the potatoes are almost tender – about 15-20 minutes.

Add the fish to the broth, cover and simmer very gently until cooked through – about 3-5 minutes depending on the thickness of the fish. Check the seasoning. Discard the orange rind, sprinkle over remaining parsley, and serve steaming hot with crusty bread.
Serves 6-8

Fish Dishes

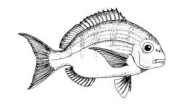

Fish is the most versatile thing in the world, happily teaming up with a myriad flavouring agents and taking well to many different cooking techniques. These recipes are perfect for any occasion, from the simplest family supper to the poshest dinner party.

Quick Fish Rissoles

A food processor means never having to pre-cook fish for rissoles ever again! Simply process the raw ingredients, mix and fry. Serve them hot with a sauce, cold with mayonnaise or make tiny ones to offer with pre-dinner drinks. Hake is marvellous for this recipe, but any white fish will do.

1 kg filleted white fish
400 g (2 large) potatoes, peeled and quartered
1 large onion, skinned and quartered
2 XL eggs, lightly beaten
60 ml chopped parsley
2 ml salt
2 ml milled black pepper
2 ml grated nutmeg
butter and sunflower oil for frying

Skin the fish and cut into manageable chunks. There is no need to worry about the small side-bones in each fillet; processing the fish mixture will take care of them for you.

Whiz the fish quickly in a food processor to chop, then transfer it to a large mixing bowl. Whiz the potatoes and onion until finely chopped and add to the fish together with the egg, parsley, salt, pepper and nutmeg. Mix well.

In a large frying pan heat plenty of butter and oil. When sizzling hot, scoop up spoonfuls of the fish mixture and drop into pan. Fry until golden-brown (approximately 3 minutes on each side), then drain briefly on absorbent paper. Transfer to a warmed serving platter while cooking the remaining rissoles.

Serve hot with creamy mashed potato and Piquant Sauce (page 98) or Herbed Tomato Sauce (page 97). If serving cold, offer with a salad and Herb Mayonnaise (page 94).

Fish Cakes

Everyone's favourite way of using left-over fish – any sort will do. Of course you're welcome to cook fish specially for the occasion if you wish.

500 g cooked fish fillets, skinned
300 g potatoes, peeled and diced
salt and milled black pepper
60 ml grated onion
45 ml chopped parsley
pinch of grated nutmeg
2 eggs, lightly beaten
toasted crumbs for coating
sunflower oil for frying

Cook the potato in a little salted water, drain, mash and season with salt and pepper. Flake the fish and mix with the mashed potato, onion, parsley, salt, pepper, nutmeg and beaten egg.

Drop spoonfuls of fish cake mixture into the crumbs and coat evenly. Form into patties with your hands, flattening them slightly.

Fry the fish cakes in hot oil until crisp and golden and drain on kitchen paper. Serve hot with chips and Herbed Tomato Sauce (page 97), or cold and nestled into mixed salad leaves.
Makes about 16

Quick Fish Rissoles, and Salpicon of Perlemoen, recipe page 79

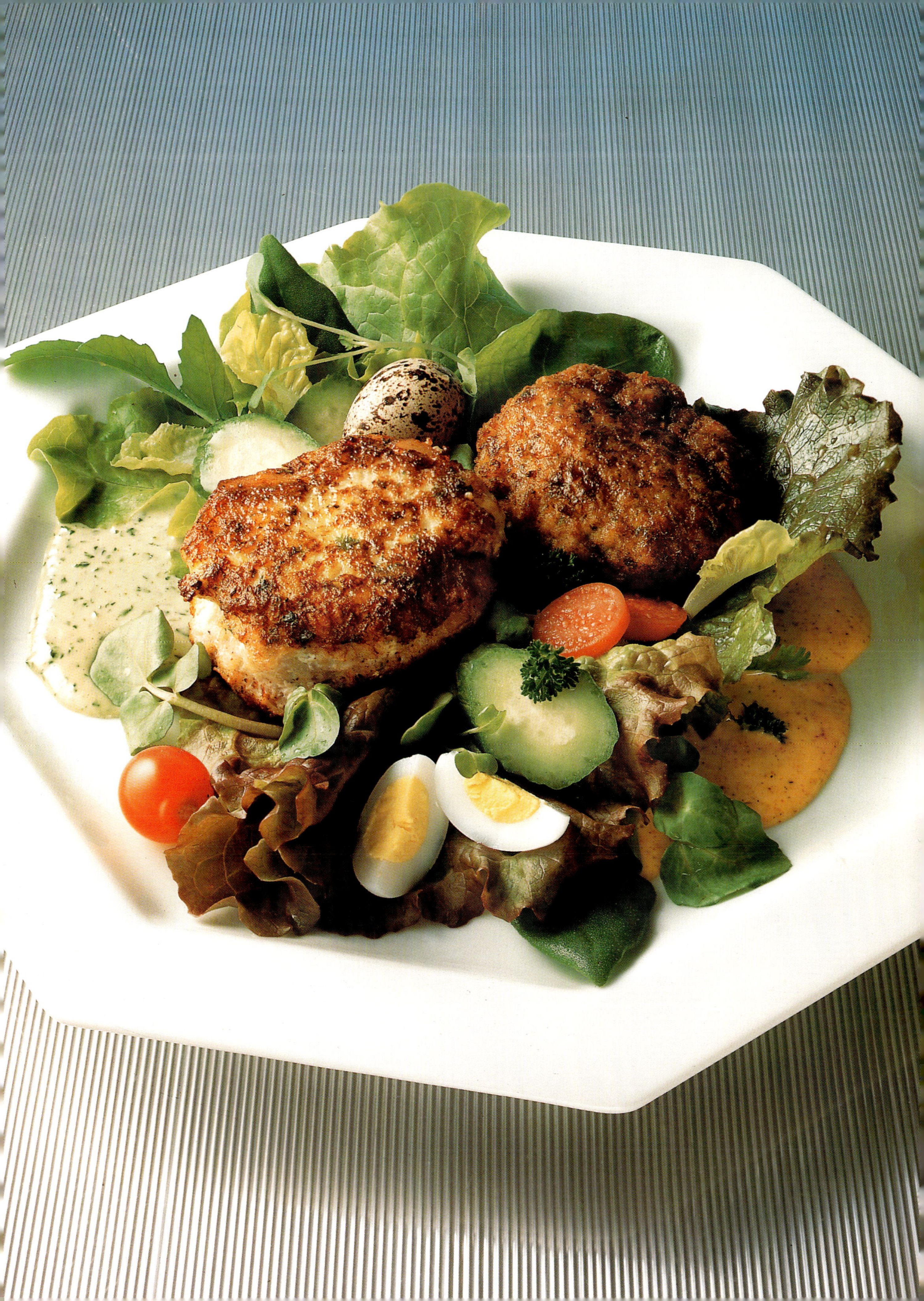

Apple and Almond Hake, recipe page 37

Spring Vegetable Hake Bake

Quick, delicious and so perfect for hake that it's unnecessary to use a more expensive fish. It may be served hot or cold.

750 g filleted white fish, cut into portions
milled black pepper
125 g button mushrooms, sliced
butter for cooking
2 carrots, grated
1 large courgette, grated
½ red pepper, seeded and finely sliced
2-3 spring onions, sliced
30 ml soy sauce
30 ml olive oil

Set the oven at 180 °C. Arrange the fish in a baking dish to fit snugly. Season with a little pepper.

Soften the mushrooms in butter and spoon over the fish. Mix together the carrots, courgettes, red pepper and spring onion and scatter on top. Drizzle evenly with soy sauce and olive oil, cover with the lid or foil and bake for 20 minutes. Uncover and cook for 10 minutes more.

Serve with mashed potato or new potatoes boiled in their jackets and a simple salad.

Serves 6

Crunchy Soufflé Hake

One of our favourite recipes for an easy and delicious meal. Other suitable fish include kob, geelbek, kingklip and steenbras.

750 g filleted hake portions
salt and milled black pepper
2 egg whites
125 ml Crème Fraîche (page 90)
or sour cream
60 ml Mayonnaise (page 94)
60 ml snipped chives
2 ml crushed garlic
250 ml soft breadcrumbs
paprika

Set the oven at 220 °C. Skin the fish and place in a single layer in a baking dish that fits snugly. Season with a little salt and pepper.

Whip the egg whites stiffly. Mix together the crème fraîche or sour cream, mayonnaise, chives and garlic. Fold in the egg white and spoon the mixture over the fish to cover completely. Sprinkle with crumbs, dust with paprika and bake uncovered for about 20 minutes until the fish is cooked through. Serve with creamed spinach.

Serves 4

HAKE ROSÉ

Delicately flavoured hake needs to be perked up with a flavoursome sauce and this recipe does the trick. Instead of hake use just about any other fish that's available – among the best are kingklip, kob and geelbek.

750 g filleted, skinless hake portions
salt and milled black pepper
flour for dusting
100 g butter
30 ml sunflower oil
150 g button mushrooms, sliced
30 ml chopped parsley
squeeze of fresh lemon juice
45 ml cake flour
125 ml Fish Stock (page 88)
125 ml cream
60 ml dry white wine
30 ml dry sherry
30 ml tomato sauce
15 ml grated Parmesan cheese
1 ml paprika

Season the fish with salt and pepper and dust with flour. In a large non-stick frying pan heat half the butter with the oil until it starts to brown. Fry the fish until cooked, making sure it's nicely browned, then set it aside and keep hot while making the sauce.

Add the remaining butter to the pan and fry the mushrooms and parsley with a squeeze of lemon juice until softened. Remove from the heat and blend in the flour. Add all the remaining ingredients and stir over high heat until the sauce thickens. Season with salt and pepper.

Place the fish on individual serving plates, ribbon the sauce on top and serve with mashed potato and vegetables or an interesting salad.
Serves 4

TOMATO AND FETA FISH

An easy recipe for just about any type of fish – hake, kingklip, kob, shark – even haddock.

Herbed Tomato Sauce (page 97)
750 g filleted, skinless fish portions
salt and milled black pepper
fresh lemon juice

TOPPING
150 g feta cheese, cut into tiny dice
4 slices white bread, decrusted
and cut into tiny cubes

Set the oven at 200 °C. Make the sauce and tip it into a suitable baking dish. Nestle in the fish, season with salt, pepper and lemon juice and scatter cheese and bread cubes on top. Bake for about 25 minutes until the fish is cooked and the topping is lightly browned. Serve at once with rice and salad.
Serves 4

APPLE AND ALMOND HAKE

Hake certainly benefits from a few tasty touches to lift it from mundane to marvellous. This recipe does just that – to hake and to any other type of fish you'd care to mention.

750 g filleted, skinless hake portions
salt and milled black pepper
flour for dusting
2 Granny Smith apples
fresh lemon juice
50 g flaked almonds

PARSLEY SAUCE
50 g (50 ml) butter
15 ml sunflower oil
30 ml cake flour
30 ml chopped parsley
60 ml off-dry white wine
125 ml cream
10 ml fresh lemon juice

Season the hake with salt and pepper and dust lightly with flour. Slice the apples into wedges and sprinkle with lemon juice to prevent discolouring.

Heat a non-stick frying pan and toast the almonds over gentle heat, tossing them to brown evenly, then set aside.

Add butter and oil to the frying pan and lightly brown the apple wedges – very quickly, please; mushy apples are not appealing. Set aside separately from the almonds.

Increase the heat and fry the fish, adding extra butter if necessary. The cooking time will be about 4-5 minutes, when the fish should be crispy-brown and perfectly cooked. Transfer it to a warmed serving platter and keep warm while preparing the sauce.

SAUCE Working off the heat, blend the flour and parsley into the pan juices. Slowly add the wine, cream and lemon juice, then stir over high heat for a couple of minutes until the sauce is smooth and thickened. Add a little water if the sauce is too thick and season with salt and pepper.

To retain the crispness of the fish, garnish the platter with apple wedges, scatter over the toasted almonds, and serve the sauce separately.
Serves 4

GRILLED FISH WITH SPICED YOGHURT

Quick and easy to do with a tangy sauce to make the dish even more special. It's a good recipe for many different fish – try hake, kingklip, kob or more flavoursome types like geelbek and red steenbras.

750 g filleted, skinless fish portions
15 ml butter
salt and milled black pepper
2 ml ground cumin
2 ml ground coriander
1 ml ground cardamom
15 ml fresh lemon juice
250 ml natural yoghurt

Lay the fish in an oven-to-table casserole. Heat the oven griller. In a small saucepan melt the butter, remove from the heat and mix in the remaining ingredients. Spoon the sauce over the fish and grill until it is cooked – the timing will depend on the thickness of the fillets. Serve with sautéed potatoes.
Serves 4

MILANESE FISH PIE

A very useful way of using up any left-over fish that may be hanging about. Or cook fish specially if you wish.

500 g cooked, flaked fish
2 ripe tomatoes, skinned and chopped
2 hard-boiled eggs
30 ml chopped spring onion or chives
30 ml chopped parsley
15 ml Worcestershire sauce
salt and milled black pepper
Mornay Sauce (page 96)
toasted crumbs for the topping

MASHED POTATO
1 kg potatoes, skinned and cubed
1 small onion, very finely chopped
butter
milk

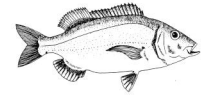

POTATO Cook the potato in a little salted boiling water until tender. Drain and mash with the onion, a knob of butter, a little milk and pepper to taste. Use half of the mixture to line a casserole.

Set the oven at 180 °C. Mix together the flaked fish, tomato, chopped hard-boiled eggs, spring onion or chives, parsley, Worcestershire sauce and seasoning. Gently mix in the sauce and spread onto the mashed potato. Cover with remaining mashed potato, sprinkle with toasted crumbs and bake for about 20 minutes until piping hot. Serve with a salad.
Serves 4-6

MAKE AHEAD Assemble the pie a day ahead, refrigerate and bake it just before serving. Remember to increase the baking time by 10 minutes if the pie has been chilled.

CREAMY FISH WITH FRIED LEEK

Delicate flavours predominate in this easy recipe. The leek garnish – though not essential – adds a nice dimension of flavour and crunch, especially if you're using hake. Kingklip, kob or any other fresh linefish makes an even more tasty dish.

750 g fish fillets
salt and milled black pepper
fresh lemon juice
250 ml Crème Fraîche (page 90)
or sour cream
6 spring onions, finely sliced
2 ml paprika
grated Parmesan cheese
1 leek, finely sliced
sunflower oil for deep-frying

Set the oven at 200 °C. Butter a suitable baking dish. Lay the fish in it in a single layer and season with salt, pepper and a good squeeze of lemon juice.

Mix together the crème fraîche or sour cream, spring onion and paprika and pour over the fish. Top with Parmesan cheese and dust with a little extra paprika. Clean the edges of the dish and bake for 20-25 minutes until the fish is cooked.

Meanwhile deep-fry the leek in hot oil just until it starts to brown. Drain on kitchen paper. Scatter the fried leek onto the fish as a garnish and serve pronto with crunchy stir-fried vegetables.
Serves 4

MAKE AHEAD Prepare the dish in the morning for serving in the evening. The fish must be baked and the leek deep-fried just before serving.

Fish Bobotie

FISH BOBOTIE

This traditional baked fish dish is as delicious and unique as its meaty counterpart. Hake is great but any white fish will do.

750 kg skinless fish fillets
2 slices day-old white bread (crusts on)
250 ml milk
1 egg, lightly beaten
finely grated rind and juice of 1 small lemon
5 ml salt
milled black pepper
butter for cooking
1 large onion, finely chopped
1 red chilli, seeded and finely chopped
10 ml fish masala, garam masala or curry powder

TOPPING
12 lemon leaves
12 almonds
2 eggs
125 ml milk
salt and white pepper

Set the oven at 180 °C. Butter a 2-litre baking dish. Trim the fish and mince or finely chop it. Crumb the bread, pour over the milk and add the egg and lemon rind and juice, and salt and pepper.

In a frying pan fry the onion and chilli in butter until lightly browned. Sprinkle over the masala or curry powder and cook for a minute more. Remove from the heat and mix into the fish with the crumb mixture.

Spoon the mixture into the baking dish and gently smooth the surface.

Roll the lemon leaves and embed them in the bobotie interspersed with the almonds. Mix the topping eggs, milk and seasoning, pour over, cover the dish and place it in a larger baking dish. Add boiling water to come half-way up the sides and bake for 40 minutes. Remove the lid for the final 15 minutes to lightly brown and set the topping. Serve with rice and sambals.

Serves 6

MAKE AHEAD Fish bobotie should be served straight from the oven, but there's nothing to stop you preparing it a day ahead. Keep covered and chilled, and don't add the custard topping mixture until just before it's baked.

Crispy Fish with Lemon and Ginger Sauce

A touch of Chinese magic to add sparkle to your life. Deep-fried fish chunks in the crispest, lightest batter, seductively sauced – and eaten with chopsticks, of course. Choose from hake, kob, geelbek, red steenbras, gurnard, kingklip, monkfish or musselcracker. If purchasing a whole fish, one with a mass of about 1,7 kg will be required, or two of about 1 kg each.

750 g filleted, skinless fish portions
flour for dusting
salt and milled black pepper
sunflower oil for deep-frying

BATTER
200 ml self-raising flour
5 ml salt
2 ml white pepper
200 ml water

LEMON AND GINGER SAUCE
1 small lemon
250 ml Fish Stock (page 88)
or chicken stock
45 ml sugar
15 ml soy sauce
2 ml crushed green ginger
30 ml dry sherry
20 ml cornflour

Cut the fish into large chunks. (Pieces which are too small will overcook.) Coat lightly with flour and season with salt and pepper. Cover and chill until just before serving time.

BATTER Sift together the flour, salt and pepper, beat in the water and allow to stand at room temperature for at least 30 minutes. During this time moisture will plump the flour, giving the batter the consistency of pouring cream.

SAUCE Grate the lemon rind, squeeze the juice and combine in small saucepan with the stock, sugar, soy sauce and ginger. Bring to the boil and stir in the combined sherry and cornflour. Stir over high heat until the sauce thickens and becomes quite clear. Check the flavour.

Dip the fish in batter and deep-fry in batches in hot oil, allowing 3-4 minutes for the batter to crisp and fish to cook through. Drain on kitchen paper, then pile into a warm serving bowl. Serve with rice or noodles and stir-fried vegetables, and offer the hot sauce separately.
Serves 4

MAKE AHEAD The sauce may be prepared a couple of days ahead and reheated. The fish must be freshly fried, although the batter remains crisp an hour after cooking.

Feta Fish in Pastry

Chunks of your favourite fish are quickly browned, wrapped in pastry with tomato and feta, then crisply baked. A superb recipe for angelfish, geelbek, gurnard, kob, kingklip, monkfish, red stumpnose and hake. Each piece of fish should be about 50 mm thick and 150 g in weight. Tail-end fillets are a trifle thin, but may be folded over before being wrapped in pastry.

Cream Cheese Pastry (page 92)
4 pieces of filleted, skinless fish
flour, salt and milled black pepper
butter and sunflower oil for frying
1 large, ripe tomato, chopped
100 g feta cheese, crumbled
30 ml chopped parsley

Prepare the pastry. Dredge the fish lightly with flour and season with salt and pepper. Heat a little butter and oil in a non-stick frying pan and brown the fish well on both sides. (No need to cook it through; baking does this to perfection.) Set the fish aside and pat dry with kitchen paper. Allow to cool.

Set the oven at 200 °C. Roll out the pastry fairly thinly. Cut squares large enough to enfold the fish portions – about 25 cm in diameter. Place fish on one side of each pastry square, top with tomato, feta and parsley and fold the pastry over, sealing edges with a little water. Trim the edges and crimp prettily with a fork.

Place the parcels on a lightly oiled baking tray and bake for 20 minutes until the pastry is crisp and golden and the fish is perfectly cooked. Serve with a simple green salad.
Serves 4

Fish Meunière

Perfectly fried fish served simply with buttery pan juices with a touch of parsley. You're welcome to add extra texture and flavour by scattering flaked, toasted almonds on top. Any fish will do – sole is traditionally cooked like this; hake and kingklip work well, small kob fillets are divine, just-caught reef fish that are large enough to fillet are perfect.

750 g filleted, skinless fish portions
salt and milled black pepper
flour for dusting
butter and sunflower oil for frying
30 ml chopped parsley
lemon wedges for garnish

Rinse the fish, pat perfectly dry with kitchen paper, season with salt and pepper and dust with flour. Over high heat melt butter and oil in a large non-stick frying pan. Just as it

Crispy Fish with Lemon and Ginger Sauce, recipe page 40

starts to brown, add one or two portions of fish and fry for a minute. Lift the fish and swish the pan with butter to prevent the fish from sticking. Cook until beautifully browned.

Turn the fish, cover the pan, reduce the heat and allow the fish to steam through. The cooking time will vary depending on the thickness and texture of the fish but the whole procedure should only take a matter of minutes.

Transfer the fish to a heated plate and tent with foil to keep warm. Add more butter and oil to the pan and fry remaining fish in the same way.

Soften the parsley in the pan juices (add extra butter if you wish), pour the buttery sauce over the fish and accompany it with lemon wedges for squeezing. New potatoes, cooked in their jackets, are the perfect accompaniment.

Serves 4

Minted Fish in Spinach

Elegant parcels of minty fish and fresh tomato wrapped in spinach. The choice of fish is all-important for flavour and texture balance; our favourites are red steenbras and fillets of large white steenbras. The proportions of the fillets are important so they may be easily wrapped in the spinach; they should be 10-12 cm in diameter and about 3 cm thick.

4 filleted, skinned fish portions,
trimmed to the correct size
4 large spinach leaves
1 large, ripe tomato, skinned and finely sliced
salt and milled black pepper
10 ml finely chopped mint
60 ml Crème Fraîche (page 90), or sour cream
30 ml dry white wine

Set the oven at 180 °C. Butter a casserole just large enough to accommodate all four fish parcels snugly. Wash the spinach and cut out the thick stalks to a quarter of the way up the leaves.

Place the spinach leaves in a large saucepan, pour over plenty of boiling water and simmer for 2 minutes. Drain and pat dry.

Place a fish portion on each leaf, season with salt and pepper and top each with chopped mint, tomato slices and 15 ml crème fraîche. Enfold the fish in spinach, nestle the parcels in the casserole and pour over the wine. Seal with foil and bake for 20-25 minutes until the fish is cooked. Serve with new potatoes tossed in parsley butter.
Serves 4

MAKE AHEAD The prepared parcels may be refrigerated for up to a day and baked just before serving.

Salmon Trout in Champagne, recipe page 43

MUSHROOM AND ALMOND FISH

A super recipe for just about any fish. Our favourites are kingklip, kob and hake.

750 g fish fillets or steaks
salt and milled black pepper
flour for dusting
100 g flaked almonds
100 g butter
sunflower oil
45 ml cake flour
125 ml Fish Stock (page 88)
125 ml cream
5 ml lemon juice
250 g button mushrooms, sliced
45 ml chopped parsley

Season the fish with salt and pepper and dust with flour. Toast the almonds in a dry frying pan (non-stick is best); set aside to cool.

In the same pan heat half the butter with a little oil and fry the fish until golden and done right through. Set aside and keep warm while preparing the sauce.

Melt the remaining butter in the pan, then remove from the heat and stir in the flour, stock, cream and lemon juice. Stir over high heat for a couple of minutes, then season to taste with salt and pepper and add mushrooms and parsley. Simmer for a few minutes more until the mushrooms are tender.

Place the pieces of fish onto individual dinner plates, pour a little of the sauce over each and garnish with toasted almonds. Mashed potato is a good accompaniment.
Serves 4

MAKE AHEAD This is best served immediately, but it's so quick to prepare that your guests won't miss you.

SALMON TROUT IN CHAMPAGNE

A classic recipe which perfectly enhances the texture and flavour of salmon trout.

6 small salmon trout, cleaned, washed and dried
750 ml dry champagne or sparkling wine
375 ml cream
24 button mushrooms, halved
small bunch spring onions, finely sliced
60 ml chopped parsley
1 bay leaf
pinch paprika
salt and milled black pepper
30 g (30 ml) butter

Set the oven at 180 °C. Place the salmon trout side by side in a buttered casserole. Pour over 500 ml of the champagne and add the cream, mushrooms, spring onion, parsley, bay leaf, paprika, salt and pepper. Cover with the lid or foil and bake for 15 minutes.

Remove the fish from the dish, remove the skin and place the fish in a warmed serving dish. Strain the sauce into a clean pot, discard the bay leaf and scatter the mushrooms over the fish. Keep warm while finishing the sauce.

Boil the sauce uncovered until reduced by half. Add the remaining champagne, whisk in the butter and check the seasoning. Pour the sauce over the fish and serve with a salad and new potatoes boiled in their jackets.
Serves 6

FISH SOUFFLÉ

A classic soufflé is easy to do and makes a lovely light meal. White fish is best – the most popular types being hake, kob, geelbek, silverfish, strepie and white steenbras.

500 g skinned fish fillets
500 ml milk
1 bay leaf
few peppercorns
sprigs of parsley
onion rings
30 g (30 ml) butter
30 ml cake flour
1 ml dry English mustard
2 ml salt
milled black pepper
3 eggs, separated

Set the oven at 150 °C. Butter a soufflé dish. In a wide saucepan heat the milk with the bay leaf, peppercorns, parsley and a few onion rings. Add the fish, cover and poach very gently until cooked. Remove the fish from the pan, flake and set aside. Strain and reserve the baking liquid to use in the sauce.

In a clean saucepan melt the butter, remove from the heat and blend in the flour and mustard, then add the baking liquid. Season with salt and pepper and stir over high heat until the sauce is smooth and thickened.

Remove from the heat, beat in the egg yolks then gently fold in the flaked fish. Allow the mixture to cool, then whisk the egg white stiffly and fold in. Pour the mixture into the soufflé dish and bake for 30 minutes.

Serve immediately with a fresh salad and a complementary sauce if you wish. Our favourites are Velouté Sauce (page 96), Fennel Sauce (page 97) and Mushroom Cream Sauce (page 98).
Serves 4

Tuna and Mushroom Casserole

1 litre cooked rice
200 g can light tuna, drained and flaked
440 g can cream of mushroom soup
1 small onion, grated
10 ml prepared English mustard
salt and milled black pepper
100 g (300 ml) grated Cheddar cheese
250 ml soft breadcrumbs

Set the oven at 180 °C. Butter an oven-to-table casserole. In a bowl mix together the rice, tuna, soup, onion, mustard, seasoning and half the cheese.

Tip the mixture into the casserole, top with the remaining cheese mixed with crumbs and bake for about 20 minutes until bubbling-hot and crispy-crusted. Serve with a Greek salad.
Serves 6

Cheat's Tuna Pizza

When a delicious end justifies the means, we're all for surreptitiously bending recipe rules. Swap ready made puff pastry for time-consuming pizza dough, and you have a quick and easy family supper. Or cut the pizza into 24 snack-sized slices to serve with drinks.

400 g frozen puff pastry
115 g can tomato paste
1 large onion, finely chopped
1 large green pepper, finely chopped
200 g can light tuna, drained and flaked
50 g can anchovies, drained and chopped (optional)
400 g grated mozzarella, Gouda or
mild Cheddar cheese
black olives
grated Parmesan cheese
milled black pepper

Set the oven at 200 °C. Defrost the pastry and lay it flat; cut in half, place each half on a lightly oiled baking tray and spread with tomato paste.

Scatter the onion, green pepper, flaked tuna and anchovy pieces on the tomato paste and top generously with grated mozzarella, Gouda or Cheddar cheese. Garnish with as many olives as you like, dust with Parmesan cheese and-season with a little pepper.

Bake for 20 minutes until the pastry is crisp and the cheese is sizzling and golden. Slice each pizza into 4 squares and serve with a green salad.
Serves 5-6

Tuna Crêpes Niçoise

This is the most elegant, tasty way of using canned tuna. For a starter or light luncheon, halve the recipe and serve with a crisp Greek salad.

10-12 Crêpes (page 91)

Tuna Filling
2 x 200 g cans light tuna, drained and flaked
1 large onion, finely chopped
2 ml crushed garlic
olive oil for cooking
4 ripe tomatoes, skinned and chopped
or a 400 g can
2 ml ground cumin
salt and milled black pepper
12 green olives, stoned and chopped
grated Parmesan cheese for topping

Cheese Sauce
80 g butter
90 ml flour
7 ml dry English mustard
1 litre milk or milk and cream
1 ml salt
80 g (250 ml) grated Cheddar cheese

Make the crêpes. Fry the onion and garlic in a little olive oil until golden. Add the tomato, cumin, salt and pepper and cook uncovered until the sauce is thick and richly coloured. Stir in the tuna and olives, heat through and check the seasoning.

SAUCE In a medium saucepan melt the butter, remove from the heat and blend in the flour and mustard. Slowly add the milk, stirring until smooth. Stir over high heat until the sauce is slightly thickened. Add salt and Cheddar cheese, stirring until it melts.

Set the oven at 180 °C. Butter a large baking dish – one measuring about 25 cm x 30 cm will do nicely. Fill each crêpe with two spoonfuls of tuna filling, roll up and place side by side in the baking dish.

Pour over the sauce, dust lightly with Parmesan cheese and bake for about 20-30 minutes until piping hot with a golden topping.
Serves 6

MAKE AHEAD Assemble the dish a day ahead, pour over the sauce but don't add the Parmesan cheese at this stage – it will be absorbed into the sauce and disappear completely. Seal with clingfilm and refrigerate.

Before baking, sprinkle over Parmesan cheese and increase the cooking time by 5 minutes to compensate for the additional chilliness.

Tuna Tagliatelle with Matchstick Vegetables

A tempting and quickly prepared pasta dish; a superb combination of textures, colours and flavours.

250 g tagliatelle (mix green and white)
olive oil

TUNA SAUCE
2 x 200 g cans light tuna, drained and flaked
2 carrots, cut into matchsticks
1 rib celery, cut into matchsticks
2 courgettes, cut into matchsticks
2 ripe tomatoes, skinned and sliced
125 g cream cheese or smooth cottage cheese
125 ml cream
15 ml cornflour
2 ml paprika
1 ml Tabasco (optional)
salt and milled black pepper
1 small onion, finely chopped
2 ml crushed garlic
chopped parsley for garnish

Cook the tagliatelle in a large pot of boiling salted water. Drain in a colander and tip into a warm serving bowl, toss with a dash of olive oil to prevent it from clumping together. Cover and keep warm while preparing the sauce.

Mix together the carrots, celery, courgettes and tomatoes. In a separate bowl mix together the cheese, cream, cornflour, paprika, Tabasco, salt and pepper.

Heat a little olive oil in a medium saucepan and fry the onion and garlic until just starting to brown. Add the vegetables and stir-fry for 1 minute. Stir in cheese mixture and reduce the heat to simmer for 2 minutes more. Add the tuna to the sauce, heat through and check the flavour.

Either keep the pasta and sauce in separate dishes, or pretty up the presentation by piling the tagliatelle round the edges of a large, flattish platter, spoon the sauce into the centre, and garnish liberally with chopped parsley.
Serves 4

MAKE AHEAD The sauce ingredients may be readied, covered and refrigerated a day ahead. Pasta may be cooked, tossed with oil, covered and refrigerated, and reheated in the microwave. The completed dish prefers to wait no more than an hour before serving, so that the texture and colour of the vegetables remain perfect.

Tuna Crêpes Niçoise, recipe page 44

SOLE VÉRONIQUE

A classic dish with a delicate flavour. Instead of sole use the fillets of small kob, barbel, gurnard, monkfish, hake or red steenbras. You'll need about 750 g. If sultana grapes aren't available use another variety, but remove the pips (the closed end of a hairclip works well).

4 large soles, skinned and filleted
salt and white pepper
100 g button mushrooms, finely sliced
butter for frying
125 ml dry white wine
125 ml Fish Stock (page 88)
large sprig of tarragon
or a pinch of dried tarragon
125 ml cream
2 egg yolks
200 g seedless sultana grapes, skinned
chopped parsley for garnish

Season the fish fillets with salt and pepper, roll them up and secure with toothpicks.

Gently fry the sliced mushrooms in butter until tender. Pour in the wine and stock, add the tarragon, cover and bring to the boil. Nestle in the fish, cover and poach very gently until cooked – 5-10 minutes depending on the thickness of the fillets.

Transfer the fish to a heated serving dish. Mix together the cream and egg yolks and add to the stock, stirring over very low heat just until the sauce thickens. Don't let the sauce boil or it will curdle.

Remove the pan from the heat, add the grapes and heat through. Pour the sauce over the fish, garnish generously with chopped parsley and serve with mashed potato and a simple green salad.
Serves 4

COCONUT BAY SOLE

A great recipe to enhance the delicate flavour and texture of sole, but any smallish fillets of fish can be given the Coconut Bay treatment: hake, kingklip, gurnard, monkfish – even suitably-sized angling fish like bream, grunter or silverfish.

4 soles, skinned and trimmed
salt and white pepper
fresh lemon juice
2 eggs, lightly beaten
60 ml toasted crumbs
60 ml desiccated coconut
butter and sunflower oil for frying
4 bananas

Season the soles with salt and pepper and a squeeze of lemon juice. Dip in egg, then coat with mixed crumbs and coconut, pressing the fish firmly into the mixture.

Peel the bananas, cut in half lengthwise and sprinkle with lemon juice. Fry gently in sizzling butter until light golden-brown. Take care not to overcook them or they'll get mushy. Remove from the pan and set aside.

Heat extra butter in the same frying pan, add a dash of oil and fry the soles until golden-brown and cooked through to the bone. Drain the fish briefly on kitchen paper, place on hot serving plates and top each one with fried banana. Serve with mashed potato.
Serves 4

PAPRIKA-GRILLED FISH

A lovely way of preparing geelbek, kob, kingklip, steenbras, angelfish and yellowtail, although any suitably-sized fish may be used. If purchasing a whole fish, one with a mass of about 1,7 kg will be required, or two of about 1 kg each.

4 large fish steaks (each about 200 g)
salt and milled black pepper
50 g (50 ml) butter
30 ml chopped parsley
15 ml chopped basil leaves
or 2 ml dried basil
squeeze of fresh lemon juice
5 ml paprika
125 ml cream

Heat the oven griller. Arrange the fish on an oiled grilling tray and season with salt and pepper.

Melt the butter in a small saucepan, mix in the parsley, basil, lemon juice and paprika. Brush half of this mixture over the fish and grill for 3-4 minutes. Turn the fish, brush with the remaining buttery mixture and grill for a further 2-4 minutes until cooked. Transfer the fish to a heated serving platter.

Pour the cream into the grilling pan and cook on the stovetop, stirring in all the buttery fish juices. Pour the sauce over the fish and garnish with an extra sprinkling of paprika. Serve with new potatoes boiled in their jackets and a green salad.
Serves 4

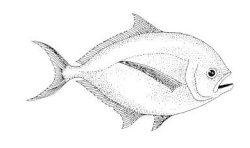

Kingklip Calamata

KINGKLIP CALAMATA

A flavoursome recipe for kingklip, yellowtail, kob or geelbek.

6 kingklip fillets (each about 200 g)
salt and milled black pepper
2 ml crushed garlic
1 fresh or dried bouquet garni
1 small onion, sliced into rings
2 large, ripe tomatoes, chopped
1 green pepper, seeded and chopped
125 ml dry white wine

CALAMATA SAUCE
50 g (50 ml) butter
45 ml cake flour
baking liquid
125 ml milk
12 calamata olives, stoned and halved
30 ml cream
chopped parsley for garnish

Set the oven at 180 °C. Skin the fish and place in a casserole. Season with pepper and a little salt. Spread a little garlic onto the fish, tuck in the herbs and add the veget-ables and wine. Cover and bake for 25 minutes until the fish is cooked; it will flake easily and lose all trace of rubberiness the moment it's done.

Transfer the fish and vegetables to a warmed serving platter, discard the herbs and strain the baking liquid into a saucepan. Boil uncovered until this has reduced to about 150 ml and reserve for the sauce.

SAUCE In clean saucepan melt the butter, remove from the heat and blend in the flour, baking liquid and milk. Stir over high heat for a few minutes until smooth and thickened. Add the olives with the cream and any liquid that has formed under fish.

Check the flavour and season to taste. Pour the sauce over the fish and garnish with chopped parsley. Serve with hot buttered noodles. A Greek salad will round off the meal in suitable Mediterranean style.

Serves 6

Orange Kingklip with Spinach Sauce

Kingklip may be substituted with filleted geelbek, kob, gurnard, monkfish, musselcracker, red steenbras – even haddock, which will give the dish a lovely smoky flavour.

1,2 kg filleted, skinless kingklip
salt and milled black pepper
125 ml fresh orange juice

SPINACH SAUCE
stock from poaching fish
100 g spinach leaves (about ½ bunch),
washed and dried
4-5 large sprigs parsley
250 g tub smooth cottage cheese
2 ml grated orange rind
30 ml cornflour
45 ml water

Cut the fish into serving portions and place in a single layer in a wide saucepan. Season lightly with salt and pepper. Pour in the orange juice, cover and simmer for about 15 minutes until the fish is just cooked through; check by piercing with a sharp knife – all traces of rubberiness will disappear the moment the kingklip is cooked. Slimmer portions cook quicker than chubbier ones, so transfer them to a warm plate the moment they're done. Tent the cooked fish with foil to keep warm. Boil the stock uncovered until reduced to about 250 ml. Set aside.

Cut off the thick spinach ribs and chop the leaves coarsely. Whiz in a food processor with the parsley, cottage cheese and orange rind. Add to the stock together with any liquid that has collected under the cooked fish. Simmer for about 3 minutes to cook the vegetables lightly.

Mix together the cornflour and water, add to the sauce and stir over high heat until nicely thickened. Remove from the heat and check the flavour, adding salt and pepper if necessary.

Spoon sauce onto warmed dinner plates, top with a portion of fish and garnish gaily with sprigs of fresh herbs.
Serves 6

MAKE AHEAD Don't! Kingklip loses moisture if kept waiting after being poached, so prepare everything ahead of time – even as far as puréeing the sauce ingredients, and cooking the dish will be simple and speedy.

Smoked Fish, recipe page 49

GRATIN OF KOB

This is a wonderful way to treat kob; or, if you prefer, skate, gurnard, hake, geelbek, monkfish, yellowtail, and red or white steenbras.

6 filleted kob portions (each about 200 g)
250 ml dry white wine
5 ml crushed garlic
salt and milled black pepper
15 ml fresh lemon juice

WINE-CREAM SAUCE
50 g (50 ml) butter
60 ml cake flour
250 ml Fish Stock (page 88)
375 ml cream or cream and milk
125 ml poaching liquid
grated Parmesan cheese for the topping
fresh chives for garnish

Combine the wine, garlic, salt, pepper and lemon juice in wide saucepan, add the fish, cover and poach until just cooked – about 3-5 minutes, depending on the thickness of the steaks. Transfer the fish to a baking dish. Boil the poaching liquid until reduced to 125 ml.

SAUCE In a medium saucepan melt the butter. Remove from the heat and blend in the flour. Slowly work in the stock, then stir over high heat until the sauce is smooth and thickened. Stir in reserved poaching liquid and cream.

Pour the sauce evenly over the fish, sprinkle generously with Parmesan cheese and brown under the griller. Garnish with chives and serve with mashed potato.
Serves 6

MAKE AHEAD Prepare the dish a day ahead, but don't add the cheese topping until just before cooking. Bake for 15 minutes at 180 °C, then brown the topping.

ITALIAN CRUNCHY KOB

A blissful blend of flavours, colours and textures. Geelbek, hake, monkfish, musselcracker, and red or white steenbras may be used instead of kob.

1 kg kob fillets
salt and milled black pepper
Herbed Tomato Sauce (page 97)

TOPPING
250 ml soft breadcrumbs
125 ml grated Parmesan cheese

Prepare the sauce. Set the oven at 180 °C. Butter an ovenproof casserole and pour in the tomato sauce. Into this nestle the fish in a single layer, season with salt and pepper and top with crumbs and cheese mixed together.

Bake for 15-20 minutes until the fish is cooked through and the topping is crunchy and golden-brown. Serve with creamed spinach and new potatoes.
Serves 6

MAKE AHEAD Prepare the dish ready for baking, but don't add the crumb topping. Cover and refrigerate up to a day, and add the topping just before baking.

SMOKED FISH

Nifty home-smokers makes smoking a breeze. Select a perfectly fresh fish, watch the smoking temperature and you can't go wrong. Just about any type of fish can be smoked, but make sure it's suitably dimensioned to fit into the smoker.

1 fresh fish
coarse salt
fennel fronds and lemon wedges for garnish

Wash, scale, gut and behead your fish. Lift the stomach flap and cut the backbone free, first on one side, then the other. Make sure the knife doesn't slip and slice the skin.

Lay the fish flat; the backbone will stand up. To improve the presentation, support it with toothpicks and lay the fish on the grid of the smoker. This is the fancy way of doing it – you could simply fillet the fish into two halves if you prefer.

Salt the fish: some types (like snoek, angelfish and yellowtail) need to be more heavily salted than delicately flavoured fish like kob or geelbek, so use your discretion.

Lie the salted fish in a cool spot for 1 hour (keep an eye out for errant cats on the prowl for a free meal), and rinse off the salt.

Sprinkle about 60 ml oak sawdust on the base of the smoker, arrange the rack (with the fish) in the box and cover with the lid. Place over medium heat (braai coals or a gas burner) until the sawdust burns. This creates the smoke that cooks the fish. Watch carefully that things don't get too hot; this will cause a bitter flavour.

After 15-20 minutes your fish should be cooked. Test it – the flesh should flake easily – and allow to cool.

Place the smoked fish on a large serving platter or tray, garnish with sprigs of fennel and serve with lemon wedges for squeezing. A mayonnaisey sauce goes well.

MAKE AHEAD Smoked fish is best served straight from the smoker. However, it doesn't suffer too greatly if prepared a day or two ahead.

SMOKED SNOEK QUICHE

Even though it may have slipped in the fashion stakes, a quiche is a popular luncheon or light supper dish, served as is or with a crisp salad. Smoked snoek or angelfish are easily obtainable for this recipe, though any smoked fish would be suitable.

Quiche Pastry (page 92)
375 ml flaked, smoked snoek
30 g (30 ml) butter
30 ml cake flour
½ ml cayenne pepper
salt and milled black pepper
250 ml milk
250 ml cream
3 eggs, lightly beaten
30 ml grated Cheddar cheese
30 ml chopped parsley

TOPPING
30 ml toasted crumbs
30 ml grated Parmesan cheese

Prepare the pastry, line a 25 cm quiche tin and bake blind. Allow to cool. Reduce the oven temperature to 180 °C.
Melt the butter in a medium saucepan. Remove from the heat and stir in the flour, cayenne pepper, salt, pepper and milk. Stir over high heat for a couple of minutes until the sauce is smooth and thick. Remove from the stove.
Mix together the cream and eggs, add the Cheddar cheese, parsley and flaked fish. Mix this lightly into the sauce and pour it into the pastry shell. Sprinkle crumbs and cheese on top. Bake for 40 minutes – the filling should be set and the topping crunchy golden-brown. Serve warm or at room temperature with a green salad. If the quiche is chilled, the flavour will be lost.
Serves 6

TWO OCEANS PASTA

Great for carbo-loaders and other athletic types. To tart up the dish, you're welcome to add a 200 g can of prawns.

600 g haddock
100 g butter
1 large onion, chopped
5 ml crushed garlic
60 ml chopped fennel
45 ml cake flour
400 ml stock (from poaching the haddock)
250 ml cream
salt and milled black pepper
snipped chives for garnish

Place the haddock in a saucepan, add just enough water to cover and poach very gently until the fish is cooked. Drain and reserve 400 ml of the liquid for the sauce. Skin the fish and break the flesh into chunks.
Heat the butter in a medium saucepan and fry the onion and garlic until softened. Stir in the fennel, then remove from the heat and blend in the flour and stock, cream and a little pepper. Stir over high heat until the sauce is smooth and thick. Check the flavour, adding a little salt if necessary. Add the haddock and heat through.
Tip the haddock into a warmed serving dish, garnish with chives and serve with just-cooked tagliatelle.
Serves 4-6

SMOORVIS

This South African dish is traditionally prepared with smoked snoek, but any smoked fish may be used. Serve it with wholewheat bread and atjar or grape jam.

500 g smoked snoek, boned, skinned and flaked
500 ml cooked rice
2 onions, finely sliced
50 g (50 ml) butter
30 ml sunflower oil
2 potatoes, peeled and cut into tiny dice
2 large, ripe tomatoes, skinned and chopped
1-2 chillies, very finely chopped
or 2 ml chilli powder
60 ml sultanas (optional)
milled black pepper
fresh lemon juice
chopped parsley for garnish

In a large, heavy frying pan fry the onion in butter and oil until golden-brown. Add the potato, tomato, chilli, sultanas and pepper and cook for a little longer until the potato starts to brown.
Stir in the fish and rice, cover and cook gently over low heat until the potato is cooked through. Tip the smoorvis into a hot serving dish, season with a good squeeze of lemon juice and garnish with chopped parsley.
Serves 5-6

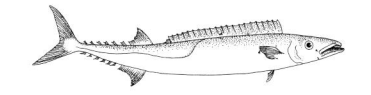

Mediterranean Tomatoes, recipe this page, Smoked Snoek Quiche, recipe page 50, and Ouma's Pickled Fish, recipe page 65

Mediterranean Tomatoes

A tasty luncheon or light supper dish.

6 large firm, ripe tomatoes
salt and milled black pepper
sunflower oil

FILLING
200 g smoked haddock
2 firm, ripe tomatoes, finely chopped
4 spring onions, finely chopped
1 clove garlic, crushed
30 ml finely chopped canned anchovies
12 black olives, stoned and finely chopped
60 ml soft breadcrumbs
30 ml olive oil

Cut the stalk ends off the 6 tomatoes and carefully remove the pith. Discard the pips and chop the pith (it will be added to the filling). Season the tomato cavities with salt and pepper, rub the skins with oil and up-end on kitchen paper to drain.

Steam or poach the haddock, drain, then remove the skin and the bones, and flake the flesh. Mix with the chopped pith and the remaining filling ingredients. Season with salt and pepper.

Set the oven at 160 °C. Lightly butter a casserole. Spoon the filling into the tomatoes, replace the 'lids', place them in the casserole and bake for 20 minutes. Serve with a mixed salad and crusty bread.

Serves 6

MAKE AHEAD The tomatoes may be filled and ready for baking up to a day ahead. Cook just before serving.

CRUSTY MUSTARD HADDOCK

Haddock bakes beautifully. Crisp it up with crumbs and into the baking liquid whip mustard and cream for a delicious sauce.

4 large haddock fillets (about 600 g)
50 g (50 ml) butter
30 ml fresh lemon juice
milled black pepper
125 ml soft breadcrumbs

MUSTARD SAUCE
baking liquid
15 ml mild prepared mustard
30 ml sour cream

Set the oven at 220 °C. Smear a large, shallow baking dish with some of the butter. Lay the haddock fillets skin down in the dish. Pour over the lemon juice, season with pepper and dot with the remaining butter.

Cover with the lid or foil and bake for 20 minutes. Sprinkle crumbs onto the fish and return to the oven, uncovered, for a further 10 minutes. Turn on the griller for a final few minutes' cooking time to toast the crumbs. Transfer the fish to warmed serving dish and keep hot while preparing the sauce.

Strain the liquid from baking dish into a small saucepan, whisk in the mustard and sour cream and boil briskly for 1-2 minutes until the sauce thickens. Pour it over the haddock and serve with new potatoes.

Serves 4

Sicilian Sardines, recipe page 53

HADDOCK MORNAY

You'll find cooking instructions on packets of frozen smoked haddock. However, if you prefer to defrost it first or can lay your hands on unfrozen haddock, here's how to poach it perfectly and blend the poaching liquid into a delicious sauce.

750 g haddock
milk
bay leaf, sprigs of parsley, fennel and thyme
6 black peppercorns
15 ml fresh lemon juice

MORNAY SAUCE
50 g (50 ml) butter
45 ml cake flour
poaching liquid plus extra milk
40 g (125 ml) grated Cheddar cheese
2 ml dry English mustard
30 ml dry sherry
salt and milled black pepper

TOPPING
250 ml soft breadcrumbs
60 ml grated Parmesan cheese

Place the haddock in a wide saucepan, add milk to cover, and the herbs, peppercorns and lemon juice. Cover and bring to simmering point. Poach very slowly (the liquid should barely move) until the fish is cooked and flakes easily. Thin fillets take about 6 minutes; fatter steaks a few minutes longer.

Remove the fish from the pan, peel off the skin, break the flesh into large blocks and place in a buttered casserole. Strain the baking liquid into a measuring jug and make up to 400 ml with extra milk. Set the oven at 200 °C.

SAUCE Melt the butter in a medium saucepan, remove from the heat and blend in the flour and poaching liquid. Stir over high heat until the sauce thickens. Remove from the heat and add the cheese, mustard, sherry and a little salt and pepper. Check the consistency: the sauce mustn't be too thick. If necessary, thin with a little milk or cream.

Pour the sauce over the fish and top with crumbs and Parmesan. Bake until bubbly-hot and the topping is crisply golden. Serve with a salad.
Serves 4

VARIATION
- Add lightly cooked vegetables to the sauce, cut into small chunks. Use broccoli, carrots and mushrooms, or mix together. In this case make extra sauce or use less fish.

MAKE AHEAD This dish may be prepared a day ahead, complete with topping. Bake just before serving.

OVEN-ROASTED SARDINES

These flavour-zapped tiddlers are delicious hot or cold.

24 sardines, cleaned, washed and dried
20 ml finely chopped garlic
125 ml olive oil
200 ml chopped parsley
500 ml soft breadcrumbs
10 ml cayenne pepper
salt and milled black pepper

Set the oven at 200 °C. Place the sardines side by side in a buttered baking dish or on a tray. Mix garlic and oil together and trickle onto the fish. Combine parsley, crumbs, cayenne pepper, and a little salt and pepper and spread on top. Bake for 15 minutes until fish are cooked and crunchy-topped.
Serves 6

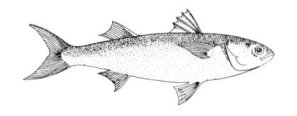

SICILIAN SARDINES

Flavours and colours of Italy in this cool summer-time stunner.

16 sardines or pilchards cleaned, washed and dried
60 ml olive oil
1 large green pepper, seeded and sliced
1 bunch of spring onions, finely sliced
10 ml crushed garlic
1 green or red chilli, seeded and sliced
400 g can tomatoes, chopped
salt and milled black pepper
20 black olives
10 canned anchovy fillets

Set the oven at 180 °C, then heat the grill. Brush the fish with olive oil and grill until crisp on both sides. Arrange them in an ovenproof baking dish. Switch off the grill.

Heat the remaining oil and fry the pepper, onion, garlic and chilli until just starting to soften. Add the tomato, salt and pepper and cook uncovered until reduced and thickened. Spoon the sauce over the fish, garnish with olives and anchovies and bake for about 10 minutes until done. Allow to cool, and serve with crusty bread.
Serves 4

JOHANN'S HARDERS

No matter how many culinary barriers we break, the foods of our childhood that spring from family traditions can prove so evocative for us all. Like this recipe for harders, prepared with affection and enthusiasm by all the men in our family whenever the trek fishermen haul their catch of superfresh harders onto the beach.

fresh, fresh harders (1-2 per serving)
coarse salt
butter and sunflower oil for frying
lemon wedges for squeezing

As soon as the fish stop wriggling, vlek by cutting through the backbone to hinge open at the belly. Clean well and rinse, then place, skin down – still dripping wet – onto a tray. Cover completely with coarse salt (substitute fine salt at your peril, and to the detriment of the fish).

Allow the harders to lie like this for 30 minutes, then rinse the salt off with cold running water. Peg the fish onto the washing line, securing with clothes pegs to foil errant breezes and mischievous seagulls. Allow to wind-dry for 4-6 hours until the surface becomes firm to the touch, keeping a watchful eye out for both flies and the neighbour's cat. (A wonderful opportunity for downing a couple of beers and swapping fishy tales.)

Panfry the harders in sizzling butter and oil until crisp and golden. Serve with lemon wedges.

JAPANESE FISH

Oriental flavours are very 'in' and here's a subtle fish dish that borrows techniques and flavours from the East. Kingklip is good in this recipe, so is any firm-fleshed linefish like geelbek, musselcracker, barracuda, marlin, Spanish mackerel or steenbras.

4 skinned fillets of fish, each about 200 g
salt and milled black pepper
butter and sunflower oil for cooking
1 onion, very finely sliced
2 cloves garlic, very finely chopped
2 ml crushed green ginger
1 chilli, seeded and very finely sliced
30 ml ketjap manis
15 ml wine vinegar
125 ml hot water

Season the fish lightly with pepper. In a large, non-stick frying pan heat butter and oil. When it starts to brown add the fish (upper side down) and brown well. Lift the fish and swish the pan with butter to prevent the fish from sticking. Turn the fish and cover the pan (use a baking sheet if necessary), reduce the heat and allow the fish to steam gently until cooked through. The cooking time will depend on the thickness and texture of the fish.

Transfer the fish to a warmed serving platter, salt it lightly and tent with foil to keep warm.

In the same pan fry the onion, garlic, ginger and chilli until soft; you may need to add a little more butter. Pour in the ketjap manis, vinegar and water and boil uncovered until the sauce thickens slightly.

Pour the sauce over the fish and serve at once with stir-fried vegetables. Or allow it to cool and serve with a salad.
Serves 4

BURMESE FISH CURRY

Seafood curries require a subtle blend of spices so that delicate flavours are enhanced and not masked. Our special curry mixture, together with a touch of garlic and ginger, will do just this. Use any firm-fleshed fish: angelfish, tuna, yellowtail, gurnard, kingklip, marlin and red steenbras are particularly suitable. If the budget will allow, mix fish and shellfish such as lobster, prawns, calamari or mussels.

750 g filleted, skinless fish
sunflower oil for cooking
1 large onion, sliced
5 ml crushed garlic
5 ml crushed green ginger
20 ml Burmese Curry Mix (page 90)
1 large, ripe tomato, seeded and chopped
5 ml brown sugar
1 ml salt
250 ml water
fresh coriander leaves for garnish

Cut the fish into large blocks. Heat a little oil in a wide saucepan, and fry the onion until lightly browned. Stir in the garlic, ginger and curry mix, cover and cook for just 30 seconds, then add the tomato, sugar, salt and water and bring to boiling point.

Nestle in the fish portions in a single layer. Cover and reduce the heat to simmer very gently for 5-6 minutes until cooked. Allow the curry to stand for a minimum of 2 hours for the wonderful flavours to penetrate every fibre of the fish.

Reheat gently, then transfer the curry to a warmed serving bowl, garnish with coriander leaves and serve with rice and sambals.
Serves 4

MAKE AHEAD Like all curries, this one is even better if it is prepared a day ahead – or at least 4-5 hours before serving. Cover and refrigerate, then reheat very gently.

Jewelled Coriander Fish

This flavoursome dish is strong on texture and appearance and needs little in the way of accompaniments – except perhaps crusty bread or a pile of buttered noodles. Use firm-fleshed fish like kingklip, geelbek, angelfish, monkfish or red steenbras.

WATCHPOINT *Inferior vinegar will ruin the flavour.*

> 800 g filleted, skinless fish
> flour, salt and milled black pepper
> 5 ml coriander seeds, lightly crushed
> 80 g butter
> 15 ml sunflower oil
> 300 g small pickling onions, skinned
> 125 ml wine vinegar
> 250 g cocktail tomatoes
> 30 ml sultanas

Cut the fish into cubes, season with salt and pepper and dredge with flour. Toast coriander in a dry, non-stick frying pan until aromatic and lightly browned – watch carefully as it's quick to burn. Set aside.

Heat the butter and oil in the pan and fry the fish until nicely browned and just cooked through. Remove the fish from the pan and set aside.

Brown the onions lightly in the same pan, add the vinegar and coriander and season with salt and pepper. Cover and cook gently until the onions are tender but still quite crisp, then add the tomatoes and sultanas. Cook uncovered over high heat for 1-2 minutes until the sauce thickens slightly. Return the fish to the pan and heat through, then tip it all into a serving dish.

Serves 4-6

VARIATION Zap things up with a chilli or two, seeded and very finely sliced, or a dash of chilli powder.

Jewelled Coriander Fish

Mahi Mahi, recipe page 57

Indonesian Fish

A very dramatic dish when catering for crowds. Suitable fish include red steenbras, stumpnose, geelbek and dageraad.

2 kg whole fish, headless and filleted
salt and milled black pepper
2 tomatoes, skinned and quartered
1 onion, peeled and quartered
100 g almonds or macadamia nuts
125 ml coconut cream
30 ml ketjap manis
15 ml oyster sauce
2 fresh chillies, seeded and chopped
5 ml turmeric
5 ml crushed garlic
2 ml crushed green ginger
fresh coriander for garnish

Rinse the fish, making sure it's free of skin, scales and suchlike. Lay the fillets in a large baking dish and season with salt and pepper.

Combine the remaining ingredients (not the garnish) in a food processor or blender and whiz until quite smooth. Pour this over the fish, cover with oiled foil and set aside in a cool spot for an hour to marinate. Meanwhile set the oven at 180 °C.

Bake the fish – still covered – for 30-40 minutes until done and the flesh is opaque right through. Lift the fillets out of the sauce and place on a warmed serving plate.

Give the sauce a stir and check the flavour and consistency. Pour it over the fish, garnish with coriander leaves and serve with sambals.
Serves 8

MAKE AHEAD If you wish, prepare the dish a day ahead, cover and refrigerate. Bake it just before serving.

SPICY SHARK WITH CREAM SAUCE

No shark? Substitute monkfish, skate wings, kingklip, yellowtail, or steenbras.

1 kg skinned shark fillets cut into 4 cm cubes
1 onion, finely chopped
butter and sunflower oil for cooking

SPICY SAUCE
60 ml brandy
15 ml tomato paste
2 ml crushed garlic
10 ml Burmese Curry Mix (page 90)
or mild curry powder
salt and milled black pepper
250 ml cream
chopped parsley and lemon wedges for garnish

Fry onion in butter and oil in a wide frying pan until golden-brown. Add the fish a few pieces at a time and brown gently in the oniony butter.

Return the cooked fish to the pan, pour over brandy, and flame. Transfer to a warmed serving platter and keep hot.

Add to the pan the tomato paste, garlic, curry powder, salt and pepper together with any juices under the cooked fish. Blend in the cream and heat through. Remove the pan from the heat, and check the flavour and consistency of the sauce.

Pour the sauce over the fish, garnish with parsley and lemon wedges, and serve at once.
Serves 6

FISH MORNAY

Use left-over fish or poach fish in the milk to be used in the sauce.

1 kg cooked fish fillets, skin removed
salt and milled black pepper
Mornay Sauce (page 96)

TOPPING
250 ml soft breadcrumbs
40 g (125 ml) grated Cheddar cheese

Butter a casserole, lay the fish in it and season with salt and pepper. Set the oven at 180 °C. Prepare the sauce, pour the sauce over the fish and top with crumbs and cheese. Bake for about 20 minutes to heat through and crisp the topping. Serve with a salad.
Serves 6

MAHI MAHI

A Hawaiian dish of subtle flavours, superb textures and stunning simplicity. It is traditionally served in individual baking dishes that retain a little sauce round each portion of fish. Alternatively, bake all four servings together in a casserole that fits perfectly under the griller.

WATCHPOINTS *Don't use any other fish but yellowtail or angelfish; their firm texture and distinctive flavour contrast beautifully with the sherry, garlic and topping. The sherry must be medium-dry. If you have none on hand, mix dry and semi-sweet in equal quantities. Lastly and most importantly: the only substitute for homemade mayonnaise for the topping is good quality, thick commercial mayonnaise.*

4 slices skinned yellowtail or angelfish fillets
each slice 150-200 g, and not more than 20 mm thick
200 ml medium-dry sherry
2 ml crushed garlic
salt and milled black pepper

TOPPING
500 ml Mayonnaise (page 94)
4 spring onions, trimmed and finely sliced
paprika

In a pan that will accommodate the fish portions closely side by side, bring sherry and garlic to simmering point. Immerse the fish in the poaching liquid, season with pepper, cover and poach for 2 minutes, turning the pieces after a minute or so.

With two forks, gently part the flesh to see if it's opaque right through. If not, simmer a while longer until done, but be very wary of overcooking the fish.

Transfer the fish to individual baking dishes or a large dish, pour over each portion 2-3 tablespoons of the poaching liquid, and salt the fish lightly. Blanket each piece with mayonnaise, smoothing it to cover the fish completely. Top with a line of sliced spring onion, dust with paprika and place under the oven griller for a few minutes until the topping is puffed and golden.

Place the baking dishes on larger plates or lift the fish portions onto warmed dinner plates. Spoon onto each plate a little of the poaching liquid. Serve with vegetables or a crisp salad.
Serves 4

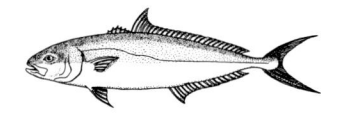

Yellowtail Steaks with Green Peppercorn Sauce

Our favourite recipes for a quick fish dish are those where the fish is quickly panfried, and a sauce is prepared in the same pan. This is such a recipe, perfect for yellowtail or tuna, but which may be used for any other fish of your choice.

6 yellowtail steaks (each about 200 g)
30 ml green peppercorns
butter and sunflower oil for cooking
30 ml brandy
salt
15 ml flour
5 ml Dijon mustard
125 ml water
250 ml cream or milk and cream
30 ml tawny port

Roughly crush half the peppercorns and spread onto the fish steaks. Heat some butter and a little oil in a heavy frying pan until sizzling hot and fry the fish a few pieces at a time. Make sure each side is golden-brown, then reduce the heat to cook through gently.

Transfer the cooked fish to a warmed platter while frying the remaining steaks, then return all the fish to the pan, pour over the brandy, warm for a few seconds and flame. Return the fish to the serving plate and salt lightly.

Working off the heat, blend the flour into the pan juices. Add the mustard and a little of the water to form a smooth paste, then stir in the remaining water. Return to the heat and stir over high heat until the sauce thickens.

Lastly add the cream, port and remaining peppercorns, together with any juices that have collected under the cooked fish. Check the flavour; add a little salt if needed.

Pour the sauce over the fish and garnish with fennel. Alternatively, transfer fish to individual heated dinner plates, garnish each serving and serve the sauce separately. Serve with sautéed potatoes.

Serves 6

Mackerel with Mustard and Orange Sauce

A delicious way to do mackerel – or choose suitably-sized maasbanker, harders or elf.

Mustard and Orange Sauce (page 98)
4 whole mackerel, cleaned and rinsed
45 ml sunflower oil
salt and milled black pepper
2 ml paprika
2 oranges, peeled and sliced

Prepare the sauce and set aside. Heat the oven griller. Cut the fish open down the backbones and place on a grilling tray. Baste with oil and season with salt, pepper and paprika. Grill until done to a turn and golden-brown – about 15-20 minutes. Turn once during cooking.

Transfer the fish to warmed serving plates, pour the sauce over while still piping hot, garnish with orange slices and serve at once with new potatoes tossed in parsley butter.

Serves 4

Baked Stump with Cream Sauce

A visual and taste sensation. Many fish types are good for baking but make sure the size is suitable: between 750 g and 2 kg. Stumpnose is our favourite, otherwise use roman, red or white steenbras, baardman, geelbek, galjoen, kob, musselcracker or silverfish.

1,5 kg white or red stumpnose
salt and milled black pepper
125 ml dry white wine
250 ml cream or sour cream
5 ml cornflour
4 spring onions, finely chopped
30 ml chopped parsley

BACON AND MUSHROOM STUFFING
50 g (50 ml) butter
3 rashers rindless streaky bacon, chopped
1 onion, finely chopped
125 g button mushrooms, finely chopped
250 ml soft breadcrumbs
15 ml chopped basil
or 2 ml dried basil
1 egg, lightly beaten

STUFFING Sizzle the butter in a frying pan, add the bacon and fry until it's quite crisp. Add the onion and mushrooms and cook until soft. Remove from the heat and stir in the crumbs, basil and egg, and season to taste with salt and pepper.

Set the oven at 180 °C. Clean the fish thoroughly inside and out, making quite sure there are no scales and other nasty bits and pieces left about. Pay particular attention to the head cavity which will also be filled with stuffing.

Season the fish with salt and pepper, fill with the stuffing and sew it up with needle and thread or close with skewers. Place it in a baking tray or casserole, pour over wine and water and cover with lightly oiled foil. (The oil prevents the foil from sticking to the fish skin – and skinless fish looks awful on a serving platter.)

Yellowtail Steaks with Green Peppercorn Sauce, recipe page 58

Bake for about 45 minutes until cooked through. Remove the foil for the final 10 minutes' cooking time. Test by sliding a sharp knife under the flesh at the thickest part and lifting carefully – the flesh should be opaque. Transfer the fish to a heated serving platter. Remove stitches or skewers. Keep warm.

Place the baking dish on the stovetop and heat. Mix together cream and cornflour and stir into the baking liquid. Add the spring onion and parsley and cook for a few minutes more. Pour the sauce into a sauce boat. Serve immediately with mashed potato and salad or vegetables.

Serves 6

SKATE WITH BLACK BUTTER

Delicate skate and a buttery sauce sharpened with capers. Shark and sole are also delicious done this way.

1 kg skinned skate wings
Court-Bouillon (page 88)
45 ml wine vinegar
100 g butter
15 ml capers
chopped parsley for garnish

Wash the skate wings and cut into serving portions. Pour the court-bouillon into a saucepan, add 15 ml of the vinegar, cover and bring to the boil. Add the fish, cover once more and reduce the heat to poach very slowly for about 10-15 minutes until done.

Lift the fish out of the stock, place on a board, remove all the bones and transfer to a warmed serving dish. Cover and keep hot.

Make the sauce by browning the butter in a small saucepan – but be careful it doesn't burn. Remove from the heat and add the capers and the remaining 30 ml vinegar. Pour the sauce over the fish and serve with boiled potatoes and lightly cooked vegetables.

Serves 6

MUSTARD CREAM SKATE

This recipe is so delicious and simple that it should encourage anyone who hasn't tried skate to do so at once. Shark steaks are a good alternative.

4 slices skinned skate wings
salt and milled black pepper
60 ml prepared English mustard
250 ml cream

Lightly butter a suitable oven-to-table baking dish. Set the oven at 180 °C.

Rinse and dry the skate wings, season with salt and pepper, spread on both sides with mustard and place in the baking dish.

Whip the cream quite thickly, pour it over the fish and bake uncovered for 20 minutes until the fish is cooked. Serve with new potatoes tossed in parsley butter and crisp, fresh vegetables.

Serves 4

MAKE AHEAD This dish must be served straight from the oven, but there's nothing to stop you from preparing it a couple of hours ahead of time. Seal with clingfilm and keep refrigerated.

Niçoise Fish, recipe page 61

Niçoise Fish

A lusty recipe for firm-fleshed fish like angelfish, yellowtail, tuna, barracuda and snoek. Geelbek, kob, dageraad, scotsman, seventyfour and kingklip may also be used.

6 steaks of filleted fish, each 2-3 cm thick
salt and milled black pepper
flour for dusting
olive oil for cooking
4 ripe tomatoes, skinned, seeded and chopped
125 ml dry white wine
18 black olives, halved and stoned
4-6 canned anchovy fillets, very finely chopped
2 cloves garlic, crushed
30 ml capers
15 ml chopped tarragon leaves
or 2 ml dried tarragon

GARNISH
4-6 anchovy fillets, halved lengthwise
lemon wedges for squeezing

Season the fish with salt and pepper, dust with flour and fry in olive oil until golden-brown – 2-3 minutes on each side. Remove from the pan, set aside and keep hot.

Soften the tomato in the same pan, adding a little more oil if necessary. Add the wine, olives, chopped anchovy, garlic, capers and tarragon. Season with salt and pepper (remember that anchovies are salty) and cook uncovered for about 5 minutes until the sauce thickens slightly.

Place the fish steaks on a large serving platter or on individual dinner plates. Top with the sauce, garnish with anchovy strips and place lemon wedges alongside.
Serves 6

Braised Gamefish

Flavoursome gamefish like tuna, marlin, barracuda, leervis, Spanish mackerel – even snoek and yellowtail – enjoy this robust treatment.

6 filleted gamefish portions (each about 200 g)
salt and milled black pepper
flour for dusting
butter and sunflower oil for frying
1 onion, sliced
2 firm, ripe tomatoes, peeled and sliced
200 g button mushrooms, sliced
1 fresh or dried bouquet garni
½ beef stock cube
60 ml hot water
60 ml dry red wine

Season the fish with salt and pepper and dust lightly with flour. In a wide saucepan brown quickly in butter and oil. Remove the fish from the pan and set aside.

Lightly brown the sliced onion in the same pan (add more butter if necessary), then add the tomato, mushrooms and herbs, and season with salt and pepper. Cover and cook the vegetables very gently for approximately 10 minutes.

Dissolve the stock cube in hot water, mix with wine and add to the saucepan with the fish. Cover and simmer gently until the fish is cooked – 8-10 minutes.

Check the flavour of the sauce, then transfer the fish and the sauce to a warmed serving platter. Serve with sautéed potatoes.
Serves 6

Foiled Tuna

There's no need to reserve this recipe for tuna. It's a great way to cook yellowtail, angelfish and marlin. Remember to reduce the baking time for thinner pieces of fish.

4 filleted tuna portions (each about 200 g)
salt and milled black pepper
butter
chopped parsley
fresh lemon juice

Set the oven at 180 °C. Butter pieces of foil large enough to wrap the fish in. Place steaks thereon, season well with salt and pepper, sprinkle on some chopped parsley (other herbs, too, if they're available) and a good squeeze of lemon juice. Top with another pat of butter and seal.

Bake for 20 minutes until done: the flesh should flake easily all the way through. Cook for 5-10 minutes longer if necessary. Serve with new potatoes, salad, and the sauce from the foil.
Serves 4

VARIATIONS
- *Bacon-Wrapped Tuna* Enfold the steaks with rindless, streaky bacon after seasoning and before wrapping. Open the foil during the final 10 minutes' cooking time to crisp the bacon.
- *Bacon and Banana-Wrapped Tuna* Place bacon rashers on a chopping board, cover with mashed banana, place the tuna steaks in the middle and wrap it all up with the bacon. Seal in buttered foil and bake as above.
- *To Braai* Easy! Simply braai your foiled tuna on a grid over medium coals. The braaiing time will depend on the thickness of the steaks – 2 cm steaks should be done in 15 minutes; adjust the time accordingly for thicker or thinner steaks.

BARBADOS FISH

A delicious recipe for any fish that tends to be dry, like marlin, yellowtail, leervis, angelfish or tuna.

1 kg filleted fish, cut into large cubes
salt and milled black pepper
juice of 1 large lemon
125 ml dry white wine
125 ml chicken stock
flour for dusting
butter and sunflower oil for frying
2 onions, finely sliced
1 fat clove garlic, crushed
1 green or red pepper, seeded and sliced
4 whole cloves
1 bay leaf
few sprigs of thyme
or 1 ml dried thyme
4 bananas

Season the fish with salt and pepper and place in a non-metal dish. Combine the lemon juice, wine and stock, pour over and set aside to marinate for about 30 minutes. Drain the fish (reserve the marinade for the sauce) and dust very lightly with flour.

Heat some butter and oil in a wide saucepan and brown the fish, a few pieces at a time. Set the fish aside. In the same pan fry the onion and garlic until lightly browned (add extra butter and oil if necessary). Add the green or red pepper, cloves, bay leaf, thyme and the reserved marinade, cover and simmer gently for about 15 minutes.

Peel and slice the bananas and add to the sauce with the fish. Cover and simmer for 5 minutes until the fish is cooked. Serve with sautéed potatoes.

Serves 6

ROAST GAMEFISH SPIKED WITH BACON

A dramatic way of cooking tuna or marlin. If you can't find a fish of the correct weight, use a chunk from a larger fish.

1,5 kg filleted, skinless tuna or marlin
250 g rindless streaky bacon
salt and milled black pepper
sunflower oil for roasting
lemon wedges for squeezing
fresh herbs for garnish

Set the oven at 160 °C. Wash the fish and pat dry. Make incisions at regular intervals with a sharp knife and into each insert a sliver of bacon. Season the fish lightly with salt and pepper and wrap with the remaining bacon, ensuring that the ends are secured well with toothpicks.

Heat a little oil in a roasting tin on the stovetop and brown the bacon-wrapped fish all over. Cover with lightly oiled foil and roast in the oven, calculating 35 minutes per kilogram. Baste occasionally with the pan juices.

Check for doneness, place the fish on a large platter and garnish with lemon wedges and fresh herbs. Serve with boiled potatoes and salad – and don't forget to offer a sauce. Choose from Peanut Pesto (page 97), Tapenade Sauce (page 97) or Herbed Tomato Sauce (page 97).

Serves 6-8

DEEP-FRIED ROMAN

Munching a whole fish is always a real Tom Jones affair – complete with tucked-in napkin and much finger licking. It's the most succulent way of enjoying surf-fresh roman, or other fish of suitable size (about 500 g), like harders, or small elf, kob, stumpnose or red steenbras deep-fried in a crunchy crust.

4 whole fish, each about 500 g
sunflower oil for deep-frying

COATING
500 ml cake flour
10 ml powdered chicken stock
milled black pepper
2 eggs
250 ml milk
500 ml toasted crumbs
lemon wedges and herb sprigs for garnish

Make sure the fish are perfectly clean – inside and out – and that there are no stray scales floating about, as these tend to put off the most devoted fish-lover.

In a large plastic bag, combine the flour, chicken stock and pepper. Grab a fish by the tail, lower head first into the bag, close the bag around the tail and shake vigorously to coat the fish with flour. Discard excess flour and set the fish aside, while giving remaining fish the flour treatment.

Beat together the eggs and milk in a flattish dish and place crumbs onto a flat plate. Dip the floured fish in the egg mixture, rolling them over to coat well, then repeat the procedure in the crumbs, gently pressing them against the fish to firm the coating.

Refrigerate the fish for 30 minutes to firm the coating, then repeat the flour, egg and crumb procedure once more – but more gently this time, so as not to disturb the first layer. More ingredients may be necessary to complete the second coating.

The fish may now be refrigerated for several hours – overnight if you wish – before deep-frying.

In your largest pot heat the oil to 190 °C (at which temperature a 3 cm cube of day-old bread will brown in 40 seconds), and lower in a fish, cooking one at a time. Should a fish tail not be completely immersed, don't fret: the bubbling oil will cook it through.

Reduce slightly the temperature of the oil, and fry the fish for 10 minutes until cooked through to the bone. Drain on a thick wad of absorbent paper, then transfer to a warm serving platter in a low oven, to keep hot while the remaining fish are cooked.

Place each fish on a bed of savoury rice, or with a pile of crisp chips. Either way, garnish the plates with lemon wedges and sprigs of fresh herbs to add a lovely splash of colour to the dish.
Serves 4

MAKE AHEAD These deep-fried, crusty fish retain succulence and crispness for quite a while after cooking, so don't rush your starter unduly; the fish will wait patiently in a low oven.

Barbados Fish, recipe page 62

Baked Stumpnose Marrakesh, recipe page 65

BAKED REEF FISH WITH AVOCADO STUFFING

Rock anglers used to have exclusive access to many species of our fish. But nowadays more and more sea-fresh fish like dageraad, stumpnose and steenbras are nabbed by professional fishermen at coastal fishing villages and find their way into fish shops. Grab one if you can and bake it immediately.

1 whole fish, 1,5 - 2 kg, well cleaned
50 g (50 ml) butter
salt and milled black pepper
125 ml dry white wine

AVOCADO STUFFING
1 ripe avocado, skinned, stoned and diced
2 slices ham, shredded
12 almonds, toasted and finely chopped
60 ml snipped chives
15 ml chopped parsley
250 ml cooked brown rice

SAUCE
baking liquid
15 ml flour
30 ml cream

Set the oven at 180 °C. If the belly cavity of the fish is on the small side, enlarge it a little with a very sharp knife, working towards the tail. Don't enlarge the belly opening, which will be sewn up after fish is stuffed. Into the cavity place a few small knobs of butter (use only about a quarter of the given quantity). Season with salt and pepper.

Mix together the stuffing ingredients and season to taste with salt and pepper. Fill the belly and head cavity and sew up the opening with a needle and thread or use thin metal skewers.

Place the fish in a large casserole or roasting tin, dot with remaining butter, pour over the wine and cover loosely with foil. Don't seal it; too much baking liquid will form, which then has to be reduced before sauce-making can commence.

Bake until cooked through – about 35-40 minutes should be sufficient. Test by inserting a knife along the dorsal fin: the flesh should flake easily to the bone. Carefully lift the fish onto a warm platter while preparing the sauce.

Strain the baking liquid into a saucepan. Spoon a little into a cup and blend in the flour, then mix this into the sauce. Bring to the boil and cook, stirring, until sauce has reduced to a creamy consistency. Season with a little salt and pepper. Add the cream and heat through. Pour the sauce over the fish or serve it separately, if you wish.

Serves 4

Baked Stumpnose Marrakesh

A whole baked fish is simply stunning. Add an interesting stuffing and the dish becomes tantalizingly exotic. If red stumpnose is unavailable, other suitable fish are white stumpnose, kob, geelbek, musselcracker or steenbras. The most important thing is that it's fresh and of suitable dimensions.

WATCHPOINT *Cooking times in this recipe are given for a 2 kg fish. If yours varies in size, adjust accordingly.*

2 kg whole red stumpnose
butter
125 ml dry white wine

MARRAKESH STUFFING
1 Granny Smith apple, skinned and finely chopped
25 g pitted dates, finely chopped
200 ml cooked brown rice
30 ml grated onion
60 ml finely chopped almonds
1 ml ground cinnamon
1 ml ground ginger
¼ ml ground cardamom
30 ml melted butter
salt and milled black pepper

SAUCE
pan juices from baking fish
15 ml flour
125 ml Crème Fraîche (page 90)
or 125 ml cream and 5 ml lemon juice

Set the oven at 180 °C. Lightly butter a casserole or roasting pan to accommodate the fish comfortably. Clean the fish thoroughly, inside and out, making quite sure there are no scales and other unlovely bits and pieces left anywhere in sight. Pay particular attention to the head cavity, which will also be filled with stuffing.

Mix together all the stuffing ingredients and season with salt and pepper. Stuff the fish, filling both the belly and the head cavity. You will enjoy every scrap, so plug it all in. Sew up the fish with needle and thread or close with metal skewers.

Place the fish in the baking dish, dot with butter, pour over the wine and seal with lightly oiled foil. Bake for 50 minutes until cooked through. Test by sliding a sharp knife under flesh at the thickest part and lifting carefully. The flesh should be opaque; if not, bake for a further 5 minutes. Carefully lift the fish onto a warmed serving platter and keep hot while preparing the sauce.

Sieve the flour onto the pan juices; it will be quickly absorbed. Blend in the crème fraîche and stir over high heat until the sauce is smooth and thickened. Season with salt and pepper and pour into a small jug.

Transfer the fish to a large serving platter and remove the stitches or skewers. Garnish with lemon wedges and – if the platter is large enough – new potatoes tossed in parsley butter. Serve at once with an exotic salad of mixed greens and fresh herbs.
Serves 6

TO BRAAI Oil a hinged grid thoroughly (the finished dish looks disgusting if bits of skin are ripped off!). Clamp the fish in it and braai for 30 minutes on each side and basting frequently with oil to make sure the skin doesn't stick to the grid. Test for doneness and serve as above.

Ouma's Pickled Fish

Yellowtail is traditionally used in this well-loved old Cape recipe, but many other types may be substituted. Alternatives include angelfish, baardman, barracuda, dageraad, geelbek, hake, kob, leervis, marlin, monkfish, red steenbras, rock cod, shark, silverfish, snoek, Spanish mackerel and stumpnose.

1 whole fish, approximately 2 kg
salt and milled black pepper
sunflower oil for frying
750 ml dark vinegar
250 ml water
200 ml sugar
15 ml turmeric
45 ml curry powder
7 ml salt
15 ml black peppercorns
4 large onions, finely sliced
6 bay leaves
250 ml sultanas (optional)
40 ml cake flour

Fillet and skin the fish, and cut into cubes about 2,5 cm in diameter. Season lightly with salt and pepper and fry in hot oil until cooked through. Drain on kitchen paper.

In a large saucepan combine the vinegar, water, sugar, turmeric, curry powder, salt and peppercorns and bring to the boil. Add the onions and the bay leaves, cover and simmer for 10-12 minutes until cooked but still ever so slightly crunchy.

Mix the flour into a little of the hot sauce and stir it into the pot. Stir over high heat until the sauce thickens.

Layer the fish, sultanas and onion in a large non-metal dish, pour sauce over, cover and refrigerate.
Serves 6-8

MAKE AHEAD If you're desperate, your pickled fish may be eaten immediately. However it's best after 3 days and will keep in the fridge for up to 6 months.

Shellfish Dishes

The shellfish found in our waters is normally reserved for special occasions – no doubt due to the high cost. Here's a tantalizing collection of recipes that will suit all cooks, whether novice or expert.

Mussel and Leek Pie

A delicately flavoured mussel pie with a crunchy topping.

Quiche Pastry (page 92)
2 kg black mussels (50-60 mussels)
75 g courgettes
75 g leeks
1 ml crushed garlic
5 ml Burmese Curry Mix (page 90)
or medium curry powder
butter for cooking
30 ml dry white wine
40 ml Fish Stock (page 88)
60 ml cream
2 eggs
salt and milled black pepper
grated Parmesan cheese for topping

Set the oven at 180 °C. Roll out the pastry and line the base of a quiche dish. Bake blind, remove from the oven and allow to cool. Reduce the oven temperature to 160 °C.

Steam the mussels open in a little water, remove from the shells, pull out the 'beards' and, unless they are really tiny, cut the mussels in half.

Grate the courgettes and soak for 30 minutes in a bowl of salted water. Drain and scatter onto the pastry. Fry the leek, garlic and curry powder in a little butter until the leek starts to get limp. Spoon over the grated courgettes as evenly as possible.

Mix together the wine, stock, cream, eggs, and salt and pepper and pour this evenly into the pie. Dust the surface with Parmesan cheese and bake for 25 minutes. Serve with a green salad.

Serves 4

Mussel Stroganoff

Delicious spooned over just-cooked pasta.

2 kg black mussels (50-60 mussels)
125 ml Fish Stock (page 88)
or chicken stock
80 ml dry white wine
80 ml water
sprigs of thyme and fennel
100 g button mushrooms, sliced
40 g (40 ml) butter
60 ml snipped chives
30 ml cake flour
80 ml cream
2 ml fresh lemon juice
salt and milled black pepper

Steam the mussels open in a little water. Drain, discard the shells, remove the beards and cut the mussels in half. Combine the stock, wine, water and herbs in a saucepan and simmer for 2-3 minutes. Set aside.

Fry the mushrooms in butter to extract the maximum flavour. Remove from the stove, add the chives and blend in the flour. Strain the stock and stir in with the cream, lemon juice and seasoning. Stir over high heat until the mixture simmers and thickens. Add the mussels and heat through – no longer than a minute, or you'll overcook the mussels. Serve with pasta and a green salad.

Serves 4

Spicy Octopus, recipe page 69, boiled crayfish, prawns, Perlemoen with Fresh Herbs, recipe page 81, Tartare Sauce, recipe page 95, Tapenade Sauce, recipe page 97, and steamed black mussels

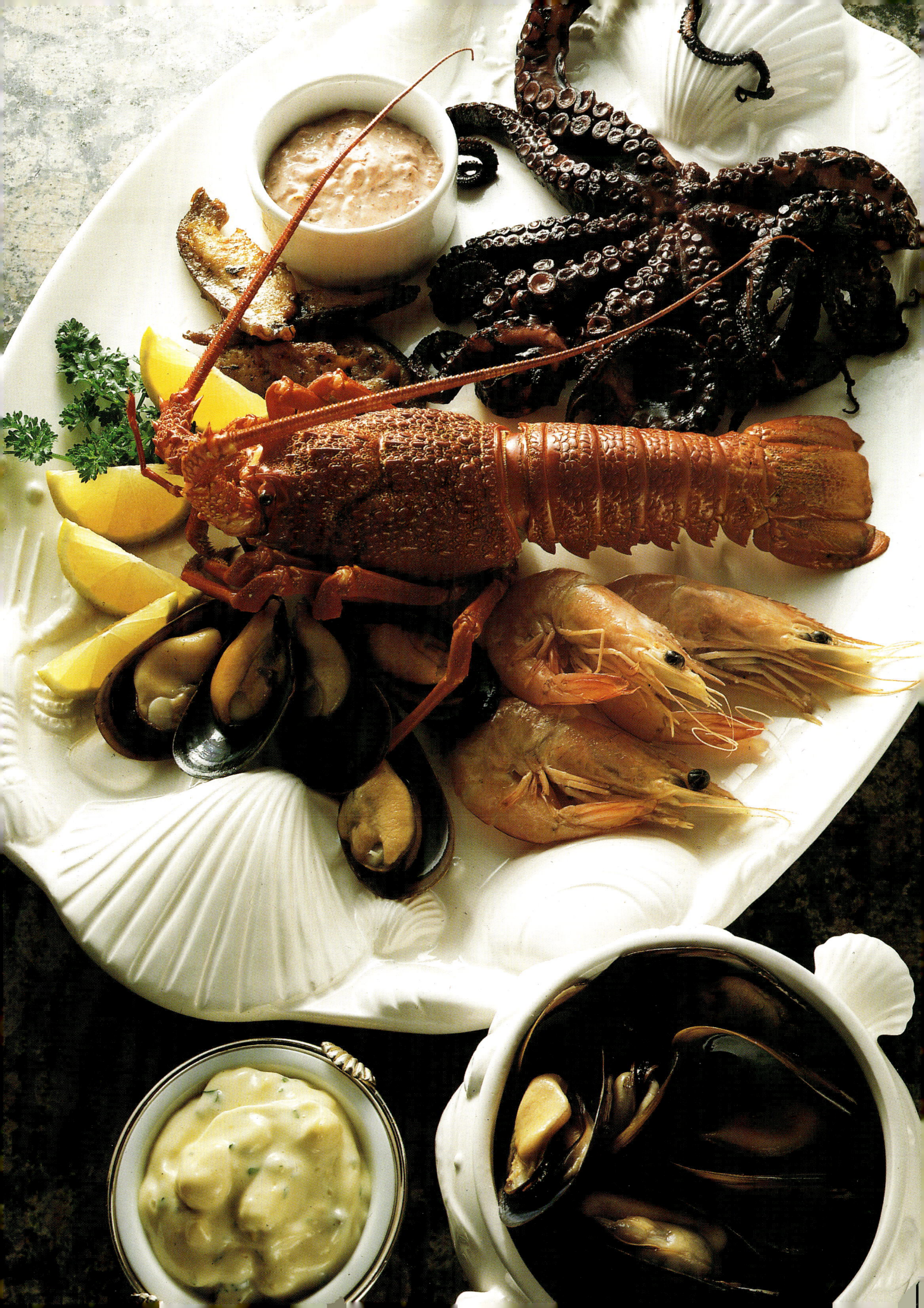

Portuguese Calamari

Whole calamari tubes filled with a herby rice stuffing and gently cooked in butter.

6-8 large, whole, cleaned calamari tubes
2 cloves garlic, finely chopped
butter and sunflower oil for frying
salt and milled black pepper
flour

STUFFING
1 onion, finely chopped
2 cloves garlic, crushed
50 g (50 ml) butter
2 ripe tomatoes, skinned and chopped
1 small green or red pepper, seeded and chopped
15 ml chopped origanum
or 2 ml dried origanum
125 ml uncooked rice
125 ml dry white wine
125 ml water

Clean the calamari thoroughly inside and out and pat dry. Chop the fins and tentacles very finely and set aside.

STUFFING Soften the onion and crushed garlic in the butter. Add the tomato, green or red pepper, origanum, and salt and pepper to taste. Cook for a minute, then stir in the rice, wine and water. Cover and simmer gently until all the liquid has been absorbed and the rice is cooked.

In a clean saucepan sizzle half the chopped garlic in a little butter and oil. Add the chopped tentacles and fins and fry for just 1 minute. Mix into the stuffing.

Lightly season the insides of the calamari tubes and fill with the stuffing – don't pack it too tightly as calamari shrinks when cooking. Secure the open ends with toothpicks. Season with salt and pepper and dust with flour.

Heat a little more butter and oil, sizzle the remaining chopped garlic and brown the calamari. Cover and cook very, very gently for about 1 hour until tender. Remove the stuffed calamari from the pan and place on a warmed serving plate. Deglaze the pan with a little water, pour over the calamari and serve at once with savoury rice.

Serves 4

Portuguese Calamari

Panfried Garlic Calamari

The secret of tender calamari lies in the cooking time. It turns from tender to tough and chewy in a flash so whip it out of the pan the moment it's done.

800 g calamari tubes, thoroughly cleaned
flour and milled black pepper
200 g butter
30 ml olive oil
10-15 ml crushed garlic
fresh lemon juice
lemon wedges for squeezing

Slice calamari according to size: tubes larger than 8 cm in rings; smaller specimens are better cut in half, lengthwise, laid flat and each piece scored lightly in a diamond pattern. Real infants may be left whole. Toss in flour seasoned with pepper.

In a large, non-stick frying pan, heat the butter and oil until it starts to brown. Stir in the garlic, add the calamari and cook for 1½-2 minutes, depending on the thickness. As it fries, press it down with a spatula to brown nicely. Remember to cook in batches, so that you don't overcrowd the pan and reduce the temperature.

Transfer the calamari to a warmed serving platter, add a good squeeze of lemon juice to the pan and pour this over the calamari. Garnish with lemon wedges and serve with rice if you like.
Serves 3 as a main course; 6 as a starter

Arniston Alikreukels

Even when you're at the sea-shore and far from a civilised kitchen you're likely to have a spare beer available for this recipe.

4-6 alikreukels
1 onion, finely sliced
1-2 cloves garlic, crushed
butter
2 ml paprika
salt and milled black pepper
340 ml can or bottle beer

Cook alikreukels in their shells in boiling, salted water for 15-20 minutes until cooked (the 'trap doors' will lift off easily). Plop them out of their shells, discard the entrails and slice finely.

Fry the onion and garlic in a little butter until just tinged with brown. Add the sliced alikreukel and season with salt, pepper and paprika. Pour in the beer, cover and simmer gently for about 5 minutes. Serve on a bed of rice.
Serves 4 as a main course; 8 as a starter

Spicy Octopus

One of the tastiest ways of preparing octopus. Serve it simply – perhaps with rice and a crisp salad.

1 large octopus or 2 small ones (about 1 kg in total)
Worcestershire sauce

After beheading, skinning and tenderizing your octopus but before cooking it (see page 112) continue as follows: cut the tentacles into 3 cm chunks and put them in a heavy-based pot (waterless is best; a well-sealing lid is essential). Splash liberally with Worcestershire sauce, cover with the lid and simmer over very low heat for about 45 minutes until the octopus is fork-tender. As it cooks it forms its own liquid, making a delicious sauce.
Serves 4-6

TO PICKLE THE LEFTOVERS Pack the pieces into a sterilized jar and top up with wine or cider vinegar and sunflower oil, calculating ⅓ vinegar to ⅔ oil. It's great for snacks and may be stored in the fridge for several weeks.

Intoxicated Octopus

A robust dish that goes well with rice and crusty bread.

1 large octopus or 2 smaller ones
(about 1,5 kg in total)
3 onions, chopped
2 fat cloves garlic, crushed
125 ml olive oil
60 ml tomato purée
250 ml red wine
125 ml water
1 chicken stock cube
2 bay leaves
15 ml chopped origanum
or 2 ml dried origanum
salt and milled black pepper
18 small new potatoes, scrubbed

Following the instructions on page 112 behead, skin, tenderize and cook the octopus. Cut the tentacles into bite-size chunks.

In a heavy pot fry the onion and garlic in oil until lightly browned. Add the octopus, tomato purée, wine, water, crumbled stock cube, bay leaves, and origanum and season with salt and pepper. Cover and simmer very slowly for about 30 minutes.

Add the potatoes, cover and simmer for 15-20 minutes more until they're cooked and the octopus is tender.
Serves 6

Seafood Sausages

If you enjoy a challenge in the kitchen, here it is. Should you not have on hand all the varieties of seafood called for, feel free to simplify matters slightly, and make up the mass by increasing the other ingredients. If there's no kingklip about, use musselcracker, geelbek, dageraad, monkfish, or white or red steenbras.

Don't be fazed by the lengthy method (sausage-making is surprisingly simple), or by the costly ingredients. The quantities of each are small, and the total cost is surprisingly low. Sausage casings may be purchased by the kilogram, but when such a small quantity is required, bribe a friendly butcher to supply and measure it for you. If you have to purchase a large quantity, store the remainder – heavily salted – in the fridge. It keeps indefinitely. But these sausages are so delicious you'll probably be making another batch quite soon!

3 metres sausage casings
50 g trimmed perlemoen, minced
375 g filleted kingklip, skinned and cubed
50 g shelled mussels
125 g shelled raw prawns, deveined and halved
120 g lobster tail (shell-on weight),
shelled and deveined
1 egg yolk
30 ml melted butter
75 ml cream
30 ml port
5 ml salt
5 ml milled black pepper
2 ml crushed garlic
20 ml chopped herbs (parsley, chives, marjoram)
butter and sunflower oil for frying
lemon wedges for squeezing

SAUCE
15 ml brandy
water
125 ml cream
salt and milled black pepper

Before sausage-making can commence, soak the casings overnight in cold water to make them pliable and easier to handle. Just before using, rinse well by fitting one end of the skin onto the tap and running fresh water through.

Mix all the seafood together and mince coarsely (use the cutting disc with the largest holes). Beat together the egg yolk and melted butter, then add cream, port, salt, pepper and garlic. Mix well into the seafood with the herbs.

The easiest way to fill the casings is through a large funnel, the hole measuring at least 2 cm. (We bought a petrol funnel, which is used only for the purpose of sausage-making.) Thread the casing onto the nozzle, leaving about 8-10 cm hanging down.

Place a few spoonfuls of the seafood mixture into the funnel and press it through the nozzle to fill the casing loosely. To prevent over-filling (which will cause the sausages to burst when cooking), flatten the sausage to a thickness of about 15 mm. Each sausage should be about 18 cm long, so be sure to leave 10 cm lengths of casing in between each, to cut and knot.

Bring water to the boil in a large saucepan, drop in the sausages and blanch for 30 seconds (this prevents them from bursting when cooking). They are now ready for frying, refrigerating or freezing.

Heat butter and oil in a large frying pan and fry a few sausages at a time over medium heat until beautifully browned and cooked through – this should take about 10 minutes. Transfer to a warmed platter and keep hot.

Pour the brandy into the pan and flame. When the flames subside, deglaze the pan with a little water to melt all the lovely browning. Stir in the cream and season with salt and pepper. Strain the sauce into a jug or sauceboat.

Allow 2 sausages per person for a main course; 1 for a starter. Pour over a ribbon of sauce, garnish with lemon wedges and serve immediately.
Makes 10 sausages

MAKE AHEAD The blanched sausages may be refrigerated for up to 3 days, or frozen for up to 6 weeks.

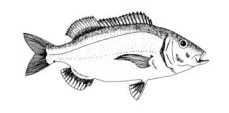

Scallops with Mushrooms and Dill

Dill has a wonderful affinity with seafood of all types, and with scallops in particular. Add mushrooms to complete the exotic trio of flavours in this memorable dish.

500 g scallops
375 ml dry white wine
1 fresh or dried bouquet garni
10 ml cornflour
15 ml cold water
30 g (30 ml) butter
300 g button mushrooms, sliced
5 ml crushed garlic
10 ml chopped dill
or 2 ml dried dill
250 ml cream
salt and milled black pepper
snipped chives for garnish

Seafood Sausages, recipe page 70

Rinse the scallops, leaving the roe intact (this is a real delicacy). If the scallops are on the large side, slice them in half. Pat dry and set aside.

In a small saucepan combine the wine and herbs and simmer uncovered until the liquid is reduced to about 250 ml. Discard the herbs. Mix together the cornflour and cold water, stir it into the flavoured wine and simmer for a few minutes until clear and thickened; set aside.

Heat the butter in a medium saucepan and quickly fry the mushrooms, garlic and dill. Cover, reduce the heat and steam for 5 minutes. Add the scallops and cook gently for 2 minutes, turning them occasionally. Add the flavoured wine and cream, season with salt and pepper to taste and heat through.

Spoon the scallops onto rice or buttered noodles and garnish with chives. Alternatively, serve simply with crusty bread and a simple salad.

Serves 4

MAKE AHEAD This dish may be prepared a day ahead and gently reheated before serving. But please don't overdo the scallops; they'll become tough and unappealing.

SPICED PRAWNS

These butterflied, basted and grilled prawns are a taste sensation. In place of prawns use langoustines or crayfish – but remember to vary the cooking time accordingly.

24-32 large prawns in shells
80 ml sunflower oil
80 ml fresh lemon juice
15 ml Dijon mustard
5 ml Burmese Curry Mix (page 90)
or mild curry powder
salt and milled black pepper
250 ml cream
lemon wedges for squeezing

Slit the prawns down their backs, devein and place shells-down on a grilling tray. Heat the oven griller.

Mix together the oil, lemon juice, mustard, curry powder and salt and pepper and brush the prawns liberally. Grill for 4-5 minutes until cooked, then transfer the prawns to a warm serving platter.

Pour the remaining basting mixture into the grilling tray, add the cream and cook on the stovetop until the sauce thickens to the correct consistency. Check the flavour and adjust if necessary.

Pour the sauce over the prawns or offer it separately if preferred. Serve with rice and a salad, and make sure there are plenty of lemon wedges for squeezing.

Serves 4

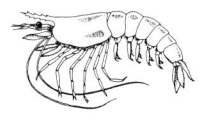

GARLIC-KISSED PRAWNS

Crisply grilled prawns are always delicious. Langoustines may also be prepared this way. Add freshly chopped herbs to the sauce if you wish.

36 large prawns in shells
100 g butter
60 ml olive oil
juice of 1 lemon
4-6 spring onions, finely chopped
3-4 fat cloves garlic, crushed
salt and milled black pepper
lemon wedges for squeezing

Heat the oven griller. Prepare the prawns by slitting down the backs to butterfly them open. Remove the vein.

Melt the butter in a shallow baking dish just large enough to take the prawns in a single layer. Mix in the olive oil, lemon juice, spring onion, garlic, salt and pepper. Dunk in the prawns, coating well, then cuddle them side-by-side, shells down.

Grill until just cooked through – 4-5 minutes should be quite long enough. Transfer the prawns to a hot serving platter, pour the sauce over and serve with lemon wedges. A scattering of chopped parsley adds a nice touch of colour. Serve with rice and salad.

Serves 6

BRANDIED PRAWNS IN CRÈME FRAÎCHE

Lazy summer evenings are for the good times, like entertaining a few close friends. Choose simple dishes that may be prepared ahead of time and reheated, and stay cool while your friends wonder how you did it!

1,2 kg prawns, heads off
60 g (60 ml) butter
milled black pepper
45 ml brandy
300 g button mushrooms, sliced
5 ml cake flour
250 ml Crème Fraîche (page 90)
7 ml soy sauce
1 ml paprika
80 ml grated mozzarella cheese

Shell and devein the prawns. In a large frying pan heat half the butter and fry the prawns for 1-2 minutes until cooked. Remove the pan from the heat and season the prawns with pepper. Warm the brandy, pour over and flame. When the flames die down transfer the prawns to a baking dish.

Melt the remaining butter in the same pan and fry the mushrooms gently until softened. Blend in the flour, then slowly stir in the crème fraîche and bring to the boil. Remove from the heat and season with pepper, soy sauce and paprika. Pour the sauce over the prawns and top with grated cheese.

Place under the griller until heated through and the topping is golden. Serve immediately with crusty bread or hot buttered noodles.

Serves 6-8

MAKE AHEAD Refrigerate the dish for a day after assembling. Bake for 10-15 minutes at 200 °C; grill the topping before serving.

PRAWNS MYKONOS

There's a Greek twist to this prawn dish which may be prepared with langoustines or crayfish as well.

24-32 large prawns, shelled and deveined
1 small onion, finely chopped
2 cloves garlic, crushed
60 ml olive oil
4 tomatoes, skinned and chopped
or a 400 g can, drained and chopped
80 ml dry white wine
15 ml chopped origanum
or 2 ml dried origanum
30 ml chopped parsley
salt and milled black pepper
75 g feta cheese, crumbled

Fry the onion and garlic in olive oil until lightly browned. Stir in the tomato, wine, origanum and half the parsley, and season with salt and pepper. Cook briskly uncovered until the mixture thickens.

Add the prawns and cook for 1-2 minutes, by which time they'll be firm, pink and just cooked through (overcook them at your peril!).

Stir in the cheese, tip the prawns into a warm serving bowl and garnish with the remaining chopped parsley. Serve with rice and a Greek salad. Some crusty bread is nice too.

Serves 4

MAKE AHEAD Prawns should always be served the moment they're cooked, otherwise they become tough and tasteless. You may, however, prepare the sauce ahead of time and add the prawns at the last moment.

Prawns Mykonos

Sweet and Sour Prawns

SWEET AND SOUR PRAWNS

Star splash-out dish of any Chinese restaurant. Chunks of crayfish may be used instead of prawns, though you're welcome to make the dish more economical by substituting fish for some of the shellfish. Or just use fish, the best types being monkfish, gurnard and kingklip.

24-32 large prawns
salt and white pepper
flour for dusting
sunflower oil for deep-frying
Chinese Batter (page 90)
Sweet and Sour Sauce (page 98)

Prepare the batter and the sauce. Behead the prawns and remove the shells, leaving the last tail-shell in situ. Slice down the backs and devein. Rinse, pat dry and season with salt and pepper. Press each prawn into flour to coat it well (this ensures that the batter sticks); set aside.

Make sure your sauce is piping hot, a bowl of rice awaits and your guests are seated before cooking the prawns. Heat the oil, dip each prawn into the batter and deep-fry for about 2 minutes, just long enough to cook through and crisp the batter. Fry in batches so as not to reduce the temperature of the oil. As soon as they're cooked drain the prawns on kitchen paper, then pile into a warmed serving bowl. Serve on rice with sweet and sour sauce separately.

Serves 4

GRILLED CRAYFISH

A deliciously simple way to do fresh crayfish. Just watch the cooking time; if you overcook the crayfish it will dry out.

4 fresh crayfish
Garlic Butter (page 91)
lemon wedges for squeezing

Heat the oven grill. Cut the crayfish in half lengthwise and clean well. Place on a baking tray, shells down. Brush liberally with garlic butter.

Grill until done, basting liberally and often. The cooking time depends on size – anything from 15-30 minutes. As soon as the flesh lifts easily from the shell and is opaque right through, it's ready to serve with plenty of lemon wedges for squeezing. Crusty bread and a salad are nice accompaniments.
Serves 4

VARIATION Perk up the baste by adding 45 ml dry sherry, 2 ml paprika and a pinch of cayenne pepper.

CRAYFISH PIE

This is our favourite way of using up the succulent leg meat of the crayfish, though there's nothing to stop you from using tail meat if you prefer. Crab meat (fresh or canned) may be used instead of crayfish. And there's no law against making the filling without the pie crust.

Quiche Pastry (page 92)
30 g (30 ml) butter
1 small onion, finely chopped
30 ml cake flour
salt and milled black pepper
2 ml finely grated lemon rind
5 ml dry English mustard
pinch of mace
500 ml milk
2 eggs
150 ml grated Cheddar cheese
500 ml chopped crayfish meat
50 g flaked almonds for the topping

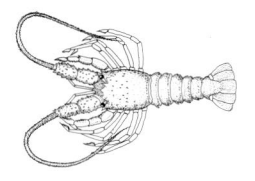

Prepare the pastry, line a 25 cm quiche tin and bake blind. Allow to cool. Reduce the oven temperature to 160 °C.

Soften the onion in butter. Remove from the heat and blend in the flour, salt, pepper, lemon rind, mustard, mace and half the milk. Stir over high heat for a couple of minutes until the sauce is smooth and thickened.

Remove the pot from the stove and add the eggs mixed into the remaining milk. Mix in the cheese and crayfish. Pour the filling into the cooked pie shell, top with almonds and bake for 30-40 minutes until the filling is cooked and almonds are nicely browned. Serve with a green salad.
Serves 6

CRAYFISH MA CHÈRE

Here's the best excuse in the world for cracking a bottle of bubbly: crayfish in a light and lively champagne sauce. Use a little in the sauce and serve the rest with the meal. If the budget won't stretch to crayfish, substitute 1,2 kg fillets of fish; sole, kob, steenbras, kingklip or monkfish are best.

6 crayfish tails (each about 200 g)
250 ml champagne or dry sparkling wine
5 ml crushed garlic
salt and milled black pepper
grated Parmesan cheese for the topping

SAUCE MA CHÈRE
50 g (50 ml) butter
60 ml cake flour
salt and milled black pepper
250 ml Fish Stock (page 88)
250 ml cream or milk and cream
125 ml champagne marinade
125 ml water
300 g grapes, skinned and seeded

Remove the crayfish meat from the shells and slice in half, lengthwise. Into the champagne mix the garlic, salt and pepper. Pour it over the crayfish and and set aside to marinate for 30-60 minutes.

Set the oven at 200 °C. Drain the crayfish (reserve half the marinade for the sauce), and place in a baking dish just large enough to accommodate the pieces.

SAUCE In small saucepan, cook the butter and flour together for 1 minute, then slowly blend in the seasoning, stock, cream, marinade and water to make a smooth, creamy sauce. Add the grapes and heat through. Pour the sauce over the crayfish, dust lightly with Parmesan cheese and bake for 20 minutes. Serve with buttered noodles or rice and salad.
Serves 6

CRAYFISH NEWBURG

4 large crayfish tails
30 g (30 ml) butter
30 ml cognac or brandy
20 ml cake flour
60 ml warm water
125 ml cream
1 ml cayenne pepper
salt and milled black pepper
paprika for garnish

Remove crayfish from the shells and devein. If you're feeling flashy, reserve the fanned part of the tail for the garnish and poach for 5 minutes in boiling water. Scrub clean.

Slice the tails lengthwise in half, then cut each half into cubes about 3 cm in diameter. Heat the butter in a medium frying pan and fry the crayfish over medium heat for 2 minutes only, turning the pieces as they cook. Remove from the heat, pour over the cognac or brandy, ignite and allow the flames to subside. Remove the crayfish from the pan and set aside in a warm bowl.

Working off the heat, blend the flour, then the warm water into the juices in the pan. When smooth, add the cream and season with cayenne pepper, salt and pepper. Stir the sauce over high heat until it thickens, then add the juices formed under the cooked crayfish.

Check the flavour and consistency – add a little more water if it's too thick; simmer briskly if it's too thin, then return the crayfish to the sauce and heat through.

Transfer it to a warmed serving platter and garnish with tail shells and a dusting of paprika.
Serves 4

CRAYFISH THERMIDOR

6 crayfish
50 g (50 ml) butter
45 ml cake flour
250 ml milk
125 ml cream
10 ml prepared English mustard
10 ml Worcestershire sauce
pinch of cayenne pepper
salt and milled black pepper
45 ml medium dry sherry
80 g (250 ml) grated Gruyère cheese

TOPPING
80 ml grated Parmesan cheese
80 ml toasted crumbs
paprika
butter

Cook the crayfish in boiling water, following the instructions given on page 117. Allow to cool. Scrub the shells clean under running water and split in half, lengthwise. Remove the flesh from the tails and bodies, discard the alimentary canal and cut the meat into chunks.

Scrub the shells nice and clean and place on a baking tray ready for filling and grilling. Melt the butter in a medium saucepan, remove from the heat and blend in the flour, milk, cream, mustard, Worcestershire sauce, cayenne pepper, and salt and pepper to taste. Stir over high heat until smooth and thickened, then remove from the heat and stir in the cheese and sherry.

Add the crayfish to the sauce, heat through and spoon into the cleaned shells. Sprinkle combined Parmesan cheese and crumbs on top, add a touch of paprika and dot with butter. Place under the oven griller to brown and crisp the topping. Serve with a green salad.
Serves 6

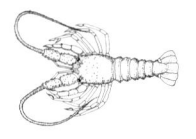

CRAB CURRY

4 large crabs (about 1 kg total weight)
45 ml sunflower oil
1 onion, finely sliced
5 ml crushed garlic
5 ml crushed green giner
30 ml Burmese Curry Mix (page 90)
or mild curry powder
10 ml fish sauce or
60 ml strong Fish Stock (page 88)
250 ml water
15 ml sesame oil
fresh coriander leaves for garnish

Clean the crabs by removing the shells from the bodies. If you wish, cut them through the centre into two halves. Disjoint the legs and crack the leg shells with a mallet. Rinse to remove bits of shell, drain and set aside.

Heat the oil in a large pot and stir-fry the onion, garlic and ginger for about 30 seconds. Add the crab pieces and curry powder and stir-fry for 1-2 minutes. Pour in the fish sauce or stock and water, cover and simmer the crab very gently for about 10 minutes until cooked. Check the seasoning: if you haven't used fish sauce, add a little salt.

Tip the curry into a warmed serving dish, drizzle over the sesame oil and garnish with coriander. Serve with basmati rice and sambals.
Serves 4

Crayfish Thermidor, recipe page 76

SULTAN'S CRAYFISH

An aromatic curry using subtly-blended spices to complement the delicate flavour of the crayfish. Serve with rice and a selection of sambals.

4 crayfish tails (each about 200 g)
50 g (50 ml) butter
2 onions, sliced
2 cloves garlic, crushed
2 ml crushed green ginger
2 ripe tomatoes, skinned and chopped
5 ml ground cumin
5 ml ground coriander
10 ml turmeric
1 ml chilli powder
500 ml milk
5 ml garam masala (optional)
7 ml salt
fresh lemon juice
coriander leaves for garnish

Remove the crayfish from the shells and cut into chunks. Discard the alimentary canals. Heat the butter and brown the crayfish pieces lightly. Remove from the pan and set aside. Fry the onion, garlic and ginger in the same pan until lightly browned, then add the tomato, cumin, coriander, turmeric, chilli powder and milk. Cook very gently uncovered until the sauce thickens – about 30-45 minutes.

Add the crayfish, salt and garam masala. Simmer for just 1-2 minutes until crayfish is cooked. Add a squeeze of lemon juice, check the seasoning and transfer the curry to a heated serving dish. Garnish with fresh coriander.
Serves 4

VARIATION
♦ *Sultan's Entrée* Make Sultan's Crayfish into a marvellous starter to serve 8: prepare a half quantity of the recipe and allow to cool while you cut 4 avocados in half. Sprinkle avocados with lemon juice and place on serving plates, cutting a sliver of skin from underneath so that they stand evenly. Spoon crayfish into the hollows, garnish with coriander and serve with crisp apple wedges.

CARIBBEAN PAELLA

A very special dish for easy entertaining and easy to double up to cater for a crowd.

6 chicken thighs
3 crayfish tails,
split in half lengthwise and
discard alimentary canals
18 large prawns
24 black mussels
300 g ham, cut into cubes
80 ml olive oil
2 onions, sliced
2 cloves garlic, crushed
2 red or yellow peppers, sliced
2 ripe tomatoes, skinned and chopped
625 ml chicken stock
375 ml uncooked rice
5 ml turmeric
250 g cooked peas
salt and milled black pepper

Skin and bone the chicken thighs and cut the chicken into large chunks. Leaving the shells on, chop each crayfish half into two. Slit the prawns down the backs of the shells and devein. Steam open the mussels, drain and pull out the beards.

Heat half the oil in a heavy frying pan and brown the chicken pieces, a few at a time. Set aside and season with salt and pepper. Fry the crayfish and prawns in the same pan; set aside with the chicken.

Add the remaining oil to the pan and fry the onion and garlic until golden. Add the red or yellow pepper, tomato and half the stock. Return the chicken to the pan, cover and cook gently until done – about 15 minutes.

Add the ham, rice, turmeric, remaining stock and a little more salt and pepper, cover and simmer until the rice is cooked and all the liquid has been absorbed.

Add the crayfish and prawns to the paella and lastly add the mussels and the peas. Stir very gently and heat through. If you like, add a dash of dry white wine to moisten the dish.

Serve with hot, crusty bread and a salad.

Serves 6

Caribbean Paella

CRUMBED PERLEMOEN

The simplest, most delicious way of serving perlemoen and one that most South Africans love best. If you prefer, coat the steaks with batter instead of egg and crumbs. See pages 90 and 91.

2 large perlemoen
flour, salt, milled black pepper
1 egg, lightly beaten
30 ml milk
toasted crumbs
butter and sunflower oil for frying
lemon wedges for squeezing

Scrub the perlemoen, cut into vertical slices about 5 mm thick and tenderize. Coat each piece lightly with flour seasoned with salt and pepper, and shake off the excess. Dip in egg mixed with milk; press into crumbs.

Heat butter and oil in a wide frying pan until sizzling hot. Fry the perlemoen, a few pieces at a time, until crisp and tender – 1-2 minutes on each side should be sufficient; overcooking will toughen it. Drain the perlemoen on kitchen paper once it's cooked.

Serve immediately with lemon wedges. A tangy sauce won't go amiss either – choose Tartare (page 95), one of the Mayonnaise variations (page 94) or Tapenade Sauce (page 97). If serving as a main course, a salad is all you'll need to go with it.

Serves 3-4 as a main course; 6-8 as a starter

SALPICON OF PERLEMOEN

Our favourite seafood croquettes, delicious served piping hot or completely cold. A food processor is essential for the preparation, unless your passion for perlemoen is so great that you're happy to chop away through the night.

500 g cleaned, trimmed perlemoen, cut into chunks
1 onion, skinned and quartered
2 rashers rindless bacon, cut into pieces
2 cloves garlic
2 eggs, lightly beaten
1 ml salt
½ ml allspice
30 ml chopped parsley
milled black pepper
100 ml soft breadcrumbs
flour for coating
butter and oil for frying
fresh chives or tiny spring onions for garnish
lemon wedges for squeezing

In the bowl of a food processor combine the perlemoen, onion, bacon and garlic and process until very finely chopped. This procedure is fairly lengthy owing to the firmness of the perlemoen. Mix in the eggs, salt, allspice, parsley and pepper. Lastly blend in the crumbs. Refrigerate for at least an hour to firm up the mixture before pattie-preparation begins.

Scoop up a spoonful of the mixture and drop it into a bowl of flour to coat lightly. Gently toss it from one hand to the other to get rid of the excess flour – a messy procedure, to be sure, demanding more than a touch of patience. Set aside on pieces of waxed paper or a lightly floured tray while completing all the patties.

In a non-stick frying pan heat butter and oil until sizzling hot. Fry the croquettes until golden-brown on each side and firm to the touch. They cook through fairly quickly, but do need to be browned really well for the best flavour. Drain on kitchen paper.

Serve hot with a crisp salad or colourful selection of vegetables. A flavourful sauce completes the feast.

If serving as a starter, arrange croquettes on lettuce leaves on a large platter or on individual serving plates. Garnish prettily with fresh chives or tiny spring onions and lots of lemon wedges for squeezing.

Serves 6 as a main course; 8 as a starter

MAKE AHEAD Uncooked croquettes may be refrigerated a day ahead. Coat with flour and fry just before serving.

PAARL LEMOEN

This is an adaptation of a classic old Cape Dutch recipe.

4 large perlemoen
250 ml water
125 ml dry white wine
50 g (50 ml) butter
salt and milled black pepper
fresh lemon juice
250 ml soft breadcrumbs
2 ml grated nutmeg

Remove the perlemoen from the shells, scrub clean, pound lightly and cut into large dice.

In a large pot combine the water, wine and butter. Season with salt, pepper and a squeeze of lemon juice. Add the perlemoen, cover, and simmer very gently until tender – this should take 1½-2 hours.

Stir in the crumbs and nutmeg to thicken the sauce. Check the seasoning and consistency – you may wish to add a little extra water. Serve in perlemoen shells, as tradition dictates.

Serves 6

Perlemoen Ragoût

Lengthy simmering produces fork-tender perlemoen.

500 g perlemoen (2-3), cleaned and trimmed
flour, salt, milled black pepper
1 bunch leeks, washed and sliced
2 rashers rindless, streaky bacon, finely chopped
60 g (60 ml) butter
5 ml crushed garlic
1 fresh or dried bouquet garni
hot water

Cut the perlemoen vertically into slices 5 mm thick, tenderize with a mallet and coat lightly with flour seasoned with salt and ground pepper. In wide saucepan soften leek in butter. Remove from the pan and set aside. Add to the pan the bacon and garlic, and fry for 1-2 minutes, then stir in half the reserved leek together with the herbs and the prepared perlemoen. Add sufficient hot water to barely cover the perlemoen, cover with the lid and simmer very gently until tender. The cooking time is about 1½-2 hours, by which time the perlemoen will be meltingly tender. Add the reserved leek to the ragoût 15 minutes before the end of cooking time.

Check the flavour and, if using dried herbs, discard before serving the perlemoen on rice or buttered noodles, or with new potatoes.
Serves 6

Perlemoen Peperonata

Perfect for perlemoen that has spent time in the freezer.

4 large perlemoen
butter and sunflower oil for cooking
3 onions, finely sliced
3 cloves garlic, finely chopped
6 ripe tomatoes, skinned and chopped
1 green or red pepper, seeded and sliced
5 ml salt
milled black pepper
15 ml chopped basil
or 2 ml dried basil
125 ml dry white wine

Scrub the perlemoen, cut into vertical steaks about 5 mm thick and tenderize. Heat the butter and oil in a large pot and lightly brown the perlemoen – a few pieces at a time, as the browning part is vital to the flavour of the dish. Remove the perlemoen from the pot, add a little more butter if necessary, and fry the onion and garlic until lightly browned.

Add the tomato, green or red pepper, salt, pepper and basil, together with the perlemoen pieces and wine. Cover and simmer very, very gently for about 1 hour until the perlemoen is tender.

Check the seasoning and consistency of the sauce – add a little more wine if it's too thick; simmer uncovered if it's too thin. Serve piping hot with rice and a crisp salad.
Serves 6

Perlemoen Fisherman's Wharf

A recipe from San Francisco's celebrated seafood emporium.

4 perlemoen
milled black pepper
1 egg
60 ml milk
500 ml soft breadcrumbs
butter and sunflower oil for frying

BEURRE BLANC
125 ml dry white wine
2 ml crushed garlic
15 ml fresh lemon juice
4 spring onions, finely sliced
50 g (50 ml) cold butter cut into small cubes
salt and milled black pepper
parsley sprigs for garnish

Clean and trim the perlemoen, and cut vertically into 5 mm thick slices, and tenderize each slice. Season with pepper. Beat together the egg and milk in a shallow dish. Place the crumbs in another dish. Coat the perlemoen steaks with egg, then with crumbs.

Heat a generous amount of butter and oil in a wide frying pan until really hot and foaming, and fry the perlemoen for about 30 seconds on each side. To ensure it cooks quickly to crisp, golden perfection, don't overcrowd the pan. Drain the cooked steaks for just 1 minute on absorbent paper, then place on a warmed serving platter. Cook the remaining perlemoen.

BEURRE BLANC In a small saucepan combine the wine, garlic, lemon juice and spring onion, cover and simmer gently for 3 minutes. Remove from the heat. Whisk in the butter bit by bit until the sauce is silky smooth. Season with salt and pepper to taste.

Garnish the platter of perlemoen with parsley and serve immediately, the hot sauce separately. Alternatively, place 4-5 slices of perlemoen onto each warmed dinner plate, pour over a ribbon of sauce and garnish with parsley.
Serves 4-6

Perlemoen with Fresh Herbs

Perlemoen with Fresh Herbs

Our favourite recipe. Remember that it is essential to work quickly. High heat and a large, heavy frying pan are essential so that frying can be done in two batches. Alternatively, cook three batches. The pan needs to be cleaned each time, as the herbs and sauce burn in a flash.

4 large perlemoen
50 g (50 ml) butter
30 ml sunflower oil
125 ml chopped herbs (parsley, tarragon, thyme, basil, origanum, chives) *
milled black pepper
water
large sprig of fresh herbs for garnish
* as a compromise, measure 125 ml chopped parsley and mix in 1 ml each of the dried herbs

Clean, slice perlemoen 5 mm thick, and tenderize. In a large frying pan heat half the butter and oil until it sizzles and starts to brown. Toss in some herbs (add a little crushed garlic too, if you wish) and fry half the perlemoen. Turn after 30 seconds when each slice will have a touch of golden-brown. The total cooking time should not exceed 1½ minutes; some pieces may cook even quicker.

Keep testing the tenderness of each slice by pressing with a fork and remove to a warm platter immediately. Lightly season the cooked perlemoen with a little pepper.

Toss in a little more herbs and deglaze the pan with 60 ml water. Boil briskly to reduce the sauce before pouring it over the cooked perlemoen.

Quickly clean the pan, add the remaining butter and oil and fry the remaining perlemoen as before.

Garnish the platter with a generous bunch of fresh herbs and serve at once with mashed potato and a crisp salad.

Serves 4

The Seafood Braai

Come summer and South Africans are to be found clustered around their braai-fires at every opportunity. With the growing popularity of fish in recent years, braaied chops have moved over for coal-sizzled seafood.

Braaied Mussels

Make a feast of braaied mussels or serve them as a starter to a fishy or meaty main course. As well as lemon wedges, serve with Garlic Butter (page 91), French Dressing (page 94) or Mustard and Orange Sauce (page 98).

freshly-gathered black mussels
lemon wedges for squeezing

Soak the mussels in fresh water for a couple of hours, scrub them and pull out the 'beards'. Place them round the edges of the grid where the heat is coolest and leave them to open. As soon as this happens, whip them off the grid and serve with a squeeze of lemon or a tasty sauce.

Braaied Alikreukels

An interesting and unusual seafoody start to a fish braai.

fresh alikreukels
Garlic Butter (page 91)
or French Dressing (page 94)

Nestle the alikreukels in moderate coals, openings upwards, and allow them to cook gently in their own juices for 20-30 minutes, depending on size. As soon as the 'trap door' lifts off easily, they're done.

When cool enough to handle, extricate the fish from their shells, discard the entrails, rinse clean, slice, and spear the pieces of alikreukel on toothpicks. Offer the sauce of your choice for dipping.

Beach Party Galjoen

An alternative braai recipe – the fish goes under the coals, not on top! Galjoen is great in this recipe, but any just-caught fish may be done this way too. It's a favourite recipe of fishermen intent on a beach-braai but without the wherewithal for fancy presentation. If the fish are single-serving size, so much the better, as everyone gets their own.

whole, fresh fish
salt and milled black pepper

Gut the fish and wash well; leave the scales on. Season with salt and pepper and wrap securely in several layers of newspaper – about 8 in all. Dampen the newspaper thoroughly.

Make a fire on the sand and allow the flames to die down until there's a good bed of coals. Down a couple of beers while you wait!

Shovel the coals to one side, dig a hole in the hot sand and bury your wrapped fish, covering them with a layer of hot sand about 5 cm thick. Shovel the coals back on top of the fish and settle back until they are cooked – 30-60 minutes depending on size.

Dig out the charred mass, unwrap your fish and discard the paper and fish skin. Tuck in with gay abandon. No-one will mind if you use your fingers!

Marinated Gamefish Kebabs, Filleted Linefish Over the Coals, recipes page 85, Braaied Crayfish, recipe page 85, and Braaied Mussels, recipe this page

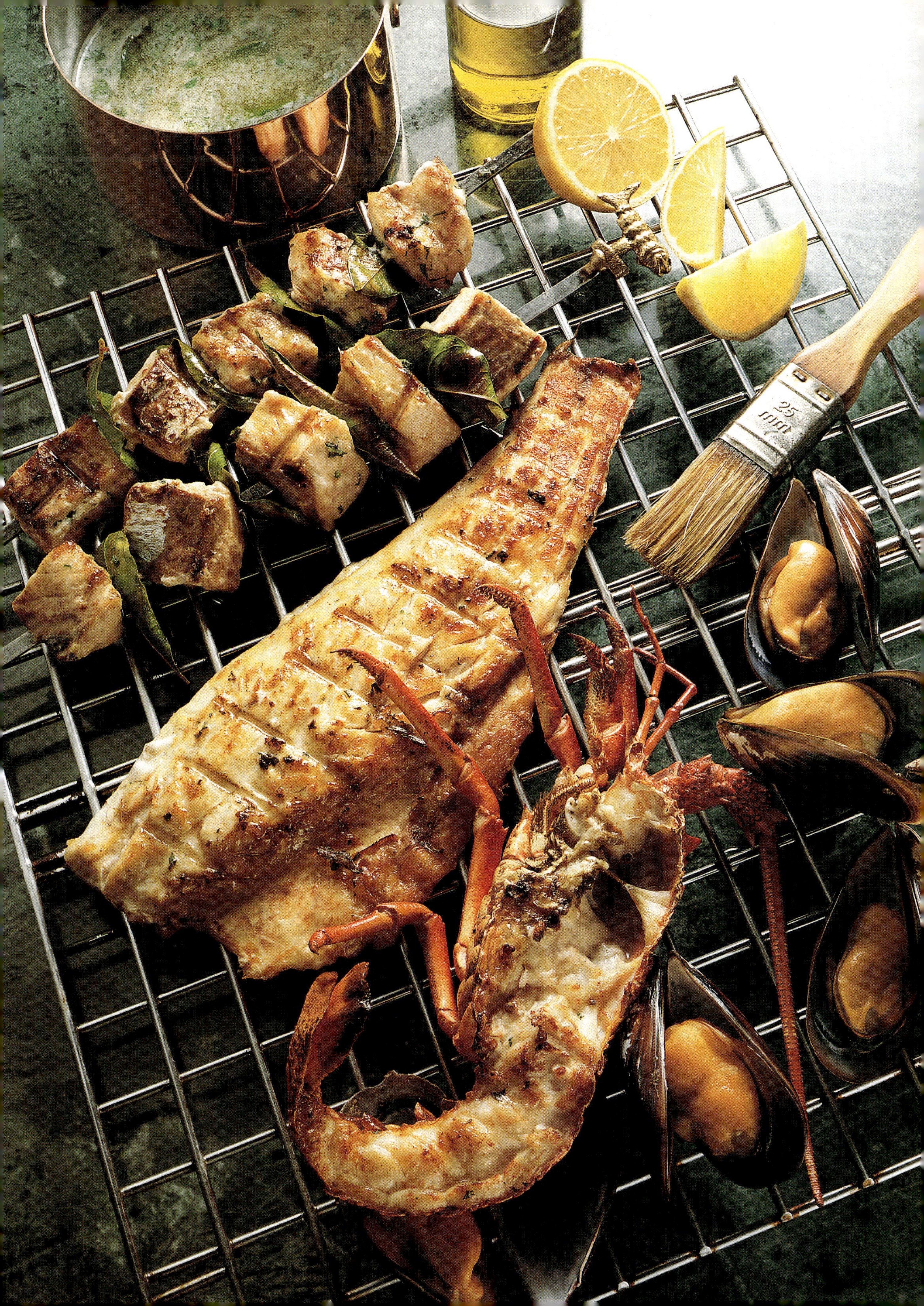
25 mm

FISH IN FOIL

A variation on the braai theme, which is suitable for any type of fish – even those with soft flesh and which would fall apart on an open grid. Smaller fish weighing less than 2 kg are ideal – choose from roman, red or white stumpnose, musselcracker, hottentot, dageraad, geelbek, kob, galjoen, bream, fransmadam, blacktail, zebra and salmon trout.

smallish, fresh fish, scaled and gutted
butter, salt, milled black pepper
finely chopped fresh herbs
or a touch of dried herbs
finely sliced tomato and onion
squeeze of fresh lemon juice and a dash of white wine

Butter pieces of heavy foil large enough to wrap the fish individually. Season the fish inside and out with salt and pepper and fill the cavities with herbs, tomato, onion and lemon juice. (If you prefer, substitute orange slices for the tomato and onion.)

Wrap securely and cook over medium coals until done. It'll take anything from 7-15 minutes per side, depending on the size and thickness of the fish. To serve, simply place the parcels on plates and tuck in.

HERB-BRAAIED REEF FISH

Reef fish that spend their time munching on shellfish are tasty, firm-fleshed and ideally suited to being braaied in this way. The best types include blacktail, zebra, galjoen, bream, harder, john brown, white steenbras, silverfish, hottentot, elf, red steenbras, roman and grunter.

4 whole reef fish
salt and milled black pepper
30 ml chopped herbs
or 5 ml dried herbs
2 leeks or 4-6 spring onions, finely sliced
4 rashers rindless streaky bacon, finely chopped
4 cloves garlic, finely chopped
oil or Garlic Butter (page 91) for basting

Clean the fish well, discarding all the yukky bits, and season well inside and out with salt and pepper. Scatter the herbs, leek, bacon and garlic inside.

Close the opening with a skewer and brush the skin with oil or garlic butter. Secure the fish in a hinged grid and braai over medium coals for about 10 minutes on each side or until cooked – the flesh will flake easily right to the bone when tested with a fork.

Serve with new potatoes or bread and butter.

Serves 4

Scored Fish Over the Coals, recipe page 85

WHOLE BRAAIED FISH

The most dramatic way to serve braaied fish – whole with head and tail intact. Stuff it if you wish, or simply fill the cavity with fresh herbs and thinly sliced lemon. Ensure your catch is secure as it cooks by bending a hinged grid to the shape of the fish. Our favourites for this method of braaiing include elf, geelbek, dageraad, galjoen, kob, musselcracker, red or white steenbras, roman, seventyfour and silverfish. Smaller species like blacktail, hottentot, bream, fransmadam, grunter and pilchard can also be braaied in this way; reduce the cooking time accordingly.

1 whole fish, about 2 kg, well cleaned
salt and milled black pepper
bunch of fresh herbs
lemon slices
oil for the fish and grid
lemon wedges for squeezing

Clean the fish very well, inside and out. Season well with salt and pepper and tuck the herbs and lemon slices inside the cavity.

Oil the fish's skin and the grid really well and braai over medium hot coals, allowing 15 minutes' cooking time on either side, or 30 minutes per side if the fish has been stuffed. Test for doneness by slicing the flesh at the thickest part with a knife. It should be opaque to the bone.

Serve simply with a sauce, an interesting salad and crusty bread.

Serves 6-8

SCORED FISH OVER THE COALS

This is a super way of braaiing tiddlers in the lightweight division – 500g-1kg. Allow one per person (two if they're feeling piggish). Cast decorum to the winds – they simply have to be eaten with the fingers! What's more no side dish is necessary. Our favourites braaied this way? Elf, white steenbras, small kob, small geelbek, silverfish, seventyfour, red steenbras, dageraad, harders, pilchards, zebra, blacktail, bream and hottentot.

whole, fresh fish, scaled and gutted
sunflower oil for the grid
fresh herbs
salt and milled black pepper
olive oil or Garlic Butter (page 91) for basting

Make diagonal slashes on each side of the fish, penetrating both skin and flesh. Season the cavities and the skin with salt and pepper and tuck herbs inside. Brush the fish with olive oil or garlic butter, and the grid with oil.

Secure the fish/es in a hinged grid and braai over medium coals for about 7 minutes on each side. The outsides should be lovely and crisp; the flesh tender and succulent.

Serve with foil-wrapped potatoes baked in the coals. A tasty sauce won't go amiss either, perhaps Tartare Sauce (page 95), Peanut Pesto (page 97) or Herbed Tomato Sauce (page 97).

MARINATED GAMEFISH KEBABS

A nice way to braai drier species of gamefish like marlin, swordfish, tuna and yellowtail.

1 kg filleted gamefish
salt and milled black pepper
Marinade Monte Mar (page 93)
fresh orange or lemon leaves

Cut the fish into cubes about 4 cm in diameter and season with salt and pepper. Place them in a bowl, pour over the marinade and set aside at room temperature for 2 hours. Thread the fish onto skewers interspersed with orange or lemon leaves to add extra flavour.

Braai over medium coals for 3-5 minutes on each side, basting occasionally with the marinade. Alternatively grill them under the oven griller. Watch the cooking time as cubed fish cooks very quickly and will dry out in a flash.

Place the kebabs on a warmed serving platter, strain the remaining marinade and serve as a separate sauce. Offer with savoury rice if you wish, and a green salad on the side to round off the feast.

Serves 6

FILLETED LINEFISH OVER THE COALS

For the best braai flavour, this is the way to go. It's ideal for larger linefish, as the heat gets quickly to all parts and the chances of it drying out are diminished. Don't try this method on smaller fish – filleting them is just too fiddly and there's simply not enough flesh (and far too many bones) to make it worth the effort. For added flavour scatter fresh herbs on the coals as the fish braais. Suitable for filleting and braaiing are elf, kob, geelbek, snoek, leervis, yellowtail, red or white steenbras, red stumpnose, dageraad, galjoen, larger bream and blacktail.

1 whole fish, about 3 kg
sunflower oil for the grid and fish
Garlic Butter (page 91)
lemon wedges for squeezing

Behead and fillet the fish, leaving the skin on and backbone in situ. Heavily oil the fish's skin and your hinged grid (there's no way you'll turn the fish on a flat grid) and place the fish in it.

Baste the fish well, using a clean paint brush. Close the grid and braai flesh-down over hot coals until beautifully browned. This will take approximately 5 minutes.

Turn the fish and cook, basting frequently, for a further 10 minutes or so until it's perfectly cooked. Raise the grid to complete the braaing over more gentle heat. Serve with the remaining garlic butter and lemon wedges.

Serves 8-10

BRAAIED CRAYFISH

Perfection in anyone's language – fresh crayfish sizzled over open coals.

4 crayfish
Garlic Butter (page 91)
lemon wedges for squeezing

Cut the crayfish in half lengthwise and clean well. Remove and discard the alimentary canal. Prepare the baste and brush the crayfish liberally. Place flesh-down on the grid over medium-hot coals and braai until nicely browned. This should only take a minute or two.

Turn, baste once more, and continue cooking at a more gentle heat (raise the grid further from the heat) for about 15 minutes more. When it's done, the flesh will lift easily from the shell.

Serve with the remaining garlic butter, lots of lemon wedges for squeezing and crisp garlic bread. A bottle of chilled sauvignon blanc completes the picture.

Serves 4

Perlemoen Parcels with Bacon and Mushrooms

Foil-braaied whole perlemoen are super-tasty and extraordinarily succulent. If you wish, add freshly chopped herbs as well. But on no account omit the mushrooms – the moisture formed as they cook are an integral part of the recipe.

2 large perlemoen
butter and olive oil
squeeze of fresh lemon juice
1-2 cloves garlic, crushed
milled black pepper
4 rashers rindless back bacon, finely chopped
100 g button mushrooms, finely sliced

Scrub the perlemoen well, cut off and discard the frilly 'skirts' and tenderise lightly, pounding on both sides and paying particular attention to the tougher outer edges.

Place each perlemoen on two layers of heavy foil cut large enough to wrap securely. Add to each a knob of butter, a little olive oil, lemon juice, garlic, pepper, bacon and mushrooms. Wrap securely and braai on the grid over hot coals for 35 minutes. There's no need to turn the parcels as they cook as this increases the risk of the precious juices being lost in the fire.

Unwrap and slice the perlemoen. Place it into a serving bowl and pour the sauce, bacon and mushrooms on top.
Serves 4-6

Fish Kebabs

Offer several different kebabs to mix and match; it stimulates the conversation as well as the taste buds. Here are two of our favourite marinades, each for 600 g of fish. Prepare the kebabs well ahead of time and braai them in a flash when guests are seated. It's important to watch the cooking time to prevent the fish overcooking and becoming dry. Steenbras, geelbek, kob, yellowtail, angelfish and tuna are excellent for this recipe, but kingklip is delicious too. Don't use hake, the flesh is too floppy.

1,2 kg filleted fish
oil or melted butter for basting

HUNGARIAN MARINADE
100 ml olive oil
100 ml fresh lemon juice
30 ml grated onion
3 bay leaves, crunched
7 ml crushed garlic
7 ml paprika
2 ml salt
2 ml milled black pepper

MARTINI MARINADE
250 ml dry Vermouth
60 ml fresh lemon juice
30 ml finely chopped fennel
10 black peppercorns, crushed
3 bay leaves, crunched
2 ml salt

Skin the fish and cut into cubes approximately 4 cm in diameter. Thinner belly-portions will need to be cut longer and doubled over when skewering.

Combine the ingredients for the two marinades in separate glass bowls, add the fish, coating well, and set aside in a cool spot to marinate for at least 1 hour.

Thread the fish cubes onto wooden skewers and brush with oil or melted butter.

Prepare a bed of hot coals and braai the kebabs quickly – about 3-5 minutes on each side. Serve straight from the grid the moment they're cooked, accompanied by hot, spicy rice and a Greek salad.
Serves 6 as a main course, 8 as a starter

Prawn and Bacon Kebabs

A mixture of prawns, crayfish and langoustines makes an even more delicious combination, or make it into a shellfish mixed grill by adding a few scallops, oysters and black mussels. Subdue the lights, open the champagne and braaied boerewors will seem light years away.

16 large prawns
milled black pepper
16 rashers rindless streaky bacon
16 button mushrooms
Garlic Butter (page 91)
lemon wedges for squeezing

Shell and devein the prawns, leaving the last tail-segment attached for appearance's sake. Rinse, pat dry and season with pepper. If adding crayfish and langoustines to the kebabs, cut into suitable-sized chunks.

Cut the bacon rashers in half and wrap the prawns and mushrooms individually. Thread onto thin bamboo skewers and brush generously with garlic butter.

Braai the kebabs over hot coals or under the oven griller, turning frequently until the bacon is crisp and the prawns are cooked to perfection – about 5-6 minutes. Baste occasionally to keep them moist.

Serve the kebabs the moment they're cooked with lemon wedges for squeezing and accompanied, if you wish, by rice and the remaining garlic butter. A simple salad rounds off the meal in style.
Serves 4

Fish Kebabs, and Prawn and Bacon Kebabs, recipes page 86

PERLEMOEN IN KELP

For flavour and tenderness, no method of cooking perlemoen can compare with this recipe that's as old as the hills – gently steaming it in a freshly-cut kelp bulb. It requires no additional seasoning (unless you're devoted to garlic and fresh herbs, in which case add as much as you like); the perlemoen cooks in its own juices.

2 large perlemoen
2 large bulbs of kelp, each about 60 cm long
2 cloves garlic, crushed (optional)
chopped fresh herbs (optional)

Scrub the perlemoen, cut off and discard the frilly 'skirt' and slice thickly. Tenderize very lightly. Pack the slices into the kelp with garlic and herbs if you wish, and plug the holes with a clean cloth. Don't use a stone as a stopper – the build-up of steam within the seaweed can cause it to become jet-propelled and a serious threat to life and limb!

Place the operative ends of the kelp right in the hot flames of the fire (no need to wait for coals to form) and cook for 20-30 minutes depending on the size of the chunks of seaweed. Turn once during the cooking time.

Slice off the top of the kelp and tip out the perlemoen and sauce into a serving dish. Serve hot with crusty bread.

Serves 4-6

SEAFOOD LOVERS PANTRY

CERTAIN THINGS SHOULD ALWAYS BE ON HAND WHEN COOKING SEAFOOD – HOMEMADE STOCKS, FLAVOURFUL MARINADES, INTERESTING BATTERS AND GOURMET GOODIES LIKE CRÈME FRAÎCHE, FRESHLY-CRUSHED GARLIC AND GINGER, AND THE BEST BLENDING OF CURRY SPICES.

FISH STOCK

A vital ingredient in many seafood dishes, it's so simple to make and freezes so well that there is no excuse not to have some on hand at all times.

1,5 litres cold water
1 kg clean fish trimmings
1 onion, quartered
1 carrot, sliced thickly
1 rib celery, roughly chopped
1 fresh or dried bouquet garni
1 strip lemon rind
12 black peppercorns

Combine ingredients in a large pot, cover and bring to the boil. Move the lid aside to partially cover the pot and reduce heat until the liquid is just moving. Skim the foam from the surface occasionally and cook for 30 minutes.
  Strain the stock into a bowl through a colander lined with several layers of muslin or kitchen wipes. Press on the solids to extract all the liquid.
Makes 1 litre

MAKE AHEAD Fish stock may be refrigerated for up to 3 days, or frozen for up to 3 months. For the sake of convenience, freeze it in 125 ml or 250 ml containers.

WATCHPOINTS
- Use lean, white varieties of fish such as kob, geelbek, sole, steenbras, stumpnose and silverfish. Avoid oily, strong-flavoured species like maasbanker, mackerel, snoek, tuna or yellowtail.
- Heads, bones and trimmings must be absolutely fresh.
- Discard gills and entrails as they're bitter.
- Don't add salt; the flavour intensifies when stock is reduced. It's safer to add salt to the dish itself.

Fish Extract Concentrate fish stock to use like stock cubes. Simply boil the strained fish stock in pots of decreasing dimensions until it is reduced and thickened. Watch carefully towards the end to prevent it burning. Remove from the heat, cool, then cut into small pieces, wrap well and freeze. Reconstitute the extract in hot water before use.

COURT-BOUILLON

1 litre water
250 ml dry white wine
1 onion, sliced
1 carrot, sliced
1 fresh or dried bouquet garni
6 black peppercorns
5 ml salt
60 ml fresh lemon juice

Combine the ingredients in a large pot, cover and bring to the boil. Reduce the heat and simmer uncovered for 20 minutes. Strain before using to poach fish.
Makes 1 litre

MAKE AHEAD Court-bouillon may be prepared up to 3 days ahead and chilled. Alternatively freeze it – before or after using to poach fish – for up to 3 months.

Fish Stock

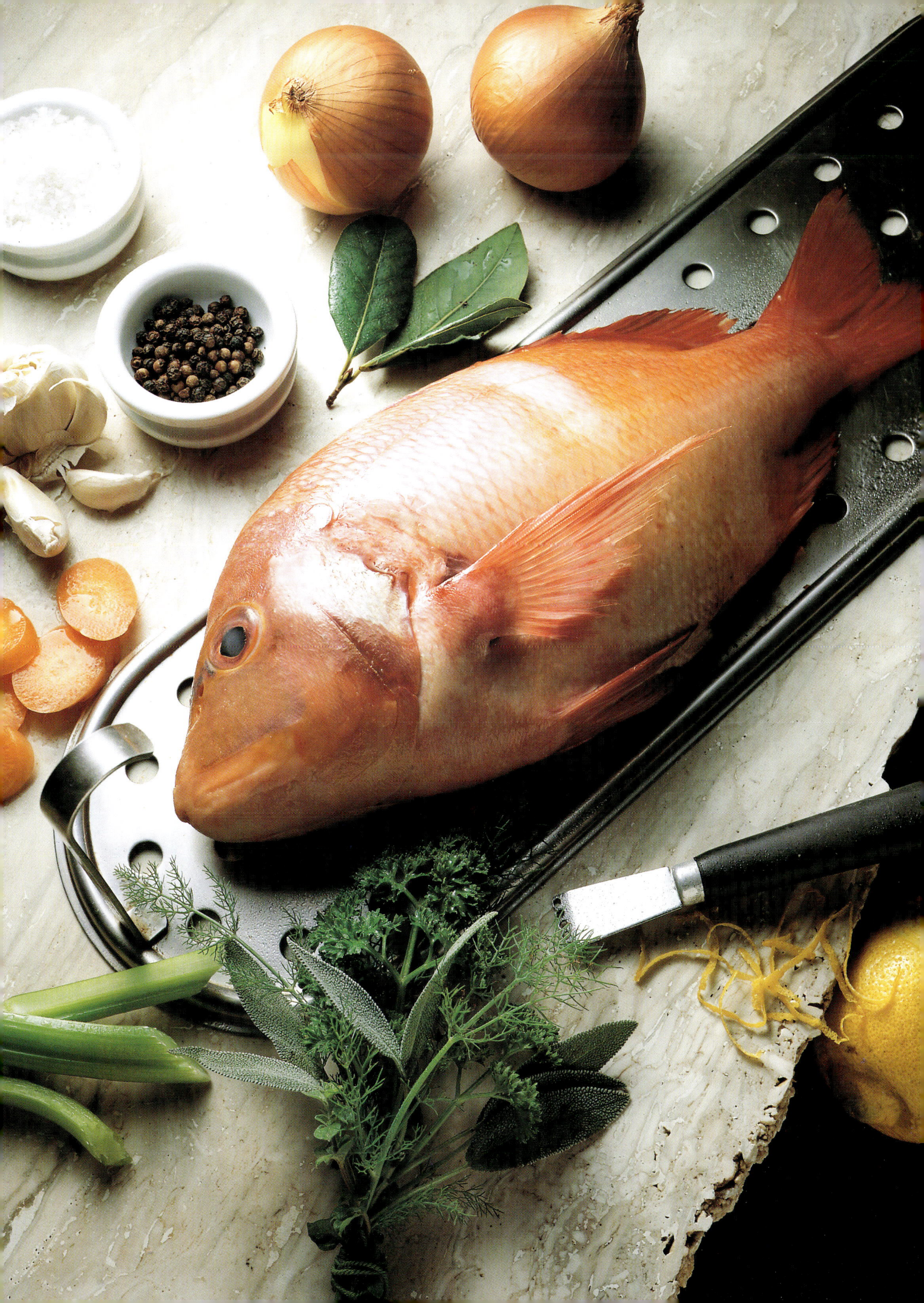

Crushed Garlic

Purchase several of the fattest, juiciest heads of garlic you can find, regardless of cost. Separate the cloves, place them in a small bowl and pour over boiling water to facilitate peeling. Whiz the peeled cloves in a food processor or blender with a little olive or sunflower oil, then transfer the pungent blend to small jars. It may be refrigerated for several months.

GARLIC IN OLIVE OIL
Instead of puréeing the garlic, simply pop the peeled cloves into small bottles and fill with olive oil.

Crushed Green Ginger

There is no comparison between this and the dried substitute. Purchase a few pieces of plump and juicy fresh ginger. (Make sure that it shows no signs of shrivelled old age.) Wash well, peel off the brown skin with a sharp knife if you wish (though there's really no need to) and whiz in a food processor or blender, adding sufficient dry sherry to make a fairly smooth paste. Fill small jars, seal and refrigerate for up to 6 months.

Burmese Curry Mix

Burmese curries are more delicately spiced than Indian curries and are well known for their piquant flavouring, which enhances all types of seafood. Here is our version of the traditional mixture. For the most authentic results, don't be shy about using plenty of onion and garlic in your curry – even tangy fish or prawn paste if it's handy.

WATCHPOINT *Before blending the spices, make sure they're nice and fresh.*

15 ml ground coriander
15 ml ground cumin
15 ml turmeric
15 ml ground ginger
10 ml chilli powder
2 ml ground cardamom
2 ml ground cinnamon
2 ml ground allspice

Mix spices together in a screw-topped jar and store in a cool, dark place. It will keep for several months. For 1 kg fish, use 20 ml of the mixture; more delicately flavoured shellfish requires only 10-15 ml.

Crème Fraîche

Making your own crème fraîche is so very easy that you'll wonder why you never attempted it before.

250 ml cream
30 ml buttermilk

Sterilize a glass jar with boiling water, drain it, then pour in the cream. Stir in the buttermilk and stand at room temperature for the crème fraîche to develop. This can take anything from 14-24 hours, depending on the freshness of the cream and the air temperature.

When the mixture is lovely and thick, put it in the fridge, where it may be stored for 1-2 weeks. The flavour will become stronger and the consistency thicker the older it gets. If you wish, add more fresh cream to dilute the mixture and to continue the culture.

Basic Batter

A standard batter that is sufficient to coat about 1 kg fish, four perlemoen or six calamari.

1 XL egg
125 ml milk
125 ml cake flour
1 ml salt

Blend the egg and milk together, add the flour and salt and mix to a smooth batter the consistency of honey. Set aside for about 30 minutes before using. If necessary correct the consistency by adding a little more milk.
Makes about 300 ml

Chinese Batter

The lightest batter imaginable that puffs up as your seafood is deep-fried. It is especially delicious as a coating for butterflied prawns and chunks of calamari.

120 g (250 ml) self-raising flour
5 ml salt
2 ml ground ginger
2 ml powdered garlic
250 ml water

Sift together the dry ingredients and blend in the water. Leave the batter to stand for about an hour before using, then check the consistency – which should be like cream.
Makes about 600 ml

Burmese Curry Mix, Crushed Garlic and Crushed Green Ginger, recipes page 90

SHANTUNG BATTER

An unusual mix of flavours that combines two types of mustard and a subtle hint of cumin.

1 egg
125 ml milk
125 ml cake flour
1 ml salt
pinch of white pepper
2 ml ground cumin
2 ml powdered garlic
5 ml prepared English mustard
5 ml prepared French mustard

Mix together the egg and half the milk. Add the flour, salt, pepper and cumin, then add the remaining milk with the garlic and mustards. Blend thoroughly and set aside for about 30 minutes. Correct the consistency, if necessary, by adding a little extra milk or water.
Makes about 300 ml

BAVARIAN BATTER

Here's a batter for the beer-lovers in the family!

120 g (250 ml) cake flour
5 ml salt
2 ml paprika
340 ml bottle or can beer

Sift together the flour, salt and paprika, then slowly add the beer, beating continually, until well blended. Set aside for about 30 minutes and correct the consistency, if necessary, by adding a little extra water.
Makes about 600 ml

CRÊPES

120 g (250 ml) cake flour
2 ml salt
300 ml milk
45 ml sunflower oil
2 XL eggs
butter for cooking

Sift together the flour and salt. Blend in the milk, oil and eggs to make a smooth batter. Refrigerate for at least 30 minutes.

Heat a little butter in a small frying pan, add a thin film of batter and cook until lightly browned. Flip the crêpe and lightly cook the other side. As the crêpes are cooked, layer them interleaved with waxed paper.
Make 10-12 thin crêpes

GARLIC BUTTER

200 g butter
juice of 1 lemon
3-4 cloves garlic, crushed
salt and milled black pepper

Melt the butter in a small saucepan, add the garlic, sizzle it for a minute or so, then mix in the remaining ingredients.
Makes 200 g

VARIATIONS
- *Garlic Herb Butter* For a terrific herby flavour, add 15 ml finely chopped fresh herbs to the garlic butter. If there are no fresh herbs around, use 2 ml dried herbs.
- *Spicy Garlic Butter* A dash of Worcestershire sauce will add spice to garlic butter.
- *Chilli Garlic Butter* Add a finely sliced fresh chilli.

Prawns cooked in Herb Butter, recipe page 93

QUICHE PASTRY

250 g (500 ml) cake flour
2 ml salt
5 ml baking powder
150 g cold butter
1 egg
15 ml sunflower oil
15 ml cold water (a little more if necessary)

Sift together the flour, salt and baking powder. Rub in the butter lightly with your fingertips (or in a food processor). Combine the egg, oil and water and mix to form a well-blended dough. Add a little extra water if necessary. Cover and chill for about an hour.

BAKE BLIND Set the oven at 200 °C. Lightly grease a 25 cm loose-based quiche tin or pie plate. Roll out the pastry and line the tin or plate with it. Prick the base with a fork.

Into the pastry and up the sides, press a piece of lightly-oiled foil and weigh down with dried beans or something similar. Bake for 15 minutes, remove the foil and beans and bake for a further 5 minutes until the pastry is lightly browned. Allow to cool before adding the filling.

CREAM CHEESE PASTRY

Whether you wish to bake fish in pastry, or wrap it around smoked fishy morsels as snacks, choose a pastry that is quick and easy to prepare and stays crisp even when it cools. Like this one.

250 g (500 ml) cake flour
2 ml salt
5 ml dry English mustard
250 g cold butter
125 g (½ tub) cream cheese
or smooth cottage cheese
1 egg

Sift the flour, salt and mustard together. Cut the butter into cubes and rub it into the dry ingredients with your fingertips or in a food processor. Add the cheese little by little, then lightly blend in the beaten egg.

Place the dough on a square of waxed paper, flatten and refrigerate for at least 30 minutes before rolling out.

Melba Toast

Melba toast couldn't be easier to make: purchase a loaf of unsliced white bread, leave it for a day, then slice thinly. Decrust and cut each slice diagonally, arrange on baking trays and bake slowly in an oven set at 140 °C. After about 20 minutes, your toast will be crisp, slightly curled and just starting to colour. Cool on a rack and store in airtight container until serving time.

Marinade Monte Mar

A delicately-flavoured marinade and basting sauce that brings the whisper of an orange grove to grilled or braaied fish.

250 ml fresh orange juice
juice of ½ lemon
80 ml olive oil
6-8 fresh orange or lemon leaves, crushed
2 cloves garlic, finely chopped
30 ml chopped parsley
15 ml chopped origanum
or 2 ml dried origanum
salt and milled black pepper

Combine the ingredients in a screw-topped jar and shake to mix. Pour over filleted fish and leave to marinate for a couple of hours before braaiing or grilling. Baste with the remaining mixture while the fish cooks.
Makes about 300 ml

Spicy Marinade and Basting Sauce

A simple, classic blend of ingredients. You're welcome to use olive oil instead of sunflower (or mix the oils half and half). And add any other fresh herb that takes your fancy.

125 ml dry white wine
125 ml sunflower oil
1-2 cloves garlic, crushed
15 ml chopped parsley
15 ml Worcestershire sauce
2 ml paprika
salt and milled black pepper

Mix all the ingredients together. Use as a marinade and basting sauce especially for drier types of fish like angelfish, snoek and yellowtail.
Makes about 300 ml

Mustard Marinade

125 ml sunflower oil
125 ml fresh lemon juice
10 ml dry English mustard
5 ml Burmese Curry Mix (page 90)
or curry powder
2 ml crushed green ginger
salt and milled black pepper

Mix the ingredients together and use as a marinade or as a sauce to drizzle over just-braaied fish or shellfish.
Makes about 250 ml

Oriental Marinade

125 ml medium dry sherry
60 ml soy sauce
5 ml brown sugar
5 ml crushed green ginger
5 ml crushed garlic
2 ml sesame oil
milled black pepper

Mix the ingredients together with a hand-whisk or in a screw-topped jar. Pour over the fish and set aside to marinate for about 1 hour before braaiing or grilling. Use leftovers to baste the fish while it cooks.
Makes 200 ml

VARIATION
♦ For a touch of heat add a seeded and finely sliced red or green chilli, or use a pinch of chilli powder.

Herb Butter

Whip this up in a food processor, chill and use as required – or freeze it for later. Add a pat to grilled, braaied or panfried fish. And remember, there's no substitute for fresh herbs here!

250 g soft butter
45 ml chopped fresh herbs
1-2 cloves garlic, crushed
squeeze of fresh lemon juice
salt and milled black pepper

Whiz all the ingredients together in a food processor until well blended. Turn out the mixture onto a sheet of greaseproof paper, roll it into a sausage shape, wrap it up and chill or freeze.
Makes 250 g

French Dressing

French dressing – also called vinaigrette – isn't exclusively for salads. Splosh it over seafood like steamed mussels, opened oysters, deshelled periwinkles or steamed and sliced alikreukels.

250 ml sunflower or olive oil
or use half and half
60 ml fresh lemon juice
60 ml wine vinegar
5 ml sugar
5 ml salt
5 ml dry English mustard
5 ml milled black pepper
5 ml crushed garlic

Combine all the ingredients in a screw-topped jar and shake vigorously to emulsify the mixture (or do it in a flash in the food processor). Store in the fridge where it will be fine for several weeks.
Makes 375 ml

VARIATION Make this into a herbed dressing: 15 ml fresh herbs or 5 ml dried herbs should be sufficient.

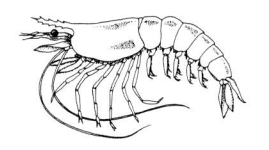

Mayonnaise

There is simply no substitute for homemade mayonnaise, the classic accompaniment to cold seafood. So make sure it is always on hand in the fridge where it may be stored for several months.

1 XL egg
2 XL egg yolks
10 ml dry English mustard
5 ml salt
2 ml white pepper
30 ml wine or cider vinegar
30 ml fresh lemon juice
750 ml sunflower oil

In a processor, blender or electric mixer, whisk the whole egg and egg yolks with mustard, salt and pepper until pale and thick. With the machine running, slowly add the vinegar and lemon juice, then pour in oil in a thin stream. If you add it too quickly your mayonnaise won't emulsify.
Makes 1 litre

MAYONNAISE VARIATIONS
To 250 ml mayonnaise add:
- *Herb Mayonnaise*
  60 ml finely chopped fresh herbs – choose your own particular favourite like parsley, dill, coriander, fennel, tarragon, thyme, marjoram, basil, origanum
- *Chilli Mayonnaise*
  30 ml tomato sauce
  5-10 ml chilli sauce (more if you dare)
- *Oriental Mayonnaise*
  30 ml soy sauce
  2 ml sesame oil
  1 ml ground ginger
  1 ml garlic powder
- *Green Peppercorn Mayonnaise*
  15 ml green peppercorns, lightly crushed
  15 ml Dijon mustard
- *Pesto Mayonnaise*
  45 ml Peanut Pesto (page 97)

Seafood Sauce

A useful mix that may be used to accompany any cold seafood (freshly cooked or canned), in cocktails or with salads. By substituting crème fraîche with cream cheese it makes a delicious dip. Fresh cream may be used instead of crème fraîche, in which case don't forget to add a squeeze of lemon juice.

125 ml Mayonnaise (this page)
125 ml Crème Fraîche (page 90),
sour cream or smetena
45 ml tomato sauce
pinch of cayenne pepper
salt and milled black pepper

Mix all the ingredients together, cover and refrigerate where it may be stored for a couple of weeks.
Makes 250 ml

VARIATIONS
Omit the tomato sauce and cayenne pepper and vary the sauce by adding instead:
- 4-6 chopped, canned anchovy fillets, 3-4 chopped spring onions, 1 chopped hard-boiled egg
- 1 cored and grated Granny Smith apple, 125 ml flaked toasted almonds, 10-15 ml chopped herbs (parsley, fennel, thyme) or 1 ml dried mixed herbs
- 1 tomato, peeled and finely chopped, 1 green pepper seeded and finely chopped, 1 clove garlic, crushed
- 2 chopped hard-boiled eggs, 60 ml finely chopped peanuts, 5 ml curry powder
- 45 ml horseradish sauce, 30 ml capers, 2 ml sugar

TARTARE SAUCE

Mayonnaise of dubious quality and derivation, with a mind-boggling array of ingredients added, is frequently found masquerading as tartare sauce. Here is a traditional recipe into which we have sneaked in a few capers to add a touch of tartness.

500 ml Mayonnaise (page 94)
3 hard-boiled eggs, finely chopped
15 ml Dijon mustard
15 ml chopped parsley
15 ml snipped chives
15 ml capers or chopped gherkin

Mix all the ingredients together and check the flavour, adding a touch of salt and pepper or lemon juice if you think it's necessary. Tip it into a serving bowl. It may be refrigerated for up to a week with no loss of flavour.
Makes about 500 ml

SPICY YOGHURT DRESSING

Add a touch of excitement to cold fish portions, or toss in a can of drained, flaked tuna to serve with salads.

250 ml Mayonnaise (page 94)
250 ml natural yoghurt
5 ml fresh lemon juice
5 ml Burmese Curry Mix (page 90)
or medium curry powder
2 ml crushed garlic
salt and milled black pepper

Mix the mayonnaise, yoghurt, lemon juice, curry powder and garlic together. Check the seasoning and add salt and pepper. Cover and refrigerate for at least an hour before serving to allow flavours to mellow. It may be refrigerated for up to a month without spoiling in any way.
Makes 500 ml

Tartare Sauce

Panfried fish served with Tapenade Sauce, and Peanut Pesto, recipes page 97

Mornay Sauce

Delicious with seafood – especially to blanket fish fillets.

50 g (50 ml) butter
45 ml cake flour
500 ml milk
or milk and cream
salt and milled black pepper
5 ml dry English mustard
80 g (250 ml) grated Cheddar cheese
30 ml dry or medium dry sherry (optional)

Melt the butter in a medium saucepan. Remove from the heat and blend in the flour. Slowly add the milk (or milk and cream), stirring until the mixture is smooth, then add salt, pepper and mustard.

Cook, still stirring, for a couple of minutes until the sauce is smooth and thickened. Remove from the heat and add the cheese, stirring until it melts. Add the sherry.
Makes about 750 ml

Velouté Sauce

One of the most stylish, classic sauces for seafood. A simple white sauce prepared with fish stock and a touch of cream.

50 g (50 ml) butter
45 ml cake flour
375 ml Fish Stock (page 88)
30 ml thick cream
salt and white pepper

Melt the butter in a medium saucepan, remove from the heat and blend in the flour. Whisk in the stock with a hand whisk, pouring it in slowly to avoid lumps forming. Cook for 1-2 minutes, stirring all the while, until the sauce is silky smooth and thickens slightly. Remove from the heat, stir in the cream and season with salt and pepper.
Makes 500 ml

VARIATION For a slightly richer sauce alter the quantities of stock and cream given above and use 200 ml of each.

PEANUT PESTO

Pesto is usually prepared with pine nuts (a ghastly price) or almonds (almost as bad). Peanuts make a satisfactory substitute for those with half an eye on the purse strings. It's a great accompaniment to braaied fish – or stir it into mayonnaise to serve with smoked fish. We also love it dolloped into Breton Fish Soup (page 26).

500 ml tightly packed basil leaves
2 cloves garlic, peeled
100 g salted peanuts
150 ml olive oil
or half olive, half sunflower oil
125 ml grated Parmesan or Pecorino cheese
salt and milled black pepper

Blend the basil, garlic and nuts together in a food processor. Add the oil, then mix in the cheese – take care you don't overmix at this stage which may cause the mixture to 'curdle' and spoil the lovely rough texture. Check the flavour and add salt and pepper to taste.
Makes about 300 ml

MAKE AHEAD Pesto keeps well in the fridge for a couple of days and may be frozen too. In this case omit the cheese, salt and pepper and add just before serving.

HERBED TOMATO SAUCE

Herbs and tomatoes make a marvellous marriage. Basil is best, otherwise opt for thyme, marjoram or origanum. If substituting dried herbs check for freshness and go easy on the quantity.

2 onions, very finely chopped
30 ml olive or sunflower oil
2 ml crushed garlic
4-5 large, ripe tomatoes, skinned and chopped
or a 400 g can
5 ml powdered beef stock
10 ml chopped fresh herbs
or 2 ml dried herbs
30 ml chopped parsley
or 10 ml dried parsley
5 ml sugar
paprika, salt, milled black pepper

Soften the onion in oil, add the remaining ingredients and cook briskly, uncovered and stirring occasionally, for 5-6 minutes until sauce thickens slightly. Check seasoning.
Purée the sauce in a blender or food processor or leave it chunky if preferred.
Serves 4

MAKE AHEAD This sauce may be made several days beforehand – and it freezes beautifully too.

VARIATIONS
Add during the last few minutes' cooking time:
◆ stoned black olives
◆ finely sliced chillies or a dash of chilli powder
◆ canned or fresh mussels
◆ finely chopped canned anchovies

FENNEL SAUCE

Fennel is one of the most perfect herbs to accompany fish, and is used here in a light, flavourful sauce.

30 g (30 ml) butter
200 ml finely chopped spring onion
30 ml chopped fennel
60 ml cream
5 ml cornflour
125 ml Fish Stock (page 88)
salt and milled black pepper

Melt the butter in a small saucepan, add the spring onion and fennel and cook over low heat until softened.
Blend the cornflour into the cream and add to the saucepan, together with the stock. Cook briskly, stirring, until the sauce thickens slightly. Check the seasoning and add salt and pepper.
Makes 350 ml

TAPENADE SAUCE

A robust sauce, especially suited to smoked fish or freshly-braaied fish.

250 ml Mayonnaise (page 94)
200 g calamata olives, stoned
6-8 canned anchovy fillets
2 fat cloves garlic, peeled
30 ml capers
2-3 spring onions, trimmed and chopped
80 ml olive oil

Pop the olives into the food processor with the anchovies, garlic, capers and spring onion. Chop finely but take care not to make too smooth a paste. Pour in the olive oil, process to mix, then blend in the mayonnaise.
If you're not using it immediately, cover and store it in the fridge. It will be fine for up to a week.
Makes about 400 ml

MUSHROOM CREAM SAUCE

Mushrooms and fish are wonderful partners, and this sauce is particularly good with fried fish. Add a touch of class by garnishing the completed dish with toasted, slivered almonds.

50 g (50 ml) butter
45 ml cake flour
5 ml fresh lemon juice
125 ml Fish Stock (page 88)
125 ml cream
salt and milled black pepper
200 g button mushrooms, sliced

Melt the butter in a medium saucepan. Remove from the heat and blend in the flour, lemon juice, stock, cream and seasoning. Stir for a couple of minutes until the sauce thickens. Add the mushrooms, cover and allow the sauce to simmer for a little longer until they are tender.
Serves 6

PIQUANT SAUCE

If you're looking for an unusual sauce to serve with grilled or braaied linefish, or a whole baked fish, here it is.

30 ml sunflower oil
15 ml finely chopped onion
2 ml crushed garlic
125 ml chopped parsley
2 ml anchovy paste
2 ml capers
30 ml white vinegar
250 ml Fish Stock (page 88)
10 ml soft butter
10 ml cake flour
salt and milled black pepper

Heat the oil in a medium saucepan and fry the onion, garlic and half the parsley for a couple of minutes until softened. Add the anchovy paste, capers, vinegar and stock and simmer for 5 minutes.
  Mix together the butter and flour and whisk it into the simmering sauce. Season with salt and pepper, stir in the remaining parsley and serve hot.
Makes 350 ml

MAKE AHEAD Refrigerate the sauce for up to 3 days. Reheat just before serving, adding a touch more freshly chopped parsley to freshen the flavour.

SWEET AND SOUR SAUCE

A tangy Oriental classic, delicious with battered and fried fish or prawns, or as an accompaniment to braaied fish. Omit the sherry if you wish and increase the quantity of water accordingly.

15 ml sunflower oil
30 ml finely chopped spring onion
2 ml crushed garlic
1 ml crushed green ginger
200 ml cold water
30 ml brown sugar
10 ml cornflour
45 ml tomato sauce
45 ml dry or medium dry sherry
30 ml vinegar
15 ml soy sauce
pinch of salt

In a medium saucepan heat the oil, add the spring onion, garlic and ginger and cook gently until softened. Mix together remaining ingredients, add and stir until the sauce thickens and becomes clear.
Serves 3-4

VARIATION
Add to the sauce chunks of green or red pepper, sliced celery, slivers of carrot or cubed pineapple. The vegetables only need a few minutes' cooking to be crisp-tender.

MAKE AHEAD This sauce may be refrigerated for up to 5 days before reheating. Stir well as you do so.

MUSTARD AND ORANGE SAUCE

An unusual flavour mix; delicious with grilled fish.

50 g (50 ml) butter
30 ml chopped parsley
30 ml finely chopped spring onion
10 ml prepared English mustard
10 ml finely grated orange rind
250 ml fresh orange juice

In a small saucepan melt the butter, add the parsley and spring onion and cook gently until softened. Add remaining ingredients and simmer uncovered for a few minutes more until the sauce thickens slightly.
Makes about 350 ml

MAKE AHEAD Store sauce in the fridge for up to 3 days and reheat before serving.

SEAFOOD A–Z

USE THIS COMPREHENSIVE A-Z TO IDENTIFY YOUR CATCH, LEARN SOME INTERESTING FACTS ABOUT IT, AND DISCOVER THE BEST WAYS TO PREPARE IT. A LIST OF RECIPES IS ALSO GIVEN IN EACH CASE.

ALIKREUKEL

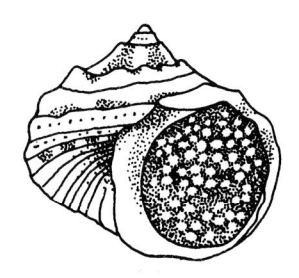

Alikreukels – sometimes called 'ollycrock' – are found all along our coastline from the Cape to Natal. They're most often plucked from underwater rocks by divers, but are sometimes found in shallow rock pools exposed at spring low tide.

They look rather like extra-large periwinkles, with hard shells protecting the flesh – tough, but very tasty and greatly enjoyed by lovers of this unusual seafood.

Preparation: Make sure your alikreukels are alive before cooking them; the protective 'trap door' will snap firmly into position when they're bothered. Wash in fresh water, then boil in their shells for about 15-20 minutes in salted water. As soon as they're cooked, the trap door will come off easily.

The fish will now plop out of the shell. Remove and discard the trap door and softish entrails and rinse clean. Slice the flesh and sizzle for a couple of minutes in butter flavoured with crushed garlic, lemon juice and chopped fresh herbs if you wish.

Another way to prepare alikreukels is by using strong-arm tactics: smash open the shells, retrieve the fish, discard the entrails, and slice the flesh. Fry gently in garlicky butter or add to a seafood casserole or curry – it'll only require a few minutes' cooking time.

SUITABLE RECIPES

Arniston Alikreukels, page 69
Braaied Alikreukels, page 82
Perlemoen Peperonata, page 80

ANGELFISH
POMFRET

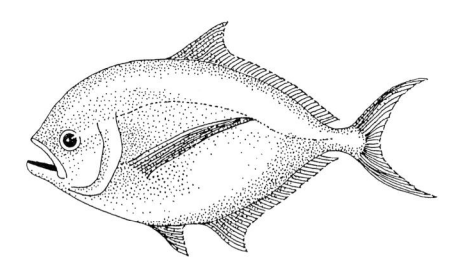

48 cm

This distinctively-shaped fish has a deep, rounded shape, compressed on each side. Not to be confused with the brightly-coloured tropical angelfishes, edible angelfish are trawled in deep water between Algoa Bay and Walvis Bay. They're a metallic silvery-black, can be slightly mottled, and attain a length of 70 cm.

Angelfish is tasty, firm and tends to be dry, for which reason it lends itself best to being ...

◆ Smoked
◆ Baked and served with a sauce
◆ Fried
◆ Braaied or grilled, but take care to baste well

SUITABLE RECIPES

Smoked Fish Pâté, page 16
Seafood in a Clay Pot, page 29
Beggar's Bouillabaisse, page 33
Smoked Fish, page 49
Milanese Fish Pie, page 38
Feta Fish in Pastry, page 40
Paprika-Grilled Fish, page 46
Jewelled Coriander Fish, page 55
Burmese Fish Curry, page 54
Mahi Mahi, page 57
Niçoise Fish, page 61
Foiled Tuna, page 61
Barbados Fish, page 62
Ouma's Pickled Fish, page 65
Fish Kebabs, page 86

BAARDMAN
TASSELFISH/CROAKER

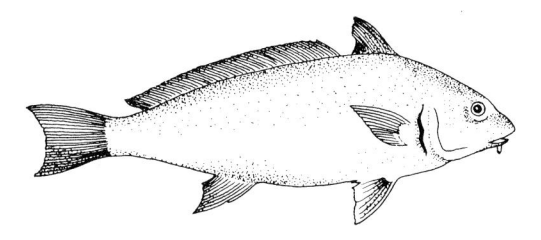

76 cm

This popular angling fish is found all along the African coastline. In appearance it's similar to kob, though the body is deeper, and it has a fleshy barbel under the chin – hence its name. The soft-bodied young have acquired an unprintable nickname from trawler-hands largely unimpressed by the quality of the meat!

Just landed, the colour ranges from silver to golden yellow, which soon darkens to a greyish-brown after the fish's demise.

Larger specimens have excellent flesh – similar to kob but slightly drier and firmer. It's best ...

- Fried
- Poached
- Baked
- Smoked

SUITABLE RECIPES

Fish Cakes, page 34
Quick Fish Rissoles, page 34
Hake Rosé, page 37
Apple and Almond Hake 37
Fish Meunière, page 40
Mushroom and Almond Fish, page 43
Fish Mornay, page 57
Paprika-Grilled Fish, page 46
Smoked Fish, page 49
Baked Stump with Cream Sauce, page 58
Ouma's Pickled Fish, page 65

BARBEL
BARBEL-EEL
CATFISH

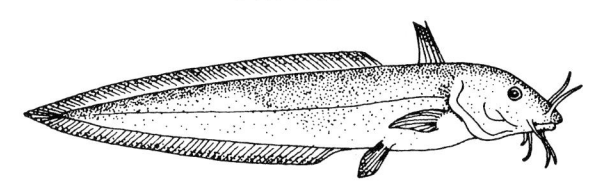

43 cm   *Barbel-eel*

36 cm   *Catfish*

Though ugly to look at, the flesh of both the barbel-eel and the catfish is surprisingly good – particularly that of the barbel-eel, which is rather like sole.

Muddy brown in colour, darker above, the distinctive long, soft body has no scales, but there are serrated spines which can cause painful lacerations and severe poisoning. So be extremely careful when handling the live fish and, if you happen to get wounded, immerse the injured part in very hot water for at least 30 minutes.

The flesh is white, rather soft, and best ...

- Dusted with seasoned flour and crisply fried
- Braaied
- Grilled
- Smoked

SUITABLE RECIPES

Fish Cakes, page 34
Quick Fish Rissoles, page 34
Hake Rosé, page 37
Mushroom and Almond Fish, page 43
Fish Mornay, page 57
Sole Véronique, page 46
Smoked Fish, page 49

BARRACUDA
SEAPIKE

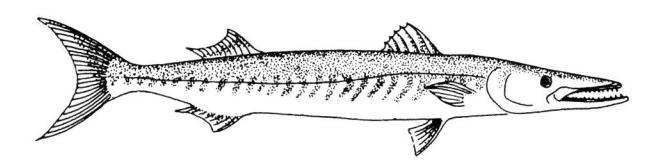

120 cm

This powerful east coast gamefish is silvery and dappled and has the dubious distinction of being known as one of the most ferocious in our seas – they kill fish seemingly for the fun of it. In addition to their anti-social aquatic activities, they're armed with rows of razor-sharp teeth. Not surprisingly, anglers and divers treat them with a great deal of respect.

Conversely, barracuda flesh is delicate of flavour and texture, though it should be bled as soon as it's caught. Eat as fresh as possible ...

- Braaied
- Grilled
- Smoked
- Fried

SUITABLE RECIPES

Paprika-Grilled Fish, page 46
Smoked Fish, page 49
Japanese Fish, page 54
Niçoise Fish, page 61
Braised Gamefish, page 61
Ouma's Pickled Fish, page 65

BLACKTAIL
DASSIE/KOLSTERT

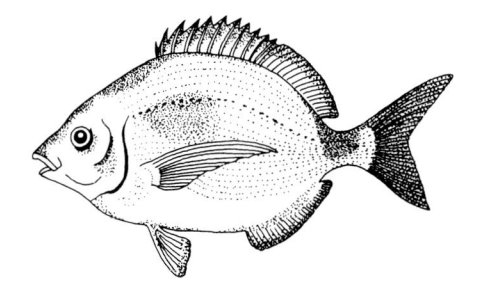

22 cm

This small but vigorous angling fish is well known to snorkelers and spearfishermen. Unique to the African coastline, and prolific in turbulent off-shore rocky areas, the young have fine bars which change as they grow to become almost black in adulthood, with their characteristic darker spot above the tail.

Despite the fact that they're on the small side, they're excellent for eating even though the texture of the flesh coarsens with age. They must be eaten fresh so cook as soon as possible after catching ...

- Filleted and deep-fried
- Filleted, dusted with seasoned flour and shallow-fried
- Basted and braaied
- Smoked

SUITABLE RECIPES

Fish Meunière, page 40
Smoked Fish, page 49
Johann's Harders, page 54
Beach Party Galjoen, page 82
Herb-Braaied Reef Fish, page 84
Filleted Linefish over the Coals, page 85
Scored Fish over the Coals, page 85
Fish in Foil, page 84
Whole Braaied Fish, page 84

BREAM

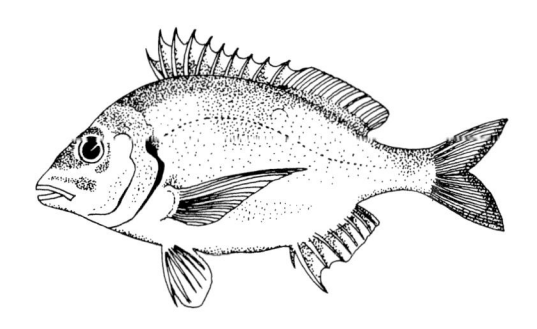

22 cm

This well-known species of angling fish comes in a variety of forms and colours – most often silvery-grey with a white belly. A master in the art of camouflage, bream can become almost black when they live in muddy waters. As the name suggests, the fish is happiest in estuaries and river mouths.

Though on the small side (they seldom get bigger than 30 cm) the flesh is excellent, and is most popular ...

- Fried
- Grilled
- Braaied

SUITABLE RECIPES

Fish Meunière, page 40
Coconut Bay Sole, page 46
Beach Party Galjoen, page 82
Herb-Braaied Reef Fish, page 84
Scored Fish over the Coals, page 85
Filleted Linefish over the Coals, page 85
Fish in Foil, page 84
Whole Braaied Fish, page 84

CRAB

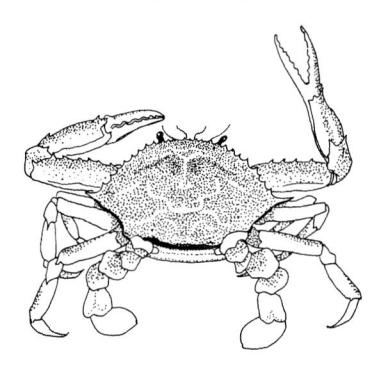

These tasty crustacea are highly prized throughout the world. Their flesh is similar to that of crayfish, though it's more delicate in texture. The flavour of fresh crab is quite different to canned crab, which is something to bear in mind when you're preparing the more delicately-flavoured fresh meat.

Although plate-sized crabs aren't plentiful on our shores, a fair supply comes from the deep waters off Natal and Mozambique and are marketed deep-frozen. All our crabs are edible and, though there seems more point in preparing the larger specimens, it is worthwhile taking the trouble to prepare the plentiful small sand crab – a fiddly, time-consuming but worthwhile task.

Preparation: Suffocate live crabs by immersing them in fresh water for a few hours before cooking, as live crabs have a tendency to lose their legs and claws when plunged straight into boiling water – a sorry state of affairs for all concerned! If your crabs have been frozen, dispense with this step and simply allow them to defrost very, very slowly in the fridge.

Place the late lamented crabs in heavily salted boiling water (at least 30 ml per 4 litres of water), cover, return to the boil, then reduce the heat to simmer for 10 minutes, not a second longer. Remove from the water and allow to drain, right side up.

To extract the flesh, remove abdomen flap and prise off upper shell. Remove gills from either side, and the intestines. Break into halves and remove flesh from each segment and from the claws.

Enjoy fresh crab with a squeeze of lemon juice or a drop of vinegar and plenty of freshly milled black pepper. It's also great in a salad with Seafood Sauce (page 94).

Crabs can be frozen for up to three months – whole (well wrapped in plastic) or the flesh stored in small containers to save freezer space. When required, thaw slowly in the fridge and drain well.

SUITABLE RECIPES

Crab Curry, page 76
Crayfish Pie, page 75

DAGERAAD
SLINGER

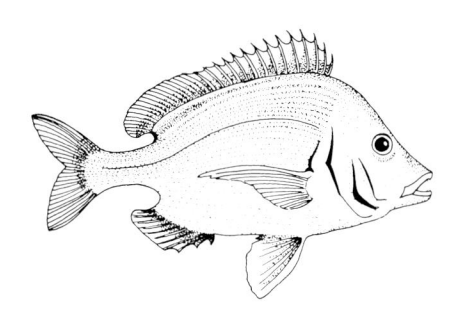

35 cm

This delicious fish belongs to the same family as roman and stumpnose. Popular amongst divers and anglers, they swim in great shoals in and about coastal reefs – dageraad being prolific in Cape waters and slinger concentrating northwards of East London.

As they die, waves of the most incredibly beautiful colours of the early-morning sky pass over their skin and scales, hence the name 'dageraad' – dawn.

These tasty fish are most popular ...

- Fried
- Baked
- Grilled
- Braaied

SUITABLE RECIPES

Hake Rosé, page 37
Fish Meunière, page 40
Mushroom and Almond Fish, page 43
Fish Mornay, page 57
Paprika-Grilled Fish, page 46
Indonesian Fish, page 56
Baked Stump with Cream Sauce, page 58
Niçoise Fish, page 61
Scored Fish over the Coals, page 85
Filleted Linefish over the Coals, page 85
Fish in Foil, page 84
Whole Braaied Fish, page 84

EEL

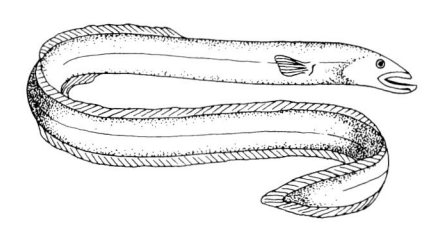

There are many species of edible eels in our waters, all tasty fish that aren't as popular here as in other parts of the world. Considering their appearance, one can imagine why – they're just not pretty! But next time you're underwater and confronted by the likes of a conger eel, sand snake or moray eel, grab it, cook it – and find out what you've been missing all these years.

They're found in all rivers flowing from east to west into the sea, as well as in the sea. Although eels freely take anglers' bait, Professor JLB Smith suggests a simple method of trapping a conger: bury bits of smelly fish along the edge of the surf at low tide. As the water rises, the fish will be enticed from their sandy homes and can easily be speared. Sounds like good fun for a summer evening!

Preparation: Beware! All eels are dangerous and they're not easy to kill – even after you've managed to extricate the hook from its powerful jaws. Whack it hard on the back of the head and make sure it's dead before proceeding any further.

Skin by slitting around the neck, cut off the tail, grip the head and pull off the skin towards the tail. Sprinkle with salt and leave for a couple of hours. Then behead it, slice it open, remove the entrails and clean well. Trim the fins, lay the fish on its back and slit through the backbone. Remove this carefully.

Warning: In some tropical regions of the world moray eels are known to be carriers of ciguatera poison – so it's wise not to eat the liver and intestines. Keeping the above in mind, and remembering as a general guide that larger eels tend to be a bit coarse and oily, enjoy your eel …

- Fried with a coating of seasoned flour or crumbs
- Smoked

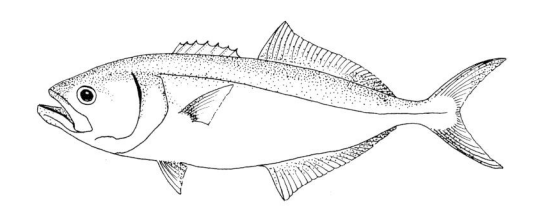

ELF
SHAD

50 cm

A vicious and powerful predator, elf (or shad, as Natal anglers prefer to call it) is one of our supreme angling and diving fish. It pounces with equal glee and gusto on its prey and a baited hook. Streamlined for speed and silvery in colour, its back is pale green, the belly white, and the colour changes to blue when it dies.

Once in danger of over-exploitation, conservation measures have been instrumental in this fine fish showing signs of now becoming more abundant.

Elf must be bled on capture to preserve the delicate flavour. Some say it's the most delicious fish in our waters – but there is a catch: it simply must be really fresh as it spoils very quickly. This is also a point worth checking on when you're offered elf at a restaurant.

Virtually every cooking method may be used. Our favourites are …

- Frying
- Braaiing
- Grilling
- Smoking

SUITABLE RECIPES

Fish Meunière, page 40
Paprika-Grilled Fish, page 46
Smoked Fish, page 49
Mackerel with Mustard and Orange Sauce, page 58
Herb-Braaied Reef Fish, page 84
Scored Fish over the Coals, page 85
Filleted Linefish over the Coals, page 85
Whole Braaied Fish, page 84

FRANSMADAM
KAREL GROOTOOG

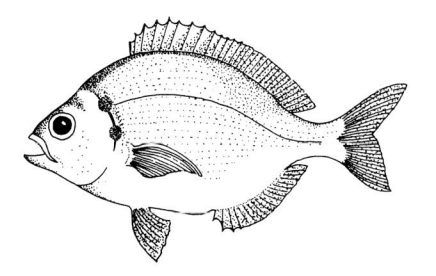

20 cm

As the name implies and the drawing shows, this is a pretty little fish. The flesh is tasty, but its diminutive size limits its usefulness as a table fish and means that it simply must be cooked whole.

- Season, dust with flour and fry
- Braai

SUITABLE RECIPES

Beach Party Galjoen, page 82
Fish in Foil, page 84
Whole Braaied Fish, page 84

GALJOEN
BANDED GALJOEN/DAMBA

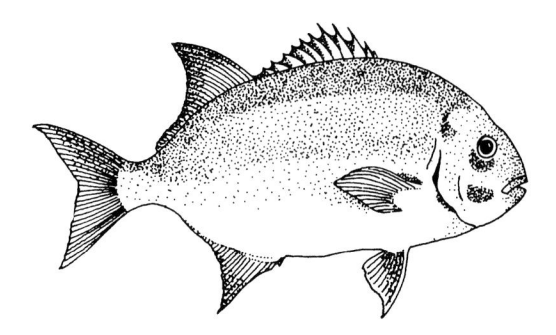

30 cm

Aptly named after that stately Spanish sailing vessel – the galleon – the galjoen is unique to South African waters and, as well as being one of our most popular angling fish, has the added distinction of being our national fish.

Sadly the fish is scarce today, even in areas where it was previously abundant, which has resulted in specific catch restrictions being applied. So for lovers of this distinctive fish, a galjoen feast is a relatively rare occurrence.

They feed very close inshore and for this reason are at their fattest and juicy best when storms have churned up the sea – and morsels of galjoen food – in late summer or early winter. Fish caught during the spring and early summer months tend to be more scrawny – but definitely still worth eating.

They range from silvery-bronze to almost black, and have been known to reach 80 cm in length, though the average is much less.

The unusual colour and flavour of the marbled, black-veined flesh means that this is a fish you either love or hate. It must be bled after being caught which improves the flavour.

Tradition dictates that galjoen is cooked – and served – with head and tail in situ. It's best ...

- Braaied
- Baked

SUITABLE RECIPES

Smoked Fish, page 49
Baked Stump with Cream Sauce, page 58
Baked Reef Fish with Avocado Stuffing, page 64
Baked Stumpnose Marrakesh, page 65
Beach Party Galjoen, page 82
Herb-Braaied Reef Fish, page 84
Filleted Linefish over the Coals, page 85
Fish in Foil, page 84
Whole Braaied Fish, page 84

GEELBEK
CAPE SALMON

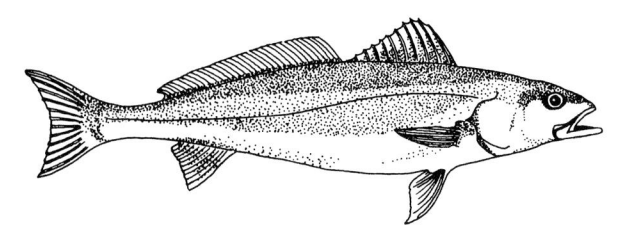

91 cm

This superb fish is similar in appearance to its close cousin, the kob, but it is brilliant yellow in the inner gill covers and mouth, from whence it gets its name. The flesh is similar to kob, though it's a trifle firmer and more flavourful.

Found in shoals all around our coastline, geelbek are eagerly pursued by ski-boat anglers and spearfishermen and are occasionally caught by trawlers.

Its excellent flesh may be prepared in just about any way imaginable ...

- Fry
- Bake
- Braai
- Grill
- Smoke
- Poach

SUITABLE RECIPES

Breton Fish Soup, page 26
Seafood in a Clay Pot, page 29
Bouillabaisse, page 30
Hake Rosé, page 37
Crunchy Soufflé Hake, page 36
Grilled Fish with Spiced Yoghurt, page 38
Creamy Fish with Fried Leek, page 38
Milanese Fish Pie, page 38
Feta Fish in Pastry, page 40
Fish Meunière, page 40
Mushroom and Almond Fish, page 43
Fish Soufflé, page 43
Fish Mornay, page 57
Paprika-Grilled Fish, page 46
Kingklip Calamata, page 47
Orange Kingklip with Spinach Sauce, page 48
Gratin of Kob, page 49
Italian Crunchy Kob, page 49
Smoked Fish, page 49
Japanese Fish, page 54
Jewelled Coriander Fish, page 55
Indonesian Fish, page 56

Baked Stump with Cream Sauce, page 58
Niçoise Fish, page 61
Ouma's Pickled Fish, page 65
Seafood Sausages, page 70
Scored Fish over the Coals, page 85
Filleted Linefish over the Coals, page 85
Fish in Foil, page 84
Whole Braaied Fish, page 84
Fish Kebabs, page 86

GRUNTER
SILVER GRUNTER/COCK GRUNTER/
SPOTTED GRUNTER

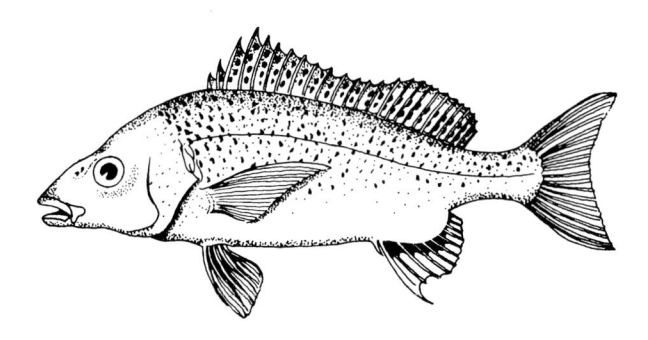

50 cm

All members of the grunter family have a distinctive elongated shape and pointy nose. Though some types are on the smallish side, which restricts their importance as a table fish, others grow to a sizable 9 kg. Anglers catch them in considerable numbers in estuaries and along sandy beaches where they congregate in shoals.

The name is derived from the sounds that a landed grunter makes by grinding its pharyngeal teeth.

Larger grunters are excellent eating (smaller ones too, but they're very bony) – best ...

◆ Braaied
◆ Fried

SUITABLE RECIPES

Hake Rosé, page 37
Fish Meunière, page 40
Mushroom and Almond Fish, page 43
Smoked Fish, page 49
Fish Mornay, page 57
Coconut Bay Sole, page 46
Paprika-Grilled Fish, page 46
Herb-Braaied Reef Fish, page 84
Whole Braaied Fish, page 84

GURNARD
CAPE GURNARD/KNOORHAAN/
CAPE SEA ROBIN

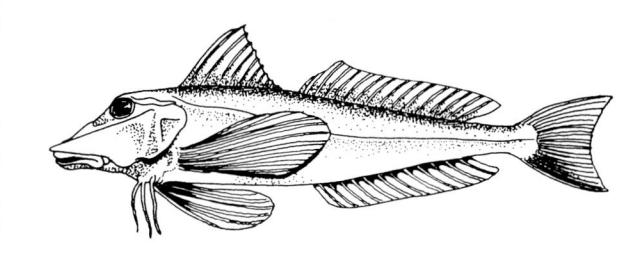

50 cm

There are seven species of gurnard in southern African waters and they're considered one of our most important commercial fish. Because they live in waters deeper than 300 metres, gurnard is not considered an angling fish, though some are taken from ski-boats and by hand-line fishermen. Most are trawled off the eastern Cape coast.

Quaint-looking, they have an elongated, red body and a broad, flattened head encased in a bony shield. Large, strikingly-patterned pectoral fins are brought into play to frighten the living daylights out of those that have the temerity to consider them easy prey.

The name is derived from an old French word, gornat, which means 'to grunt' – the sound the fish makes as it's captured. Excellent eating, gurnard is nicknamed 'poor man's sole' and it can, indeed, be used in dishes devised for the more costly sole.

To clean, simply slit open, bend the head backwards, give a tug and pull off the skin. The fillets can then be cut off the bone.

◆ Fry with a coating of seasoned flour, batter or crumbs
◆ Poach whole, then fillet and serve with a sauce
◆ Wrap the fillets in bacon and grill or braai

SUITABLE RECIPES

Beggar's Bouillabaisse, page 33
Hake Rosé, page 37
Crispy Fish with Lemon and Ginger Sauce, page 40
Feta Fish in Pastry, page 40
Fish Meunière, page 40
Mushroom and Almond Fish, page 43
Fish Mornay, page 57
Sole Véronique, page 46
Coconut Bay Sole, page 46
Gratin of Kob, page 49
Orange Kingklip with Spinach Sauce, page 48
Burmese Fish Curry, page 54
Sweet and Sour Prawns, page 74

HAKE
STOCKFISH

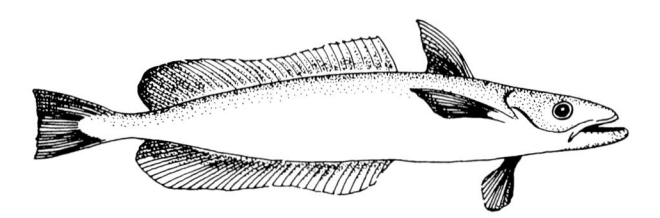

60 cm

Without doubt this is South Africa's most important and economical table fish – available fresh (very occasionally) and conveniently filleted and frozen.

Smoked hake (haddock) is also readily available and popular for a quick meal – a very useful stand-by to have in the freezer. It merely requires a quick poaching, a squeeze of lemon and a touch of pepper. Defrost it and place skin down in a wide saucepan. Add just enough cold water or milk to cover, cover with the lid and simmer very gently for about 5-10 minutes (depending on the thickness of the cut), until the fish is opaque right through and flakes easily.

But back to hake: a bottom-feeder, hake is prolific off our coastline, though often at great depths which is why it isn't considered a sport-fish. Trawling is the most common form of capture.

Hake is fairly soft to the touch and the flesh is equally soft and delicate of flavour. Though it is incredibly versatile and can be prepared in a variety of ways, we like it best ...

- Coated with flour, crumbs or batter and crisply fried
- Poached and served with a tasty sauce
- Baked
- Grilled

SUITABLE RECIPES FOR HAKE

Fish Cakes, page 34
Quick Fish Rissoles, page 34
Hake Rosé, page 37
Spring Vegetable Hake Bake, page 36
Crunchy Soufflé Hake, page 36
Apple and Almond Hake, page 37
Tomato and Feta Fish, page 37
Grilled Fish with Spiced Yoghurt, page 38
Creamy Fish with Fried Leek, page 38
Milanese Fish Pie, page 38
Fish Meunière, page 40
Crispy Fish with Lemon and Ginger Sauce, page 40
Feta Fish in Pastry, page 40
Mushroom and Almond Fish, page 43

Fish Mornay, page 57
Fish Souffle, page 43
Sole Véroniqué, page 46
Coconut Bay Sole, page 46
Paprika-Grilled Fish, page 46
Gratin of Kob, page 49
Italian Crunchy Kob, page 49
Ouma's Pickled Fish, page 65

SUITABLE RECIPES FOR HADDOCK

Haddock and Leek Roulade, page 16
Haddock Salad O'Neill, page 25
Haddock and Orange Broth, page 26
Mediterranean Tomatoes, page 51
Two Oceans Pasta, page 50
Crusty Mustard Haddock, page 52
Haddock Mornay, page 53

HARDER
MULLET, RED MULLET

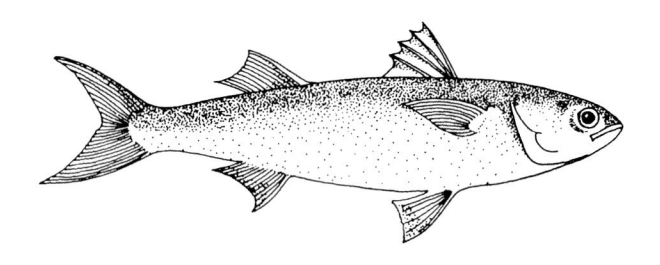

35 cm

One of our most important food fishes, these little wrigglers are oily, firm-fleshed and well flavoured, though on the small side and very bony. They may be prepared in many different ways like ...

- rolled in brown paper and baked
- poached
- smoked
- vlekked and braaied after salting and wind-drying for a few hours

SUITABLE RECIPES

Oven-Roasted Sardines, page 53
Johann's Harders, page 54
Mackerel with Mustard and Orange Sauce, page 58
Beach Party Galjoen, page 82
Herb-Braaied Reef Fish, page 84
Scored Fish over the Coals, page 85

HOTTENTOT

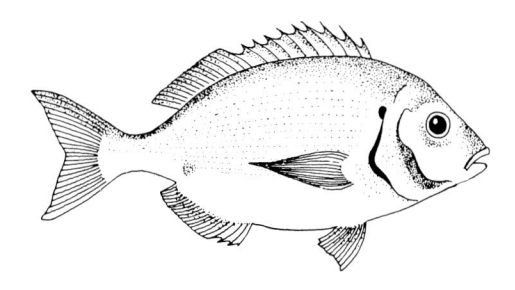

22 cm

These dusty-faced fish have a distinctive flavour – not to everyone's liking. The flesh is not very firm and remains moist even during grilling and smoking. We enjoy it ...

- Poached in strong court-bouillon
- Well-seasoned and baked; in both cases serve with a tasty sauce

SUITABLE RECIPES

Fish Cakes, page 34
Quick Fish Rissoles, page 34
Hake Rosé, page 37

JACOPEVER

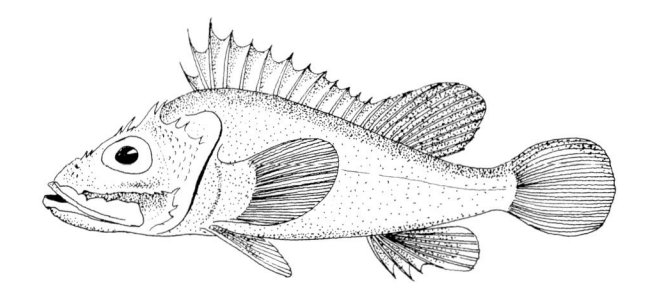

25 cm

This funny-looking fish has a ruddy complexion and bulbous eyes – features which prompted its name: the sailing mates of one Jacob Evertsen, an early Dutch sailor with a certain fondness for the bottle, named the fish after him!

In addition to its strange face, the jacopever has spiny fins and sharp spines on its head and gill covers too. Seldom caught by boat anglers, it is trawled quite abundantly off the southern and western Cape coast. Much of the catch ends up in animal feeds, though some gets through to the domestic market.

Similar identifying features are found in the false jacopever, which is taken by line-fishermen on the Cape west coast and in False Bay.

The flesh is quite firm and delicately flavoured, and the best way to enjoy it is ...

- Filleted and fried

SUITABLE RECIPES

Hake Rosé, page 37
Fish Meunière, page 40
Mushroom and Almond Fish, page 43

JOHN BROWN
JANBRUIN

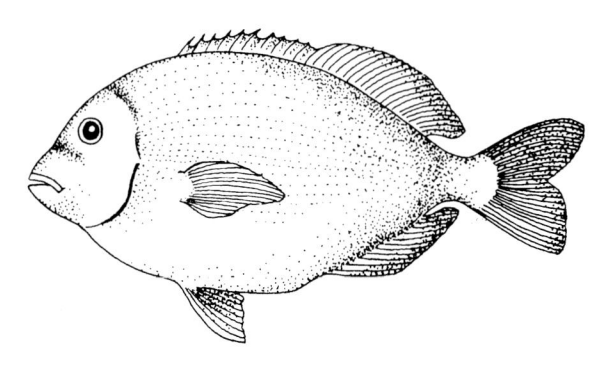

25 cm

This plump, shapely, bream-like fish is typically South African and is found in rocky parts of the coastline between the Transkei and False Bay. It most often swims alone or in pairs, and is less abundant now than before. A distinctive fish, it has a dark brown body, bright blue eyes and large, comical teeth.

The flesh is firm, almost tough, and should be skinned. Then ...

- Fry in butter and olive oil with a squeeze of lemon juice added
- Grill
- Braai, basting continually
- Smoke

SUITABLE RECIPES

Hake Rosé, page 37
Mushroom and Almond Fish, page 43
Fish Mornay, page 57
Paprika-Grilled Fish, page 46
Smoked Fish, page 49
Beach Party Galjoen, page 82

John Dory

30 cm

The John Dory is nicknamed St Peter's Fish because the distinctive dark spots on each side are said to be the marks left by St Peter's thumb and forefinger as he plucked it from the waters of the Sea of Galilee to remove a coin from its mouth for the tax collector.

This deep-water fish is a dull greyish-green colour and very slim when viewed head-on. Commercial trawl-nets land most of the catch, though some are caught by ski-boat anglers.

Its raggedy-looking appearance belies delicately flavoured flesh, which is rather like trout, though not quite as tasty. It is traditionally grilled or braaied, always with herbs and a basting sauce to enhance the flavour. The head is considered a delicacy, so it is usually left on.

- Fillet, season well, coat with egg and flour or crumbs, and fry in butter and oil
- Poach and serve with a sauce
- Bake
- Grill
- Braai

Suitable recipes

Hake Rosé, page 37
Fish Meunière, page 40
Mushroom and Almond Fish, page 43
Fish Mornay, page 57
Paprika-Grilled Fish, page 46
Baked Stump with Cream Sauce, page 58

Kingklip

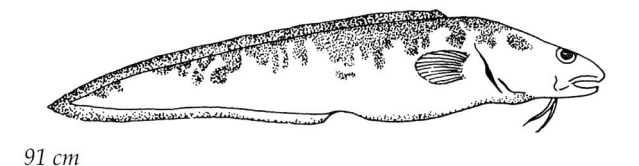

91 cm

Quite unmistakable with its long, scaleless, eel-like body and mottled in shades of pink, kingklip is one of our most important commercial fishes and is trawled in the deep waters off our western and east Cape coasts. It is also caught in considerable numbers on long lines.

Soft and slimy to the touch, its appearance does nothing to deter kingklip devotees from eating it with relish. There's probably not a restaurant in the country that doesn't have kingklip on the menu.

- Fry
- Poach
- Bake
- Grill

Suitable recipes

Breton Fish Soup, page 26
Seafood in a Clay Pot, page 29
Bouillabaisse, page 30
Hake Rosé, page 37
Crunchy Soufflé Hake, page 36
Tomato and Feta Fish, page 37
Grilled Fish with Spiced Yoghurt, page 38
Creamy Fish with Fried Leek, page 38
Crispy Fish with Lemon and Ginger Sauce, page 40
Feta Fish in Pastry, page 40
Fish Meunière, page 40
Mushroom and Almond Fish, page 43
Coconut Bay Sole, page 46
Paprika-Grilled Fish, page 46
Orange Kingklip with Spinach Sauce, page 48
Japanese Fish, page 54
Jewelled Coriander Fish, page 55
Burmese Fish Curry, page 54
Spicy Shark with Cream Sauce, page 57
Niçoise Fish, page 61
Seafood Sausages, page 70
Sweet and Sour Prawns, page 74
Crayfish Ma Chère, page 75
Fish Kebabs, page 86

Kob
KABELJOU
SQUARETAIL KOB/KING KOB

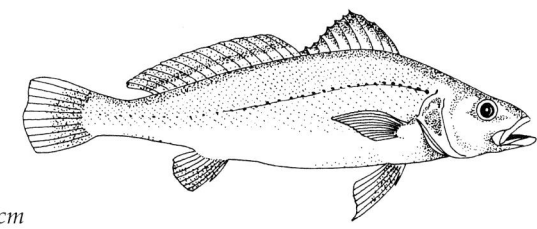

83 cm

Kob (kabeljou – derived from the ancient Dutch word 'kabeljauw', a stockfish) is one of our most important and versatile food fishes and so prolific that it's invariably the 'linefish of the day' you'll be offered at restaurants. All but the very largest have firm and tasty flesh that can be prepared in many different ways.

Its cousin, the squaretail or king kob, swims in large shoals off the Natal coast where it is enthusiastically fished by ski-boat anglers.

It is distinctively coloured – palest silver, and with a row of 'portholes' along the lateral line which accentuates the sleek lines of the fish.

Commercially caught by trawlers and line-boat fishermen, it's also popular with anglers and divers alike.

- Fry
- Braai
- Grill
- Bake
- Smoke

SUITABLE RECIPES

Ceviche, page 15
Breton Fish Soup, page 26
Seafood in a Clay Pot, page 29
Bouillabaisse, page 30
Beggar's Bouillabaisse, page 33
Hake Rosé, page 37
Crunchy Soufflé Hake, page 36
Tomato and Feta Fish, page 37
Grilled Fish with Spiced Yoghurt, page 38
Creamy Fish with Fried Leek, page 38
Milanese Fish Pie, page 38
Crispy Fish with Lemon and Ginger Sauce, page 40
Feta Fish in Pastry, page 40
Fish Meunière, page 40
Mushroom and Almond Fish, page 43
Fish Soufflé, page 43
Fish Mornay, page 57
Paprika-Grilled Fish, page 46
Sole Véronique, page 46
Kingklip Calamata, page 47
Orange Kingklip with Spinach Sauce, page 48
Gratin of Kob, page 49
Italian Crunchy Kob, page 49
Baked Stump with Cream Sauce, page 58
Niçoise Fish, page 61
Ouma's Pickled Fish, page 65
Crayfish Ma Chère, page 75
Scored Fish over the Coals, page 85
Filleted Linefish over the Coals, page 85
Fish in Foil, page 84
Whole Braaied Fish, page 84
Fish Kebabs, page 86

LEERVIS
LEERFISH/GARRICK

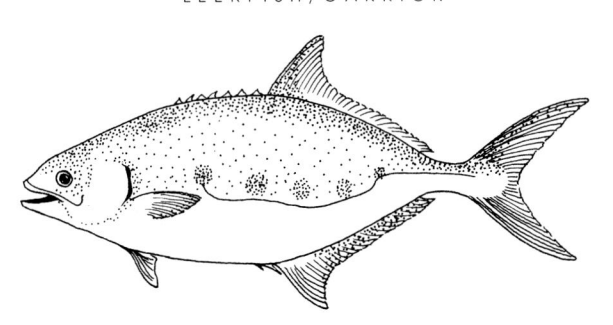

76 cm

Most shore-anglers and spearfishermen agree that this is, without doubt, the best gamefish in our seas, although it has little commercial significance. A large and aggressive predator, it hunts near the surf where it feeds off shoals of smaller baitfish. The name refers to the tough, leathery skin that appears scaleless, although minute scales are, in fact present.

Smaller leervis are good eating, but the flesh becomes coarser and drier as the fish gets bigger, when it's best skinned and pickled. Leervis must be bled on capture.

- Fry in butter and serve with lemon-butter sauce
- Bake in foil to retain succulence
- Grill with a basting sauce
- Braai

SUITABLE RECIPES

Paprika-Grilled Fish, page 46
Braised Gamefish, page 61
Barbados Fish, page 62
Ouma's Pickled Fish, page 65
Filleted Linefish over the Coals, page 85

MAASBANKER
HORSE MACKEREL

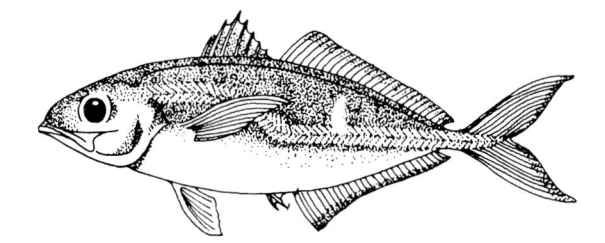

45 cm

This small, bony pelagic fish has dark, rich, tasty flesh and a characteristic strip of prickly, spiked scales down each side of its body. Make sure these scales are cut out completely and jettisoned before you begin to cook the fish.

The maasbanker has great commercial value and is trawled in great numbers. Ski-boat anglers catch it too, more often to use as bait than to take home for supper. We like it best ...

- Smoked
- Cured
- Fried
- Braaied

SUITABLE RECIPES

Mackerel with Mustard and Orange Sauce, page 58
Beach Party Galjoen, page 82

MACKEREL

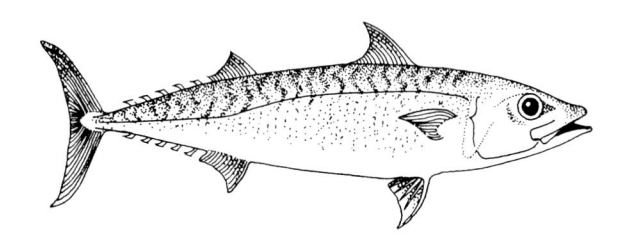

30 cm

This is one of the smallest members of the tuna family that occurs in large shoals – to the infinite delight of ski-boat anglers who hunt it with much enthusiasm. One of our most important commercial fish, catches in excess of 10 000 tonnes end up, literally, in tins to feed the nation.

Mackerel has rich, oily flesh that must be bled on capture and eaten fresh. It's wise not to handle it too much or to leave it in the sun, as the flesh spoils easily, and the strongly flavoured red meat should be cut away along the sensory line. Then it may be prepared and eaten in a variety of ways ...

- Panfry in a little oil and butter
- Grill or braai – a particularly good method of preparation as the flesh is oily and the skin is thick
- Poach and serve with a sauce
- Smoke
- Pickle

SUITABLE RECIPES

Mackerel with Mustard and Orange Sauce, page 58

MARLIN
BLACK MARLIN, BLUE MARLIN, STRIPED MARLIN, SAILFISH, SWORDFISH

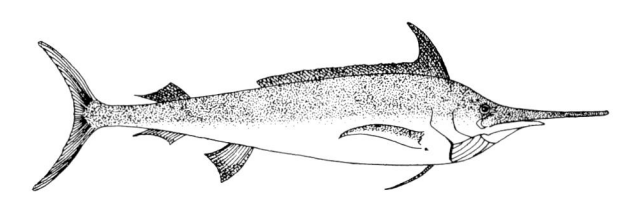

300 cm

Members of the billfish family are among the world's most famous gamefish and, to the delight of the local ski-boat fraternity, are being caught in increasing numbers in South African waters.

Seven different species have been recorded off our shores, among them the blue marlin, the striped marlin, the highly-prized black marlin and the sailfish, which is the one most commonly caught.

Swordfish, the marlin's famous and pugnacious cousin, is not usually caught as frequently, but its flesh is just as highly esteemed.

Flavour-wise, marlin and swordfish steaks cannot be compared with any other type of fish, but the texture is similar to tuna. And, like tuna, all billfish should be bled.

In Japanese cuisine these are the fish most often used for sashimi, when it is served raw, very finely sliced and offered with a dipping sauce.

But for local tastes the time-honoured method of grilling cannot be improved upon. Simply season with pepper, baste well with melted butter and fresh lemon juice, grill quickly over high heat and serve immediately. Don't overcook it whatever you do – it dries out very easily.

- Grill
- Braai
- Smoke
- Roast

SUITABLE RECIPES

Ceviche, page 15
Paprika-Grilled Fish, page 46
Japanese Fish, page 54
Burmese Fish Curry, page 54
Braised Gamefish, page 61
Foiled Tuna, page 61
Barbados Fish, page 62
Roast Gamefish Spiked with Bacon, page 62
Ouma's Pickled Fish, page 65
Marinated Gamefish Kebabs, page 85

MONKFISH

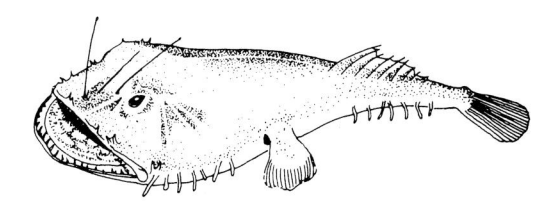

91 cm

Rather odious-looking with its huge head and softish body, monkfish has gained considerable popularity locally. It is often used as a substitute for crayfish, for the texture is quite firm, though it's not nearly as flavoursome.

- Poach and serve with a tasty sauce
- Fry

SUITABLE RECIPES

Crayfish Cocktail, page 15
Beggar's Bouillabaisse, page 33
Hake Rosé, page 37
Milanese Fish Pie, page 38
Crispy Fish with Lemon and Ginger Sauce, page 40
Feta Fish in Pastry, page 40
Mushroom and Almond Fish, page 43
Fish Mornay, page 57
Sole Véronique, page 46
Coconut Bay Sole, page 46
Spicy Shark with Cream Sauce, page 57
Orange Kingklip with Spinach Sauce, page 48
Gratin of Kob, page 49
Italian Crunchy Kob, page 49
Jewelled Coriander Fish, page 55
Ouma's Pickled Fish, page 65
Seafood Sausages, page 70
Sweet and Sour Prawns, page 74
Crayfish Ma Chère, page 75

MUSSEL
BLACK MUSSEL, BROWN MUSSEL, WHITE MUSSEL, CLAM

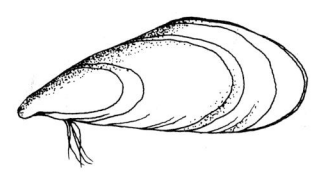

Mussels are among our most tasty molluscs and great favourites among lovers of seafood. They may be collected from the seashore (black and brown mussels attach themselves to rocks where they stay put and wait for their food to come along, filtering it through their systems; white mussels are found beneath the sand) and black mussels are also cultivated and sold fresh, frozen and canned.

There's no such thing as a safe season for collecting and eating mussels, but like all molluscs, they take in water from the sea around them as well as anything in the water, which accumulates in their systems. If these substances are poisonous, such as bacteria from a sewerage system or from a toxic tide, molluscs themselves will be dangerous to eat. And will remain so until they've had a chance to cleanse their systems.

It follows, therefore, that a few simple rules apply to safe mussel-eating. Never collect them from areas which may be polluted. In tidal zones, collect them from the deepest areas, where they are in clean water and further from the influence of shore pollution.

Most important of all, watch for toxic tides. If you're in any doubt check with the Department of Fisheries; they constantly monitor the situation.

Discard any with broken or cracked shells and those that remain open after you've tapped them. (If they don't close pretty smartly, they're dead.) Keep mussels cool and cook as soon as possible – preferably within a few hours.

Clams: These molluscs, of American clam chowder fame, are quite different to black mussels in appearance, looking more like white mussels. Their shells are almost circular, smooth and white, some exquisitely criss-crossed with beige and brown stripes. They have a flavour and texture all their own – slightly firmer than mussels and, to some, tastier. Prepare them in exactly the same way as mussels – though in some parts of the world aficionados prefer to eat them raw, like oysters.

Preparation: Scrape shells clean, de-beard, rinse well in cold water, then leave in a bucket of fresh water for at least 30 minutes. During this time they will 'spit out' any sand that may be trapped inside. Sandier white mussels may have to be soaked for a longer period.

To cook: Fill a large saucepan half-way up with cleaned mussels. Add just enough water to cover the base of the pot, cover and bring to the boil.

As soon as they open, they're cooked and ready for eating, so remove them immediately with a pair of tongs. Discard any that remain shut.

When cool enough to handle, remove one or both shells, depending on how you wish to serve them, and carefully pull out any beards which may have been too difficult to extract while cleaning. Strain the stock for use in your sauce or soup, or freeze it for later use.

To freeze: Steam mussels open as described above, discard shells and freeze in strained stock. Don't attempt to freeze them dry as they rapidly lose flavour and texture.

Remember, too, to remove them from the pot the moment the shells open, as overcooked mussels don't keep well.

Mussels are among our most versatile seafoods, and can be prepared in a variety of ways. There is nothing more delicious, though, than freshly-steamed, hot mussels generously dipped in French Dressing (page 94) or drizzled with hot Garlic Butter (page 91). If you've got a fire on the go for a braai, open the mussels round the edges of the grid where it's coolest.

Another useful tip from those in the know: never use a fork to eat mussels. Pluck them out with another shell – they're ready-hinged for the job.

SUITABLE RECIPES

Marinated Mussels, page 12
Pandora's Mussels, page 16
Scallops in Creamy Leek Sauce, page 21
Black Mussel Soup, page 28
Bouillabaisse, page 30
Red Sails in the Sunset, page 33
Mussel Stroganoff, page 66
Mussel and Leek Pie, page 66
Braaied Mussels, page 82
Seafood Sausages, page 70
Caribbean Paella, page 78
Prawn and Bacon Kebabs, page 86

MUSSELCRACKER
BLACK MUSSELCRACKER/POENSKOP
WHITE MUSSELCRACKER/BRUSHER/
WHITE BISKOP

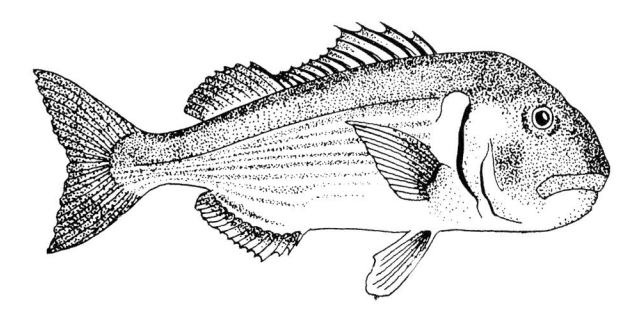

76 cm

Between them, black and white musselcrackers once had the distinction of sharing more common names than any other fish in our seas. When *Free From The Sea* was first published in 1979, we recorded a total of 17 different names! Most of these have fallen into disuse and will now pass into the mists of memory.

Both black and white musselcrackers are enthusiastically fished by rock anglers and spearfishermen, for they are robust fish and powerful fighters. So strong are their jaws that the musselcracker is most often 'the one that got away' – having first straightened your hook!

Musselcrackers have characteristically large heads, the flesh of which is considered a great delicacy. The younger fish are good eating, though the flesh coarsens with age.

Firm, white musselcracker steaks are best ...

- Fried
- Poached
- Smoked
- Baked
- Braaied

SUITABLE RECIPES

Breton Fish Soup, page 26
Bouillabaisse, page 30
Hake Rosé, page 37
Milanese Fish Pie, page 38
Crispy Fish with Lemon and Ginger Sauce, page 40
Fish Meunière, page 40
Mushroom and Almond Fish, page 43
Fish Mornay, page 57
Paprika-Grilled Fish, page 46
Orange Kingklip with Spinach Sauce, page 48
Italian Crunchy Kob, page 49
Japanese Fish, page 54
Baked Stump with Cream Sauce, page 58
Seafood Sausages, page 70
Fish in Foil, page 84
Whole Braaied Fish, page 84

OCTOPUS
SEACAT

This multi-legged cephalopod, oddities of the sea that include squid and cuttlefish, hide their lives away in shallow rocky pools along our coastline.

Masters of camouflage that they are, seeking them out isn't easy. The best way is to lure them with something orangy-red (the colour of the crabs that octopuses feed on). Try tying strips of a tyre's inner tube to the end of a stick or gaff and jiggle it under likely-looking ledges. With a bit of luck an octopus will take the lure and you can grab it with your hand – or gaff it if you're not into arm-wrestling an occy.

Murder it with a couple of whacks on the rocks, turn the head inside out and cut out the beak – the hard black bit at the base of the head.

Toughness and octopus flesh are synonymous and there are two ways of dealing with it. Continue bashing it on the rocks – 99 times in all. The 100th throw is into the pot, for by this time it will be skinless as well as tenderized. Remember to pause between every few bashes to 'scour' it on the rock until it foams.

Alternatively, if you're against making a spectacle of yourself on the beach, hang your occy on a nail (or ask a friend to hold it for you) and skin it with a sharp pair of scissors, removing the suckers at the same time. Cut off the head if you wish, together with the guts and the ink sac too, if that's your preference (though aficionados always use it in the dish, saying it adds immeasurably to the flavour). Now tenderise the tentacles with the back of an axe, cut it into pieces and put in into a heavy-based pot with a well-fitting lid. Cook it in its own juices until tender – about 30-45 minutes should do the trick.

Then gently fry the pieces for a few minutes in garlicky butter and serve with a squeeze of lemon. Or make one of these delicious recipes:

SUITABLE RECIPES

Pickled Winkles, page 12
Spicy Octopus, page 69
Intoxicated Octopus, page 69
Perlemoen Croquettes, page 18
Perlemoen Peperonata, page 80

OYSTER

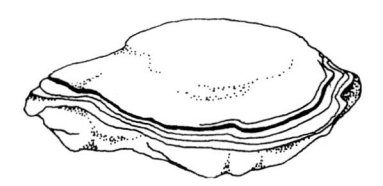

Oyster worshipers the world over agree – these marvellous molluscs should be eaten kneeling! And we must concur, for to find a far-flung shore and a clustering of wild oysters clinging to wave-washed rocks for the taking, is a seafood treat without compare.

We are well catered for in the oyster line, with the delicious bivalves being found along many parts of our coast. The main sources of supply for the domestic and restaurant market are Natal (wild oysters in deep, oblong shells), Knysna (cultivated in the lagoon and with a valuable export market), Algoa Bay (where they are cultivated on ropes in the deep sea), and the West Coast as far as Namibia, where the oysters are usually larger and tastier than their east-coast counterparts.

Oysters must be kept chilled to ensure they're still alive when eaten out of the shell. Refrigerated, they'll remain perfectly fresh for up to seven days and in cold weather may be safely stored unrefrigerated for up to three days. It's a simple matter to check for freshness – the shells must be tightly shut, or should close when tapped.

Preparation: Prise the shell open with an oyster knife, being careful to avoid spilling the liquid. Never, ever rinse your oyster with clean water, as this washes away all the natural sea liquor entrapped in the shell. Purists wouldn't dream of anointing their oysters with anything, though for a change of pace you may enjoy a squish of fresh lemon juice and a smidgen of black pepper or cayenne pepper. A drop of Tabasco sauce or a touch of horseradish sauce appeals to those with more adventurous inclinations. Buttered brown bread and a glass of stout are the preferred accompaniments.

Cooked oysters are often served in the deeper half of their shells. To keep them upright, settle them in a layer of coarse salt on a baking tray before grilling.

SUITABLE RECIPES

Marinated Mussels, page 12
Oysters Kilpatrick, page 18
Nut-Crust Oysters, page 21
Cheese Crust Oysters, page 20
Smoked Oyster Bites, page 19
Quissico Bisque, page 30
Prawn and Bacon Kebabs, page 86

PERIWINKLE
WINKLE

They look just like miniature alikreukels and are similar in taste too. In many parts of the world periwinkles are eaten raw, but most people prefer them cooked.

Gather periwinkles from rock pools at low tide – choose the largest you can find, which makes the task of winkling them out of their shells less arduous.

Preparation: Soak in fresh water for about 30 minutes, rinse in cold running water and drain. Poach for 5 minutes in boiling, salted water, timed from when the water starts to boil. Drain, allow to cool and remove periwinkles from their shells with a pin – bend the pin first to make the job easier. Pull off the protective disc and the soft stomach, rinse again and enjoy as is or with Garlic Butter (page 91) or doused with French Dressing (page 94).

Prepare periwinkles as above for use in the recipe.

Suitable recipe

Pickled Winkles, page 12

Perlemoen
ABALONE/KLIPKOUS

Elsewhere in the world, perlemoen is known as 'ormer' – a corruption of the French oreille de mer or 'sea ear'. South Africans have been partial to this delicious (if toughish and extraordinarily expensive) univalve since the earliest times. Shells have been unearthed in the midden heaps of the Strandlopers who lived on our shores before the first White man even dreamed about making this his home. We have since learned to mince it, braai it in the coals in the belly of freshly-cut kelp, and fry it with a coating of fresh or toasted crumbs.

The western and southern Cape coastal areas are rich in perlemoen, with the focus centred at Hermanus. Although the industry is the smallest in the fishing sector, it generates big bucks abroad, with most of the annual quota snaffled up by the East.

Many perlemoen cooks like to use a pressure-cooker; we don't find it necessary, though perlemoen must be beaten to tenderize it. Nor should it ever be overcooked, for this toughens it too.

Preparation: Remove the fish from its shell as soon as possible after diving it from the deep – preferably while it's still alive. Scrub off the black slime under cold running water, using a hard brush or a pot-scourer, trim off the frilly 'skirt' if you wish (though some prefer to cook this too, especially if making soup) and your perlemoen is ready for storing.

To prepare for cooking, slice vertically into steaks not thinner than 5 mm, then beat each one carefully with a mallet, especially around the hard outer edges. How much to tenderize depends largely on each individual perlemoen – you'll feel when it's enough.

Freezing: Like all seafood, perlemoen is best when it's never been frozen. But sometimes there's no way round it and into the freezer they must go. We prefer to freeze them whole, after cleaning and trimming. It may be kept frozen for up to six months, though the flavour and texture deteriorates as time goes by. It's best to use frozen perlemoen in a recipe with a sauce.

Suitable recipes

Perlemoen Croquettes, page 18
Perlemoen Timbales with Pink Hollandaise, page 22
Cream of Perlemoen Soup, page 29
Seafood Sausages, page 70
Crumbed Perlemoen, page 79
Salpicon of Perlemoen, page 79
Paarl Lemoen, page 79
Perlemoen Peperonata, page 80
Perlemoen Ragoût, page 80
Perlemoen Fisherman's Wharf, page 80
Perlemoen with Fresh Herbs, page 81
Perlemoen Parcels with Bacon and Mushrooms, page 86
Perlemoen in Kelp, page 87

Pilchard
HERRING, SARDINE, WHITEBAIT, ANCHOVY

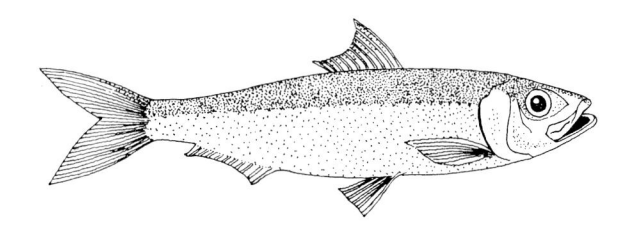

17 cm

Just as the herring was once the mainstay of the fishing industry in Northern Europe, so the pilchard and sardine have long been equally important in South Africa.

Overfishing in both hemispheres has, however, resulted in catch restrictions in an effort to protect the species from further dwindling.

All these fish swim in large shoals and are captured in purse-seine nets. However, you'll often find ski-boat anglers in hot pursuit, intent on catching the little fish for bait to lure the gamefish that hunt the tiddlers.

Small fish all, they're best known as canned fish, but – though very bony – there are many ways of preparing them fresh that makes the most of the rich and tasty flesh. In most recipes they're best left whole. Larger fish may be baked or grilled – or floured and fried.

The tiniest members of the family are best made into rollmops, or dipped in flour and deep-fried. Gourmets wouldn't dream of topping or tailing them – etiquette demands that they're eaten whole.

Kippers are smoked herrings. The simplest way of preparing them is to place them, heads down, in a deep jug. Fill to the brim with boiling water, leave for about 5 minutes, then drain and serve with a pat of butter.

All these fish may be ...

- Fried
- Baked
- Smoked
- Pickled

SUITABLE RECIPES

Rollmops, page 14
Kipper Pâté, page 15
Oven-Roasted Sardines, page 53
Sicilian Sardines, page 53
Scored Fish over the Coals, page 85
Whole Braaied Fish, page 84

PRAWN, SHRIMP AND LANGOUSTINE

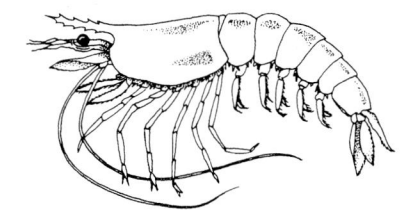

For our purposes, these delicious shellfish are grouped together. Though they differ in appearance, texture and size, all may be similarly prepared.

They're usually purchased fresh, frozen in blocks of ice, snap frozen or canned. Like crab, the canned variety differs in flavour and texture.

Preparation: If they're to be cooked in the shell, first remove the alimentary canal (vein) down the back. Cut the shell with a tiny pair of scissors and pull it out carefully. Langoustines or large prawns may be cut right through which makes them even easier to clean. If you like, remove and discard the head too.

To remove the shell, pull off the head, slit the shell along the underside between the legs, then bend off towards the back. Straighten the fish and devein from the head end. If the vein refuses to budge, make a small incision along the back and remove that way. Rinse and dry.

To cook: For use in salads or cocktails: shell and devein, then drop them into boiling, salted water. Cook the tiniest shrimps for 1 minute only, timing from when the water starts to boil once more. Add a little extra time for larger prawns and langoustines.

Overcook prawns, shrimps and langoustines at your peril – they become powdery and flavourless. Otherwise they're delicious ...

- Grilled
- Fried
- Braaied

SUITABLE RECIPES

Crayfish Cocktail, page 15
Perlemoen Croquettes, page 18
Bouillabaisse, page 30
Red Sails in the Sunset, page 33
Velvety Scallop Soup, page 33
Seafood Sausages, page 70
Spiced Prawns, page 72
Sweet and Sour Prawns, page 74
Garlic-Kissed Prawns, page 72
Prawns Mykonos, page 73
Caribbean Paella, page 78
Prawn and Bacon Kebabs, page 86
Brandied Prawns in Crème Fraîche, page 72

REDBAIT

Intrepid redbait munchers cut fresh pods of their favourite snack from the rocks at low tide and guzzle the morsels raw. Others (like us) prefer it cooked – and deep-fried is the nicest way to do it.

It is vital that only the freshest of fresh redbait is used for cooking. If it's kept for any length of time rather use it for bait, catch a fish – and eat that!

SUITABLE RECIPE

Redbait Poffertjies, page 18

Red Steenbras

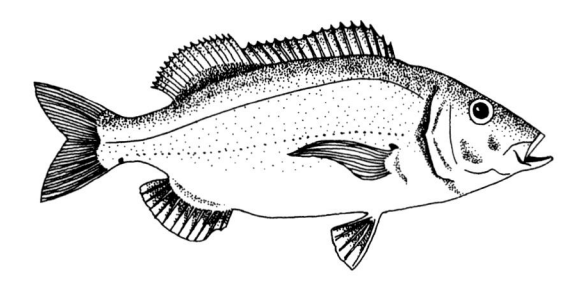

76 cm

This is one of the finest angling fish in our seas – and one of the most delicious too. Once abundant, numbers have dwindled drastically during recent years, resulting in restrictions in when they may be caught.

Aggressive fish, the largest of which ferociously defend their territory, they're exciting to catch, fight and land. They frequently remain in a fighting frame of mind out of the water and the angler needs to be careful and steer clear of the vicious teeth.

The flesh is tasty and firm, and it's one of the few species that doesn't coarsen with age. Prepare it any way you like, but we like it best ...

- Fried
- Baked
- Braaied
- Grilled
- Smoked

Suitable recipes

Breton Fish Soup, page 26
Seafood in a Clay Pot, page 29
Bouillabaisse, page 30
Hake Rosé, page 37
Crunchy Soufflé Hake, page 36
Grilled Fish with Spiced Yoghurt, page 38
Creamy Fish with Fried Leek, page 38
Fish Meunière, page 40
Mushroom and Almond Fish, page 43
Fish Mornay, page 57
Sole Véronique, page 46
Paprika-Grilled Fish, page 46
Japanese Fish, page 54
Jewelled Coriander Fish, page 55
Smoked Fish, page 49
Burmese Fish Curry, page 54
Indonesian Fish, page 56
Spicy Shark with Cream sauce, page 57

Baked Stump with Cream Sauce, page 58
Ouma's Pickled Fish, page 65
Herb-Braaied Reef Fish, page 84
Scored Fish over the Coals, page 85
Filleted Linefish over the Coals, page 85
Whole Braaied Fish, page 84

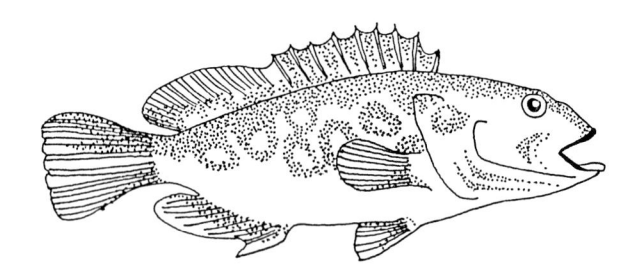

Rock cod

120 cm

More than seventy species of rock cod are found in our waters, most of which make great eating, though some are much too small to bother with. At the other end of the scale, the massive brindle bass – a ferocious fish with a reputation for attacking divers and shipwreck survivors – has been known to exceed 3,6 metres in length.

Most rock cods reside in rocky reefs and range widely in colour, though most are mottled to blend in with their surroundings. Wreckfish (also called stonebass) are so named because their favourite dwelling places are in the vicinity of sunken wrecks.

Firm of flesh and delicately flavoured, rock cod should first be skinned, then ...

- Coated with seasoned flour, batter or crumbs and fried
- Grilled with a basting sauce

Suitable recipes

Fish Cakes, page 34
Quick Fish Rissoles, page 34
Hake Rosé, page 37
Apple and Almond Hake, page 37
Grilled Fish with Spiced Yoghurt, page 38
Milanese Fish Pie, page 38
Mushroom and Almond Fish, page 43
Fish Soufflé, page 43
Fish Mornay, page 57
Paprika-Grilled Fish, page 46
Ouma's Pickled Fish, page 65

Rock Lobster
LOBSTER/CRAYFISH/KREEF

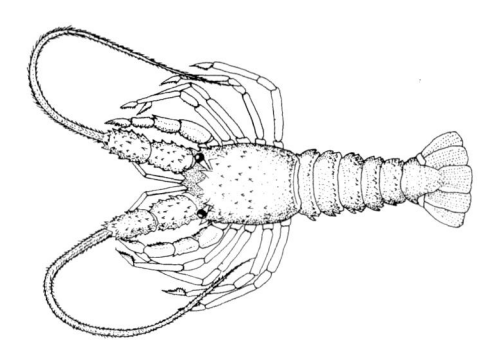

When he first landed at the Cape, Jan van Riebeeck was offered 'fine large crayfish' by resident Strandlopers already adept at catching all manner of sea goodies. The rest, as they say, is history, with these marvellous shellfish gaining in popularity as the years have passed, even though the cost has increased in equal measures.

Our early cookbooks called them 'kreeft' (mercifully shortened to kreef as time went by). Cooks today know them as crayfish. The Department of Sea Fisheries insist on them being named Rock Lobster, the idea being to prevent international confusion in the export market. Crayfish or crawfish are smaller types of lobster and are not found in our waters.

At one time crayfish was one of our cheapest seafoods but, as its value has escalated on the export market, so the cost has increased locally. Still one our most desirable edibles, nothing – not even price – will keep a lobster-lover from enjoying his favourite meal.

Three types are fished and marketed here, each with its own habitat and each controlled by specific regulations pertaining to catch, bag and size limits: West Coast Rock Lobster (Jasus lalandii) are found from Cape Cross north of Walvis Bay to Cape Hangklip, and occasionally on the Agulhas Bank. South Coast Rock Lobster (Palinurus gilchristie) proliferate from Cape Hangklip to the Great Kei River, and the smaller, mottled East Coast Rock Lobster (Palinurus homarus) found in the waters of Natal.

Storage: No-one would deny that fresh (as in never-been-frozen) is best, so if you're not going to eat them immediately, crayfish may be stored in the fridge until they expire. Fridge life may be a couple of hours or a few days, depending on their condition at the start.

When faced with a crayfish glut (wonderful thought!) you may have to resort to freezing. Separate tails from bodies and freeze individually, tucking them tightly in freezer bags. They'll be fine for a couple of months and are best used in recipes with sauces.

We don't advocate freezing the bodies; it's not that easy to extricate the flesh afterwards. Rather cook them in boiling, salted water for 6 minutes and tuck into a leg-cracking and body-picking session immediately.

Nor do we like to freeze cooked crayfish; the flavour and texture is lousy.

Preparation of live crayfish: The least distressing way (for the cook) is to drown them by immersing in cold, fresh water. This will take about 30 minutes. But those who have researched the matter from the crayfish's point of view suggest it's best to kill them by shock – like piercing the head with a thin knife.

To cook: Gone are the days when all crayfish were boiled in seawater for 20 minutes irrespective of size. In order to cook them to perfection weigh beforehand, then place in a large pot of boiling water or Court-Bouillon (page 88) and cook for 6 minutes per 500 g. Remember to start timing only when the liquid comes back to the boil. The flesh in the legs, claws and tail will be cooked to perfection.

After a quick shell-scrub under running water, your crayfish is ready to serve. If your guests are picky (or you're trying to impress), present it in two halves: lay it belly-down on a chopping board and cut lengthwise with a large, sharp knife, giving the back of the knife a whack with a mallet to facilitate matters.

Clean out the alimentary canal before serving.

To extricate the tail meat for use in a salad or cocktail, cut along both sides where the softer underside meets the back shell. Peel off the underside shell, lift out the meat and discard the alimentary canal.

The traditional accompaniment to cold crayfish is Seafood Sauce (page 94), although homemade Mayonnaise (page 94) or any other mayonnaise-based sauce would be perfectly acceptable.

Suitable recipes

Crayfish Cocktail, page 15
Steamed Crayfish with Tangy Butter, page 21
Crayfish Mousseline with Red Pepper Purée, page 22
Bouillabaisse, page 30
Crayfish Bisque, page 32
Seafood Sausages, page 70
Spiced Prawns, page 72
Prawns Mykonos, page 73
Sweet and Sour Prawns, page 74
Grilled Crayfish, page 75
Crayfish Pie, page 75
Crayfish Ma Chère, page 75
Crayfish Newburg, page 76
Crayfish Thermidor, page 76
Braaied Crayfish, page 85
Sultan's Crayfish, page 77
Caribbean Paella, page 78
Prawn and Bacon Kebabs, page 86

ROE

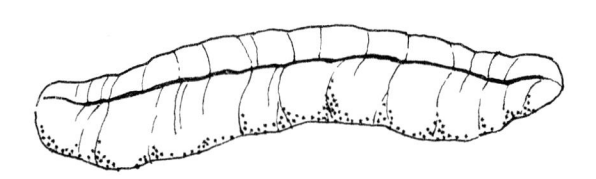

Roe is the spawn of the fish; when cooked it has a delightful texture and with careful seasoning can be prepared in many interesting ways. One of our earliest recipes was for fish roe soup which, besides being delicious, was reputed to have medicinal value. The roe was first soaked, the membranes removed, and then simmered very gently in a mirepoix of onions, green ginger, herbs and vinegar. It was then cut into pieces and cooked with stock and green peas and finished with a little white wine and nutmeg.

A word of warning: poisoning can result from eating the roe or liver of several species of fish which have a high vitamin A content, or as a result of fish being in contact with pollution from the land. Play safe and don't eat the liver or roe of the red steenbras, kob, wreckfish or shark, or of any species which is unfamiliar.

Caviare is the roe of the European sturgeon, and extracting it requires skill acquired through experience. Immediately the fish is caught it is bled and gutted and the eggs are carefully removed. They're then placed on a sieve and washed, drained and salted.

The sturgeon, like many other species of fish, is becoming more and more rare, so Russian scientists have developed an operation which allows the fish to be returned to the water after the removal of the roe. No wonder caviare is so costly! Only the true gourmet eats it as it should be enjoyed – a goodly portion, as is, with a mere sprinkling of lemon juice to enhance the flavour. Lesser mortals like you and me must be content with an occasional smattering on our canapés.

Preparation: Wash fresh fish roe under cold running water, then pop it straight into the frying pan with sizzling butter – add garlic and a squeeze of lemon juice if you wish. Or simmer intact for 5 minutes in water with a teaspoonful of vinegar. Drain, split in two, season with salt and pepper and fry in hot butter for a minute or two. Serve with lemon wedges.

Alternatively, remove the skin of simmered roe, slice it and add to a salad, or use it in one of these recipes:

SUITABLE RECIPES

Mock Caviare, page 15
Aegean Island Pâté, page 16

ROMAN
RED ROMAN/DAGGERHEAD

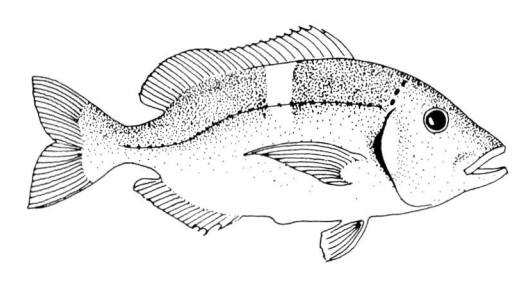

25 cm

A beautiful, bright orange fish with a bold white saddle over its back. It is particularly delicious stuffed and baked. The flesh is firm and the flavour is robust.

Prolific off the Cape coast where it congregates off reefs, roman is caught by spearfishermen, anglers and commercial line-boat fishermen with equal enthusiasm.

- Bake
- Grill
- Braai
- Fry

SUITABLE RECIPES

Hake Rosé, page 37
Paprika-Grilled Fish, page 46
Baked Stump with Cream Sauce, page 58
Beach Party Galjoen, page 82
Herb-Braaied Reef Fish, page 84
Fish in Foil, page 84
Whole Braaied Fish, page 84

SALMON TROUT

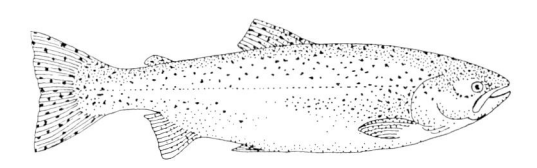

30 cm

This superior table fish starts life in fresh water – as a rainbow trout – whereafter it is transferred to the salt-water environment of hatcheries of salmon trout farmers. Superb marketing has resulted in the fish gaining popularity with diners since it was introduced to us in the early eighties and it is regularly found on restaurant menus.

A beautifully plump fish with flesh that is succulent, firm and very delicately flavoured, it can be adapted for many different ways of cooking.

- Poach
- Bake
- Smoke
- Grill
- Braai

SUITABLE RECIPES

Hake Rosé, page 37
Fish Meunière, page 40
Mushroom and Almond Fish, page 43
Salmon Trout in Champagne, page 43
Baked Stump with Cream Sauce, page 58
Fish in Foil, page 84

SCALLOP

Around the world, scallops are a delicacy. Costly, for sure, but whether you find it fresh or frozen you'll agree it is a superlative seafood.

Scallops live in deep water which, luckily for them, precludes them from being easily gathered by divers. They're sometimes landed in the fishing nets of trawlers, where they're immediately frozen and brought in to the fish shops. Other than these, imported frozen scallops are our most likely source of supply.

Preparation: If you're lucky enough to come across fresh scallops, scrub the shells and place them on a baking tray in a hot oven. As soon as the top shell shows signs of rising, lift it off with a knife. Remove the flesh – the tasty white part with the bright orange roe attached – trim away the beard and the black intestinal thread, and rinse the flesh, then drain and dry it.

The scallops are now ready for use: place them in a saucepan of cold water, bring to the boil and simmer for 2 minutes. Alternatively season with salt, white pepper and a pinch of cayenne pepper, dip in batter or crumbs, deep-fry in hot oil and serve with a sauce.

SUITABLE RECIPES

Scallops in Creamy Leek Sauce, page 21
Bouillabaisse, page 30
Velvety Scallop Soup, page 33
Scallops with Mushrooms and Dill, page 70
Prawn and Bacon Kebabs, page 86

SCOTSMAN

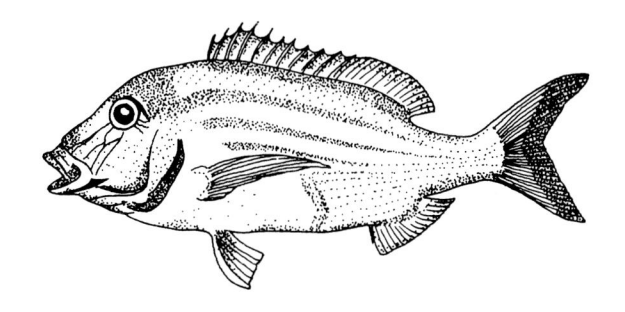

45 cm

This long-faced fish, a member of the seabream family, is pinkish-red with blue stripes around the eyes and along each side.

Normally found alone, it frequents deep offshore reefs – too deep for spearfishermen – to be caught by ski-boaters who consider it a fine angling and table fish.

Though not abundant, a scotsman is a real taste treat. It's best when it's ...

- Fried and served with a sauce
- Baked
- Grilled

SUITABLE RECIPES

Hake Rosé, page 37
Fish Meunière, page 40
Mushroom and Almond Fish, page 43
Fish Mornay, page 57
Paprika-Grilled Fish, page 46
Baked Stump with Cream Sauce, page 58
Niçoise Fish, page 61
Scored Fish over the Coals, page 85

SEA URCHIN

Fanciers of these spiky delicacies comb rock pools at low tide armed with a pair of scissors and lemon wedges, to enjoy their dozen at their freshest. Gourmet urchin-eaters are recognized by the fact that they carry cayenne pepper, brown bread and butter – and a bottle of cold white wine as well!

Sea urchins are seasonal – best collected at spring tide and beneath the full moon. The deeper under the water they live, the better (less likelihood of contamination from the land) and they must be fresh. Don't refrigerate them or leave them in the sun. There is a freshness test if you're not going to eat them on the rocks – sprinkle salt into the hollow mouth; if they start moving, they're still alive – and safe to eat.

A pair of pruning gloves makes opening them easier. Cut right round the shell and discard the top. Turn the urchin upside down, rinse quickly in seawater, and you'll see the edible portion inside – brightly coloured and looking like caviare (the female is brighter than the male). Season with salt, pepper and a touch of cayenne or Tabasco, if you wish, and eat them raw.

Watchpoint: If you find the inside mushy and black, don't eat it – the urchin is out of season!

Sea urchins may also be lightly boiled – it'll only take 4-5 minutes, after which they may be cut open with a pair of scissors. You could also try the way they were prepared by the ancient Greeks (who, of course, taught the ancient Romans a thing or two about food): wrap them in fig leaves and place them in the ashes of the fire.

SEVENTYFOUR

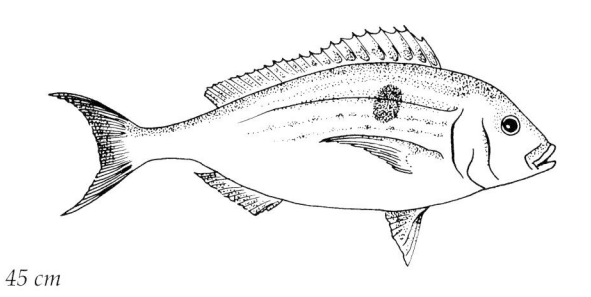

45 cm

This elegant and tasty fish, once abundant, has become scarce in recent years – even since this book was first published. In recent years size restrictions and a closed season have been introduced which, hopefully, will correct the imbalance.

The seventyfour got its name from the lines on its body which resemble the rows of gun ports of an old warship. Shoals frequent reefs and pinnacles in deep water, normally well out of the reach of shore anglers and spearfishermen. They're most often captured by commercial fishermen and ski-boat anglers.

The superlative flesh may be prepared in many different ways, the best being …

- Fried
- Baked
- Grilled
- Braaied
- Smoked

SUITABLE RECIPES

Hake Rosé, page 37
Fish Meunière, page 40
Mushroom and Almond Fish, page 43
Fish Mornay, page 57
Paprika-Grilled Fish, page 46
Baked Stump with Cream Sauce, page 58
Niçoise Fish, page 61
Scored Fish over the Coals, page 85
Whole Braaied Fish, page 84

SHARK

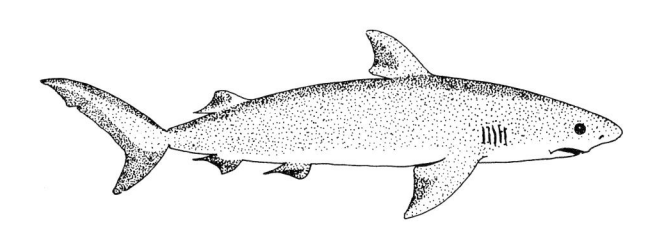

Many different species of shark in our water are edible – and delicious, too. Elsewhere in the world shark is highly esteemed and forms the bulk of the fish sold at fish 'n chips outlets.

Edible sharks include copper shark (also called the bronze whaler), Zambezi shark, blackfin or blacktip shark, dusky shark, blackspot shark, soupfin shark (more commonly known as the vaalhaai), St Joseph shark, sandshark, spiny dogfish and spotted spiny dogfish.

When your shark is landed, kill and bleed it by cutting the head off and hanging it up by the tail. Skin and fillet it, taking steaks from the tail section. Lay the steaks in seawater or salted fresh water. After 20 minutes or so a frothy substance will have floated to the surface. Change the water three or four times more until no more froth appears. Your shark will now be free of the ammonia odour and you may proceed to prepare it in any of the following ways …

- Coat with egg and flour and fry
- Bake
- Poach and serve with a sauce

Suitable recipes

Fish Cakes, page 34
Quick Fish Rissoles, page 34
Hake Rosé, page 37
Crunchy Soufflé Hake, page 36
Tomato and Feta Fish, page 37
Mushroom and Almond Fish, page 43
Spicy Shark with Cream Sauce, page 57
Skate with Black Butter, page 60
Mustard Cream Skate, page 60
Baked Reef Fish with Avocado Stuffing, page 64
Ouma's Pickled Fish, page 65

Silverfish
Carpenter/Kaapenaar

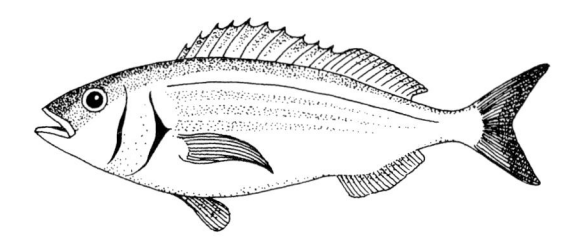

38 cm

This pretty, silvery-pink fish is quite prolific and often found at fish shops, mostly brought in by line-boats and trawlermen.

The flesh is fairly firm, moist and tasty. Smaller specimens usually end up in fish cakes or fish soup; larger fish may be …

- Fried
- Baked

Suitable recipes

Breton Fish Soup, page 26
Bouillabaisse, page 30
Fish Cakes, page 34
Quick Fish Rissoles, page 34
Hake Rosé, page 37
Crunchy Soufflé Hake, page 36
Fish Meunière, page 40
Mushroom and Almond Fish, page 43
Fish Soufflé, page 43
Fish Mornay, page 57
Baked Stump with Cream Sauce, page 58
Ouma's Pickled Fish, page 65
Herb-Braaied Reef Fish, page 84
Scored Fish over the Coals, page 85
Whole Braaied Fish, page 84

Skate
Spearnose Skate/Ray

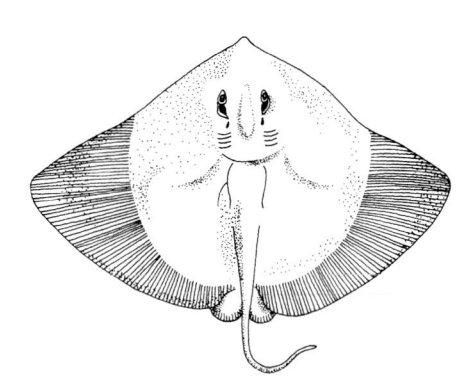

The wings of these large, floppy-finned denizens of the deep are quite delicious, and widely acclaimed throughout the world.

Preferring cooler water and sandy areas, most are caught by trawlers along the Cape coast and some are captured off Natal. Occasionally they may be hooked by shore-anglers, but, being enormously strong, most break free and live to tell the tale.

You're most likely to purchase skate wings skinned and ready for cooking, but there's an interesting freshness test for the recently-landed skate: for about ten hours after landing, it continues to form a sticky coating over its skin, so by wiping it you'll soon see whether the coating reforms and whether or not it's fresh.

Skinning the wings is no easy task (you may have to call on someone stronger and more adept – like your fishmonger). They may then be cut into convenient portions and …

- Poached
- Fried

SUITABLE RECIPES

Hake Rosé, page 37
Mushroom and Almond Fish, page 43
Fish Mornay, page 57
Gratin of Kob, page 49
Spicy Shark with Cream Sauce, page 57
Skate with Black Butter, page 60
Mustard Cream Skate, page 60

SNOEK
BARRACOUTA

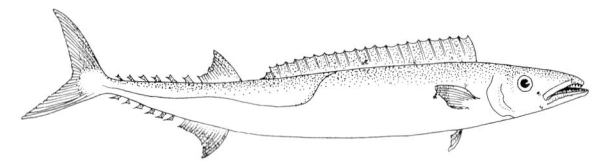

76 cm

This migratory and predatory fish migrates in a southerly direction from Namibia in autumn, massing off the West Coast, then continuing on to the Cape Peninsula during the winter months and early spring, and causing much excitement among commercial fishermen during the 'snoek run'. Their migration follows the seasonal distribution of its prey – anchovies and pilchards.

During the 'run' great numbers are captured by handlines and are sold fresh to the public who gather at coastal harbours to await the snoek boats' return from the sea. Vendors expertly gut and vlek the fish for you at lightning speed. Much of the catch is smoked, frozen and dried, and a fair amount is canned.

During winter, which coincides with the breeding season, the condition of the flesh deteriorates and a low protein and oil content of the flesh is recorded. You may notice worm-like parasites in the flesh. Don't be put off – they're completely harmless.

A vicious fighter, the snoek's mouth is well protected by sharp serrated teeth, much feared by fishermen who take care to kill the fish the moment it's boated to avoid the risk of injury.

The tasty flesh should be tinged with pink (the older it gets, the greyer) and do test the texture before buying. Overhandling causes it to become soft quickly – some believe that this also happens if the fish is exposed to the rays of the moon. Whatever the reason, a *pap* snoek is no use to anyone!

The flesh is rich and rather oily. Here's a tip that the *Kaapenaars* have used for years: soak your filleted snoek in salted, luke-warm water for a couple of hours before cooking. The oil will separate from the flesh and float to the surface. Pat dry with kitchen paper and ...

- Fry without any coating
- Grill
- Braai
- Smoke

SUITABLE RECIPES

Ceviche, page 15
Smoked Fish Pâté, page 16
Smoked Fish, page 49
Smoked Snoek Quiche, page 50
Niçoise Fish, page 61
Braised Gamefish, page 61
Ouma's Pickled Fish, page 65
Filleted Linefish over the Coals, page 85

SOLE

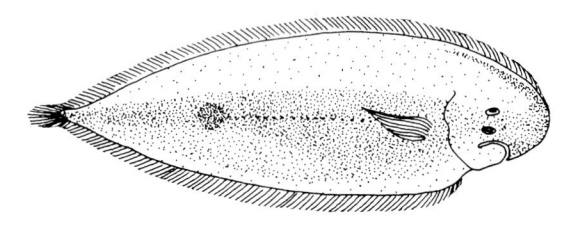

25 cm

Two types of flatfish in our waters find their way onto our tables – the west coast sole and the east coast sole, which is considerably smaller, more prolific and more highly esteemed. And while the catches from the west coast have decreased during recent years due to over-fishing, an important industry of east coast soles has developed off Mossel Bay, carefully controlled by permit and quota.

A much smaller variety, the blackhand sole, is fished in small quantities along the east coast – usually by tribal people using primitive spears to bag them.

Sole is delicately flavoured and finely textured. It is versatile and rather expensive, and can be filleted or cooked whole as whim dictates. Simple, classical dishes bring out the flavour best.

- Fry
- Grill, brushing first with butter

SUITABLE RECIPES

Hake Rosé, page 37
Fish Meunière, page 40
Mushroom and Almond Fish, page 43
Sole Véronique, page 46
Coconut Bay Sole, page 46

Paprika-Grilled Fish, page 46
Skate with Black Butter, page 60
Crayfish Ma Chère, page 75

Spanish Mackerel
KING MACKEREL/COUTA

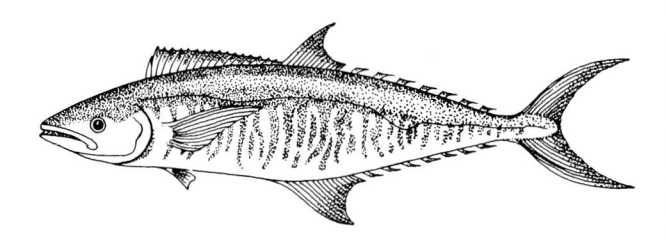

100 cm

This, the largest of the mackerel family (2 metre specimens aren't uncommon), is a sleek and ferocious predator, eagerly hunted by east coast game fishermen and spearfishermen. Commercial anglers also pursue it with enthusiasm, for it's a valuable food fish. After capture it must be bled. The meat is rich, dark and oily; it's best ...

- Fried without a coating
- Grilled
- Braaied
- Smoked

SUITABLE RECIPES

Hake Rosé, page 37
Paprika-Grilled Fish, page 46
Japanese Fish, page 54
Indonesian Fish, page 56
Braised Gamefish, page 61
Ouma's Pickled Fish, page 65

Squid
CALAMARI/CHOKKA/INKFISH
CUTTLEFISH

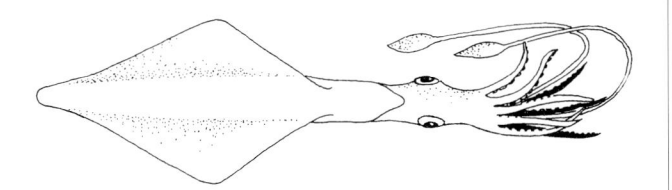

Squid and cuttlefish shouldn't be confused. Though they're close cousins and are both called calamari on restaurant menus, they look quite different. Our line drawing is of a squid; the cuttlefish has a shorter head and tentacles, and a much larger body which yields steaks that are considerably thicker and much more tender than calamari. Also, the cone of the cuttlefish contains a chalky cuttle bone unlike the transparent, flexible pen of the squid.

The cone and tentacles may be prepared in many different ways, in rings and steaks which are fried, grilled, stir-fried or casseroled.

Preparation: Catching squid with special lures on handlines is great sport. They have a sneaky habit of squirting their ink as they're yanked aboard and, if it's aimed in your direction, you'll return splattered and stained.

To clean: Grasp the head and tail sections firmly and pull them apart. Lift the ink sac from inside the tail cone and set aside (it's a delicacy and can be used in your dish, if you wish). With a sharp knife cut tentacles free, just beyond the eyes. Discard eyes and entrails. Remove the small, round cartilage from the base of the tentacles and pull out and discard the tail skeleton. Pull the fins from the tail cone and remove the mottled membrane from fins, tail cone and tentacles. Wash everything and dry well.

If you wish to freeze it, clean, dry and pack in airtight freezer bags. It may be frozen for up to three months without deteriorating too much.

When cooking, tenderness is a matter of timing – and lots and lots of practice! It cooks in the shortest time – fry for as little as 15 seconds, just until the edges start to curl. Over-cooked squid is tough, dry and tasteless.

- Panfry in garlic butter
- Deep-fry with a coating of flour, crumbs or batter

SUITABLE RECIPES

Calamari Crackling, page 12
Cool Calamari Salad, page 25
Panfried Garlic Calamari, page 69
Portuguese Calamari, page 68

Strepie
KARANTEEN

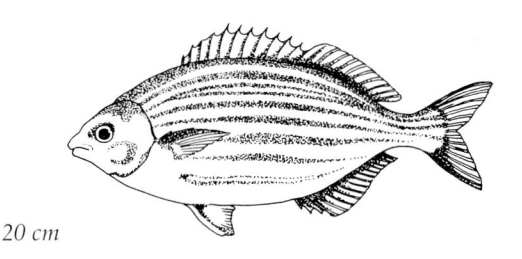

20 cm

Shoals of strepies frequent rocky regions close to the shore and rock anglers know them well, though they're far too small to rate as a serious source of food.

The flesh, though, is tasty – but fiddling about filleting them is a complete waste of time. Leave whole and ...

- Fry
- Smoke
- Braai

Suitable recipes

Fish Cakes, page 34
Quick Fish Rissoles, page 34
Fish Soufflé, page 43
Beach Party Galjoen, page 82

STUMPNOSE
WHITE STUMPNOSE/CAPE STUMPNOSE
RED STUMPNOSE

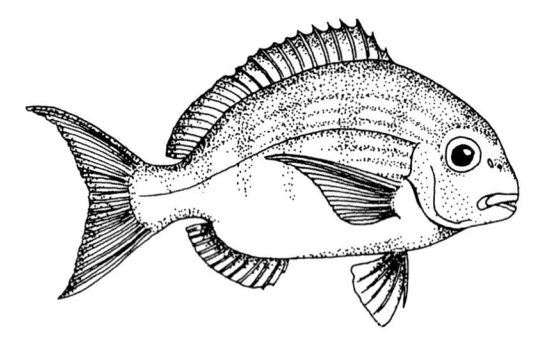

35 cm

The red stumpnose and all the white stumpnose species have superlative flesh, and for this reason are eagerly sought by amateur and professional ski-boat anglers.

The red stumpnose is a beautiful fish – pointy-snouted and deep-bodied with a distinctive hump on the head that grows more bulbous the older the fish gets. The colour is a distinctive shimmery red, darker above, with some blotching to add interest. When caught off deep reefs it smells like iodine.

The white stumpnose (illustrated above) and its close cousin, the Cape stumpnose, are silvery-white and don't develop the head hump. A good sport fish, it frequents coastal waters and estuaries, where it swims in shoals.

Though different in flavour, red and white stumpnose can be prepared in similar ways ...

- Baked
- Filleted and fried or grilled
- Braaied

Suitable recipes

Breton Fish Soup, page 26
Bouillabaisse, page 30
Hake Rosé, page 37
Crispy Fish with Lemon and Ginger Sauce, page 40
Fish Meunière, page 40
Minted Fish in Spinach, page 42
Mushroom and Almond Fish, page 43
Fish Mornay, page 57
Sole Véronique, page 46
Paprika-Grilled Fish, page 46
Indonesian Fish, page 56
Spicy Shark with Cream Sauce, page 57
Kingklip Calamata, page 47
Orange Kingklip with Spinach Sauce, page 48
Gratin of Kob, page 49
Italian Crunchy Kob, page 49
Baked Stump with Cream Sauce, page 58
Baked Stumpnose Marrakesh, page 65
Ouma's Pickled Fish, page 65
Seafood Sausages, page 70
Filleted Linefish over the Coals, page 85
Fish in Foil, page 84
Fish Kebabs, page 86
Crayfish Ma Chère, page 75

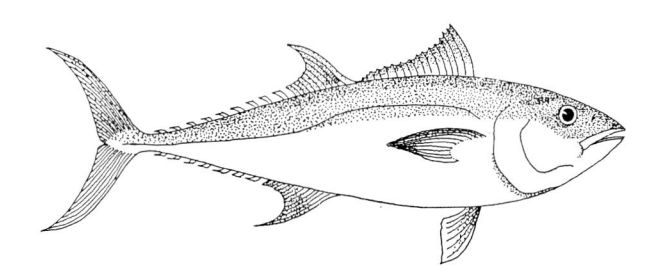

TUNA
TUNNY

182 cm

Of the many species of this supreme gamefish, twenty four are found in southern African waters. Among the fastest swimmers, the tuna is migratory, travelling vast distances on the way to wherever it's headed. The return of tuna to within striking distance of the shore is an annual event eagerly anticipated by sports fishermen.

Of the species caught in our waters, the following are the best eating: bluefin tuna, longfin tuna, yellowfin tuna, bonnito (katonker) and skipjack.

Much of the annual catch ends up in cans, and becomes one of South Africa's most important pantry standby's. In the East, of course, fresh tuna is a very important ingredient of sashimi, thinly sliced raw fish – a trend gaining popularity in the West as well.

Tuna must be bled on capture. The flesh is rather dry, very flavourful and tends to be rich and reasonably oily. We like it best ...

- Braaied, with lots of basting on the way
- Grilled
- Roasted
- Braised

SUITABLE RECIPES

Ceviche, page 15
Salad Niçoise, page 24
Tuna and Mushroom Casserole, page 44
Tuna Crêpes Niçoise, page 44
Cheat's Tuna Pizza, page 44
Tuna Tagliatelle with Matchstick Vegetables, page 45
Burmese Fish Curry, page 54
Paprika-Grilled Fish, page 46
Yellowtail Steaks with Green Peppercorn Sauce, page 58
Niçoise Fish, page 61
Braised Gamefish, page 61
Foiled Tuna, page 61
Barbados Fish, page 62
Roast Gamefish Spiked with Bacon, page 62
Marinated Gamefish Kebabs, page 85
Fish Kebabs, page 86

WHELK

For a long time, spoilt by an abundance of relatively cheap fish and shellfish, South Africans didn't explore other delicacies that were there for the taking.

As the cost of crayfish, perlemoen, calamari and mussels escalated, goodies like the humble whelk started gaining popularity. It is a creamy-coloured sea snail with a flavour not unlike a mixture of mussels and perlemoen – delicate and not too fishy.

Preparation: For the retail market they are purged and frozen raw or steamed. If you'd like to collect your own, however, boil them for 8-10 minutes, extract the meat from the shells and discard the gut. Scrub the foot lightly, rinse in cold water and they are ready to sizzle in garlic butter or dressed in French dressing for a quick and tasty snack.

Alternatively, dip them in egg, roll in seasoned crumbs and deep-fry quickly in hot oil. Drain and serve with a squeeze of lemon juice, or a suitable sauce: Tartare Sauce (page 95), or Seafood Sauce (page 94) are best.

WHITE STEENBRAS
PIGNOSE GRUNTER
WESTCOAST STEENBRAS

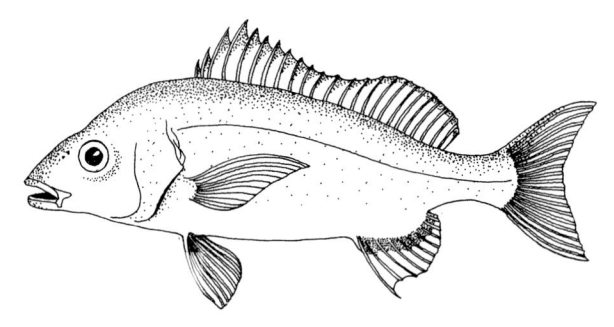

50 cm

Not only are the white steenbras and its close cousin, the westcoast steenbras, delicious table fish, they're great angling fish, easily caught from the shore. They're often seen in the shallow waters of estuaries, snout in the sandy sea-bed burrowing for food, tails jiggling away out of the water. When hooked on light tackle, they put up a memorable fight.

Though both species can attain 1 metre in length, most are considerably smaller than that. Silvery in appearance, they are nicknamed ghostfish by skindivers, because they are wily and difficult to see underwater.

White steenbras flesh is white, firm, delicately flavoured and has large flakes when cooked.

- Fry
- Grill
- Braai
- Bake

SUITABLE RECIPES

Beggar's Bouillabaisse, page 33
Hake Rosé, page 37
Crunchy Soufflé Hake, page 36
Crispy Fish with Lemon and Ginger Sauce, page 40
Fish Meunière, page 40
Minted Fish in Spinach, page 42
Mushroom and Almond Fish, page 43
Fish Soufflé, page 43
Fish Mornay, page 57

Sole Véronique, page 46
Paprika-Grilled Fish, page 46
Kingklip Calamata, page 47
Orange Kingklip with Spinach Sauce, page 48
Gratin of Kob, page 49
Italian Crunchy Kob, page 49
Japanese Fish, page 54
Spicy Shark with Cream Sauce, page 57
Baked Stump with Cream Sauce, page 58
Baked Stumpnose Marrakesh, page 65
Crayfish Ma Chère, page 75
Filleted Linefish over the Coals, page 85
Seafood Sausages, page 70
Beach Party Galjoen, page 82
Herb-Braaied Reef Fish, page 84
Scored Fish over the Coals, page 85
Whole Braaied Fish, page 84
Fish Kebabs, page 86

YELLOWTAIL

CAPE YELLOWTAIL

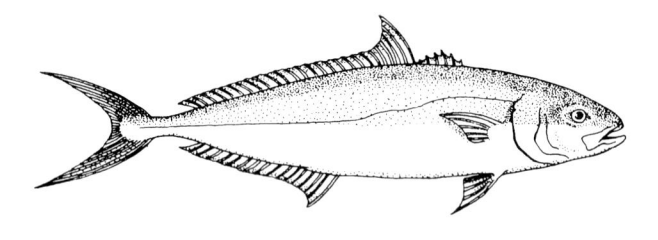

76 cm

This fine seasonal gamefish is one of the most respected in our seas – not only for the quality of its fight when hooked, but also for its meat which can be prepared in many different ways.

Besides its yellow tail and the distinctive torpedo shape, the yellowtail's brilliant blue-green colour is noteworthy, especially when just landed and the broad yellow stripe from head to tail stands out in bright contrast.

Bleed yellowtail on capture. The flesh is very firm, tasty and tends to be coarse, especially in older and larger specimens. Overcooking and cooking over too high heat tends to make it even drier, so watch out on both these counts.

Soak in heavily salted milk, drain, dip in flour and fry in olive oil and butter; alternatively …

- Grill
- Braai
- Pickle
- Smoke

SUITABLE RECIPES

Ceviche, page 15
Breton Fish Soup, page 26
Bouillabaisse, page 30
Paprika-Grilled Fish, page 46
Kingklip Calamata, page 47
Gratin of Kob, page 49
Burmese Fish Curry, page 54
Spicy Shark with Cream Sauce, page 57
Mahi Mahi, page 57
Niçoise Fish, page 61
Yellowtail Steaks with Green Peppercorn Sauce, page 58
Braised Gamefish, page 61
Foiled Tuna, page 61
Barbados Fish, page 62
Ouma's Pickled Fish, page 65
Filleted Linefish over the Coals, page 85
Marinated Gamefish Kebabs, page 85
Fish Kebabs, page 86

ZEBRA

WILDEPERD/STREEPDASSIE

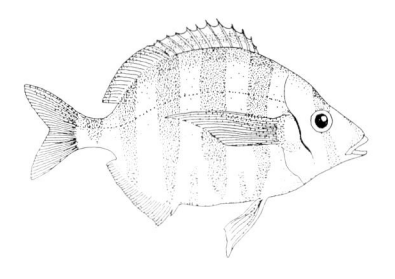

25 cm

This is one of the most attractive reef-fishes which is also great to catch on light tackle. Easily reached by rock anglers, ski-boat fishermen and spearfishermen, the family are equally pleased when it reaches the kitchen, so delicious is its flesh.

The zebra's most distinctive features are the bold black bars on its silvery-gold body. It also has a black bar across the eyes. Its close cousin is the blacktail, and though both can be prepared similarly, the flesh of the zebra is tastier.

- Fry
- Braai
- Salt lightly and smoke heavily

SUITABLE RECIPES

Smoked Fish, page 49
Beach Party Galjoen, page 82
Herb-Braaied Reef Fish, page 84

Index

Abalone 114
Aegean Island Pâté 16
Alikreukels 99
   Arniston 69
   Braaied 82
Anchovy 114
   Avocado, Baked 19
Angelfish 99
Apple and Almond Hake 37
Arniston Alikreukels 69

Baardman 100
Baked
   Anchovy Avocado 19
   Reef Fish with Avocado
     Stuffing 64
   Stump with Cream Sauce 58
   Stumpnose Marrakesh 65
Banded Galjoen 104
Barbados Fish 62
Barbel 100
Barbel-Eel 100
Barracouta 122
Barracuda 100
Basting Sauces, see Marinades
Batter
   Basic 90
   Bavarian 91
   Chinese 90
   Shantung 91
Beach Party Galjoen 82
Beggar's Bouillabaisse 33
Black Marlin 110
Black Mussel 111
Black Musselcracker 112
Black Mussel Soup 28
Blacktail 101
Blue Marlin 110
Bluefin Tuna 124
Bobotie, Fish 39
Bonnito 123
Bouillabaisse 30
   Beggar's 33
Braaied
   Alikreukels 82
   Crayfish 85
   Fish, Whole 84
   Mussels 82
Braised Gamefish 61
Brandied Prawns in Crème
   Fraîche 72
Bream 101
Breton Fish Soup 26
Brown Mussel 111
Brusher 112
Burmese Curry Mix 90
Burmese Fish Curry 54

Calamari 123
   Cool Salad 25
   Crackling 12
   Panfried Garlic 69
   Portuguese 68
Cape Gurnard 105
Cape Salmon 104
Cape Sea Robin 105

Cape Stumpnose 124
Cape Yellowtail 126
Caribbean Paella 78
Carpenter 121
Catfish 100
Caviare, Mock 15
Ceviche 15
Cheat's Tuna Pizza 44
Cheese-Crust Oysters 20
Chilli Mayonnaise 94
Chinese Batter 90
Chokka 123
Clam 111
Cock Grunter 105
Coconut Bay Sole 46
Cool Calamari Salad 25
Court-Bouillon 88
Couta 123
Crab 102
   Curry 76
Crayfish 117
   Bisque 32
   Braaied 85
   Cocktail 15
   Grilled 75
   Ma Chère 75
   Mousseline with Red Pepper
     Purée 22
   Newburg 76
   Pie 75
   Steamed with Tangy Butter 21
   Sultan's 77
   Thermidor 76
Cream Cheese Pastry 92
Cream of Perlemoen Soup 29
Creamy Fish with Fried Leek 38
Crème Fraîche 90
Crêpes 91
Crispy Fish with Lemon and
   Ginger Sauce 40
Croaker 100
Crumbed Perlemoen 79
Crunchy Soufflé Hake 36
Crusty Mustard Haddock 52
Curry
   Burmese Fish 54
   Crab 76
   Mix, Burmese 90
Cuttlefish 123

Dageraad 102
Daggerhead 118
Damba 104
Dassie 101
Deep-Fried Roman 62

Eel 102
Elf 103

Fennel Sauce 97
Feta Fish in Pastry 40
Filleted Linefish over the
   Coals 85
Fish
   Barbados 62
   Bobotie 39
   Braaied Whole 84
   Cakes 34
   Creamy with Fried Leek 38

   Crispy with Lemon and
     Ginger Sauce 40
   Curry, Burmese 54
   Feta, in Pastry 40
   Grilled with Spiced Yoghurt 38
   Herb-Braaied Reef 84
   Indonesian 56
   in Foil 84
   Japanese 54
   Jewelled Coriander 55
   Kebabs 86
   Meunière 40
   Minted, in Spinach 42
   Mornay 57
   Mushroom and Almond 43
   Niçoise 61
   Paprika-Grilled 46
   Pâté, Smoked 16
   Pickled 65
   Pie, Milanese 38
   Rissoles, Quick 34
   Scored over the Coals 85
   Smoked 49
   Soufflé 43
   Soup, Breton 26
   Stock 88
   Tomato and Feta 37
   Whole Braaied 84
Foiled Tuna 61
Fransmadam 103
French Dressing 94

Galjoen 104
   Beach Party 82
Gamefish
   Braised 61
   Kebabs, Marinated 85
   Roast with Bacon 62
Garlic
   Crushed 90
   Butter 91
   Herb Butter 93
   -Kissed Prawns 72
Garrick 109
Geelbek 104
Ginger, Crushed Green 90
Gratin of Kob 49
Green Peppercorn
   Mayonnaise 94
Grilled
   Crayfish 75
   Fish with Spiced Yoghurt 38
   Paprika-Grilled Fish 46
Grunter 105
Gurnard 105

Haddock
   and Leek Roulade 16
   and Orange Broth 26
   Crusty Mustard 52
   Mornay 53
   Salad O'Neill 25
Hake 106
   Apple and Almond 37
   Crunchy Soufflé 36
   Rosé 37
   Spring Vegetable Bake 36
Harders 106
   Johann's 54

Herb-Braaied Reef Fish 84
Herb Butter 93
Herbed Tomato Sauce 97
Herb Mayonnaise 94
Herring 114
Horse Mackerel 109
Hottentot 107

Indonesian Fish 56
Inkfish 123
Intoxicated Octopus 69
Italian Crunchy Kob 49

Jacopever 107
Janbruin 107
Japanese Fish 54
Jewelled Coriander Fish 55
Johann's Harders 54
John Brown 107
John Dory 108

Kaapenaar 121
Kabeljou 108
Karanteen 123
Karel Grootoog 103
Katonkel 124
Kebabs
   Fish 86
   Marinated Gamefish 85
   Prawn and Bacon 86
Kingklip 108
   Calamata 47
   Orange with Spinach Sauce 48
King Kob 108
King Mackerel 123
Kipper Pâté 15
Klipkous 114
Klipkous ...
Knoorhaan 105
Kob 108
   Gratin 49
   Italian Crunchy 49
Kolstert 101
Kreef 117

Langoustine 115
Leerfish 109
Leervis 109
Lobster 117
Longfin Tuna 124

Maasbanker 109
Mackerel 110
   with Mustard and Orange
     Sauce 58
Mahi Mahi 57
Marinades and Basting Sauces
   Marinade Monte Mar 93
   Mustard Marinade 93
   Oriental Marinade 93
   Spicy 93
Marinated Gamefish Kebabs 85
Marinated Mussels 12
Marlin 110
Mayonnaise 94
   Chilli 94
   Green Peppercorn 94
   Herb 94
   Oriental 94
   Pesto 94

Mediterranean Tomatoes 51
Melba Toast 93
Milanese Fish Pie 38
Minted Fish in Spinach 42
Mock Caviare 15
Monkfish 111
Mornay Sauce 96
Mullet 106
Mushroom
   and Almond Fish 43
   and Tuna Casserole 44
   Cream Sauce 98
Mussel 111
Musselcracker 112
Mussels
   and Leek Pie 66
   Braaied 82
   Marinated 12
   Pandora's 16
   Soup, Black 28
   Stroganoff 66
Mustard and Orange Sauce 98
Mustard Cream Skate 60
Mustard Marinade 93

Newburg, Crayfish 76
Niçoise Fish 61
Nut-Crust Oysters 21

Octopus 112
   Intoxicated 69
   Spicy 69
Orange Kingklip with Spinach
   Sauce 48
Oriental
   Marinade 93
   Mayonnaise 94
Ouma's Pickled Fish 65
Oven-Roasted Sardines 53
Oysters 113
   Cheese-Crust 20
   Kilpatrick 18
   Nut-Crust 21
   Smoked Bites 19

Paarl Lemoen 79
Paella, Caribbean 78
Pandora's Mussels 16
Panfried Garlic Calamari 69
Paprika-Grilled Fish 46
Pasta, Two Oceans 50
Pastry
   Cream Cheese 92
   Quiche 92
Pâté
   Aegean Island 16
   Kipper 15
   Smoked Fish 16
Peanut Pesto 97
Periwinkles 113
   Pickled 12
Perlemoen 114
   Croquettes 18
   Crumbed 79
   Fisherman's Wharf 80
   in Kelp 87
   Paarl Lemoen 79
   Parcels with Bacon and
     Mushrooms 86

Peperonata 80
Ragoût 80
Salpicon 79
Soup, Cream of 29
Timbales with Pink
   Hollandaise 22
with Fresh Herbs 81
Pesto Mayonnaise 94
Pesto, Peanut 97
Pickled Fish, Ouma's 65
Pickled Winkles 12
Pie
   Crayfish 75
   Milanese Fish 38
   Mussel and Leek 66
Pignose Grunter 125
Pilchard 114
Piquant Sauce 98
Pizza, Cheat's Tuna 44
Poenskop 112
Pomfret 99
Portuguese Calamari 68
Prawns 115
   and Bacon Kebabs 86
   Brandied in Crème Fraîche 72
   Garlic-Kissed 72
   Mykonos 73
   Spiced 72
   Sweet and Sour 74

Quiche Pastry 92
Quissico Bisque 30

Ragoût, Perlemoen 80
Ray 121
Redbait 115
Redbait Poffertjies 18
Red Mullet 106
Red Roman 118
Red Sails in the Sunset 33
Red Steenbras 116
Red Stumpnose 124
Roast Gamefish with Bacon 62
Rock Cod 116
Roe 118
Rock Lobster 117
Rollmops 14
Roman 118
Roman, Deep-Fried 62

Sailfish 110
Salad
   Cool Calamari 25
   Haddock O'Neill 25
   Salad Niçoise 24
   Salmon Chantilly 25
Salmon Trout 118
   in Champagne 43
Salpicon of Perlemoen 79
Sardines 114
   Oven-Roasted 53
   Sicilian 53
Sauces
   Chilli Mayonnaise 94
   Fennel Sauce 97
   French Dressing 94
   Garlic Butter 91
   Green Peppercorn
     Mayonnaise 94

Herb Butter 93
Herbed Tomato Sauce 97
Herb Mayonnaise 94
Mayonnaise 94
Mornay Sauce 96
Mushroom Cream Sauce 98
Mustard and Orange Sauce 98
Oriental Mayonnaise 94
Peanut Pesto 97
Pesto Mayonnaise 94
Piquant Sauce 98
Seafood Sauce 94
Spicy Yoghurt Dressing 95
Sweet and Sour Sauce 98
Tapenade Sauce 97
Tartare Sauce 95
Velouté Sauce 96
Sausages, Seafood 70
Scallops 119
   in Creamy Leek Sauce 21
   Soup, Velvety 33
   with Mushrooms and Dill 70
Scored Fish over the Coals 85
Scotsman 119
Seacat 112
Seafood
   in a Clay Pot 29
   Sauce 94
   Sausages 70
Seapike 100
Sea Urchin 120
Seventyfour 120
Shad 103
Shantung Batter 91
Shark 120
   Spicy with Cream Sauce 57
Shrimp 115
Sicilian Sardines 53
Silverfish 121
Silver Grunter 105
Skate 121
   Mustard Cream 60
   with Black Butter 60
Skipjack 124
Slinger 102
Smoked
   Fish 49
   Fish Pâté 16
   Oyster Bites 19
   Snoek Quiche 50
Smoorvis 50
Snoek 122
   Quiche, Smoked 50
Sole 122
   Coconut Bay 46
   Véronique 46
Soufflé
   Crunchy Hake 36
   Fish 43
Soup
   Beggar's Bouillabaisse 33
   Black Mussel Soup 28
   Bouillabaisse 30
   Breton Fish Soup 26
   Crayfish Bisque 32
   Cream of Perlemoen Soup 29
   Haddock and Orange Broth 26
   Quissico Bisque 30
   Red Sails in the Sunset 33

Seafood in a Clay Pot 29
Scallop Soup, Velvety 33
Spanish Mackerel 123
Spearnose Skate 121
Spiced Prawns 72
Spicy
   Marinade and Basting Sauce 93
   Octopus 69
   Shark with Cream Sauce 57
   Yoghurt Dressing 95
Spotted Grunter 105
Spring Vegetable Hake Bake 36
Squaretail Kob 108
Squid 123
Steamed Crayfish with Tangy
   Butter 21
Stockfish 106
Stock, Fish 88
Streepdassie 126
Strepie 123
Striped Marlin 110
Stumpnose 124
Stump, Baked with Cream
   Sauce 58
Stumpnose, Baked Marrakesh 65
Sultan's Crayfish 77
Sweet and Sour Prawns 74
Sweet and Sour Sauce 98
Swordfish 110

Tapenade Sauce 97
Tartare Sauce 95
Tasselfish 100
Thermidor, Crayfish 76
Tomato and Feta Fish 37
Tomatoes, Mediterranean 51
Tomato Sauce, Herbed 97
Tuna 124
   and Mushroom Casserole 44
   Crêpes Niçoise 44
   Foiled 61
   Pizza, Cheat's 44
   Tagliatelle with Matchstick
     Vegetables 45
Tunny 124
Two Oceans Pasta 50

Velouté Sauce 96
Velvety Scallop Soup 33

Westcoast Steenbras 125
Whelk 125
Whitebait 114
White Biskop 112
White Mussel 111
White Musselcracker 112
White Steenbras 125
White Stumpnose 124
Whole Braaied Fish 84
Wildeperd 126
Winkle 113
Winkles, Pickled 12

Yellowfin Tuna 124
Yellowtail 126
Yellowtail Steaks with Green
   Peppercorn Sauce 58

Zebra 126